Authors' Note

Since the first print run of *After Suicide*, the authors have recognized we must stress that the spiritual principles presented herein are not only useful for those who have suffered the impact of a suicide. Rather, the principles apply to anyone who has died by any means (Part One), as well as anyone who has experienced a heart-wrenching loss of a loved one (Part Two). In fact, the book could have been accurately titled *After a Death: There's Hope for Them and for You*. While suicide remains the primary type of tragic loss we address in order to demonstrate the spiritual principles, we want to emphasize these principles can help those struggling with any kind of difficult loss.

If you are having suicidal thoughts,
please call the suicide hotline immediately at
800-273-8255 (TALK) or 800-SUICIDE.
Understanding professionals are on standby
ready to help you.

For a list of warning signs and risk factors
that are common in those contemplating suicide,
please see Appendix A.

**Please visit
SuicideAndHope.com**

BOSTON COLLEGE

May 20, 2019

Dear Fr. Alar,

Thank you for thinking of me and sending me your book. I am impressed by its simplicity, honesty, and power, and am very happy to recommend it.

I can think of absolutely no possible greater sorrow in this world than the suicide of someone we love. I can think of no better answer to it than this book.

This is a "must" book. Like no other, it fills a terribly deep need with a terribly deep clarity, charity, and wisdom borrowed from the saints, and without the slightest sentimentality, patronizing, or condescension but also without the slightest deviation from orthodoxy. Fr. Alar shares with us the *real* teaching of the Church and her saints and theologians about suicides, which is startlingly and life-changingly different from what you probably thought it was.

Peter Kreeft

Peter Kreeft

Advance Praise

This book is so uniquely moving that once you begin, you won't stop. Death is a hard fact of life, and we all have to face it, but when we lose someone to suicide, we oftentimes face death with even more pain. We look for answers in the midst of darkness; we look for hope in the midst of despair, in the midst of shame, in the midst of so many unanswered questions and feelings of guilt. Many believe that suicide automatically condemns one to hell. That was what Fr. Chris Alar believed when his grandmother took her own life. For many, this may even cause them to question their faith.

In response, Fr. Chris eloquently brings this whole tragic experience to life — reliving it and supplying enlightened answers to many lingering questions. To do this, Fr. Chris and Jason Lewis masterfully dig deep into their faith in God, into the mystery of the Incarnation, into ecclesiology and eschatology, into science and psychology, and even into history and the life of the saints.

They interweave this all together with their personal experience, research, and deep understanding and hope in Jesus, the Divine Mercy. Through this, there is hope for the salvation of those who have died by their own hand and for those "left behind." While there are many books offering help regarding suicide, Alar and Lewis have dared to deal with such a tough and very sensitive subject in a way few others have: from the perspective of Church teaching and from the aspect of spirituality, which many abandon or fail to see in the midst of such a tragedy.

After Suicide is deeply charged in scholarly research, but is quite readable. For all those needing depth and convincing affirmation in their devotion to Divine Mercy, this is the book to read. I won't be surprised if you, too, will be awakened by your own personal "epiphany of hope," as I personally was while reading this work. There is hope because God's mercy is greater than any sin — even suicide. As such, this book is a "must read" and I could not recommend it more highly.

— **CARDINAL SOANE PATITA PAINI MAFI,**
Bishop of Tonga

In this theologically innovative and pastorally sensitive volume, Fr. Chris Alar and Jason Lewis provide justifiable hope for those grieving the loss of relatives and friends from suicide. Acknowledging the gravity of suicide's sinfulness, Fr. Alar and Jason draw on the *Diary of Saint Maria Faustina Kowalska* and other saints to show the unconditional merciful love of Jesus manifest in the New Testament. By synthesizing the Lord's merciful love with His power to transcend time (as shown in St. Augustine's brilliant explication of God's "Eternal Present"), Fr. Alar and Jason reasonably and responsibly justify the efficacy of prayer for those who have died from suicide in the past. Recounting the same belief (in the efficacy of prayers for events in the past) by Padre Pio, C.S. Lewis, Dorothy Day, and others, Fr. Alar and Jason Lewis point to an indispensable, hope-filled, effective response to suicide for those who have been sorely afflicted by it.

— **FR. ROBERT J. SPITZER, SJ, President, Magis Center of Reason and Faith**

After Suicide: There's Hope for Them and for You by Fr. Chris Alar and Jason Lewis is an extraordinarily comprehensive, hopeful, and well written book. It makes manifest God's infinite mercy for each of us and in a special way for those who sorrowfully take their own lives, as well as for those who mourn their passing. As a college president and psychologist, I believe that this book will be a special blessing, comfort, and grace to those who have lost a loved one to suicide. Father Alar and Jason's book is mercy itself. Jesus, I trust in You!

— **DR. BILL THIERFELDER, President, Belmont Abbey College and clinical psychologist**

After Suicide might be the most important book that you will ever read! Your fears about the fate of life lost to suicide will be allayed. The great theology of hope is emphasized in this comprehensive examination of suicide, which affects not only the lost life, but everyone left behind. The knowledgeable authors gracefully approach a most difficult, sorrowful, and unsettling subject with love and dignity. They share intimately the sorrows, grief, and hope in their own lives. As well, in addition to providing Church teaching, spiritual aids, and compelling stories, the authors lay out three spiritual principles to guide you to hope and healing, leading you to trust in God's merciful love. I highly recommend this powerful and important book!

— **DONNA-MARIE COOPER O'BOYLE, EWTN TV host and author,** *52 Weeks With Saint Faustina*

Father Chris Alar and Jason Lewis offer a well-written and comprehensive overview of the teaching of the Catholic Church on Divine Mercy and compassion offered to those whose loved ones have died by suicide, pastorally assuring them with a profound sense of hope and peace that their prayers for them are efficacious.

— MOST REVEREND MARTIN D. HOLLEY,
Bishop Emeritus of Memphis

Suicide, along with the fragility in mental health that is often its cause, is still very misunderstood within our culture. It is still a taboo that cannot be talked about. No obituaries ever state that the death was by suicide. It would seem too shameful. We desperately need a literature of understanding around the issue of suicide and, as Christians, a literature that helps us understand what happens to our loved ones who die by suicide when they meet God face-to-face. Chris Alar and Jason Lewis address those questions. Their answers will come as a consolation to anyone who has lost a loved one to suicide.

— FR. RONALD ROLHEISER, OMI

The night before Fr. Alar invited me to write an endorsement for this book, I was told about three people who had committed suicide in our local community just last week. This book couldn't be more timely, and it couldn't come from a better priest. Father Alar understands well the pain and anguish surrounding suicide, and he effectively applies the soothing hope and healing balm of Divine Mercy to that wound.

— FR. MICHAEL GAITLEY, MIC, author, *33 Days to Morning Glory* and *33 Days to Merciful Love*

Grief and anguish cannot begin to describe the emotions swirling around the loss of family or friends through suicide. Today it has become almost epidemic. Suicide is so final, so shocking, so regrettable. It is surprising that a book like *After Suicide* has not yet been written — but thanks to Fr. Chris Alar and Jason Lewis, we now have this excellent and timely resource to help us cope, but not *just* to cope, but to provide hope for them and for us. A leading expert on the devotion of the Divine Mercy, Fr. Alar brings to bear his knowledge and experience with the mercy of God to provide hope in the darkest hours. This book will be a godsend for thousands of people seeking solace and consolation.

— STEVE RAY, author of *Crossing the Tiber*

Oftentimes when tragedy strikes, those trying to comfort us will say they know how you feel. But often they don't. They're just at a loss for words and have no idea how to react to the pain, especially of something as horrific as losing a loved one through suicide. Father Chris Alar, however, really does know how you feel. In his book, *After Suicide*, coauthored with Jason Lewis, Fr. Chris draws on that pain through his own personal experience and the beautiful teachings of the Catholic Church. Father Chris and Jason show us how the love of God can and does break through even the most unthinkable circumstances, providing hope, not only for you, but those loved ones who left us much too soon.

— **TERESA TOMEO, syndicated Catholic talk show host of "The Catholic View for Women"**

The topic of suicide is an uneasy one. When a loved one takes their own life, many questions arise: "Is my loved one lost forever?" "How can I live with such heartache and loss?" "Who can I talk to?" The questions can seem endless, the pain unending, and sometimes statements made by others can be confusing and hurtful. For this reason, *After Suicide* is probably one of the most important books of our generation. It offers to the many people affected by the suicide of a loved one a consoling message of hope and an incredible message of God's timeless mercy. I very highly recommend it.

— **FR. DONALD CALLOWAY, MIC, author,** *No Turning Back: A Witness to Mercy*

A balanced mix of personal experience and Church teaching, this book has much to offer — not only to those who have lost a loved one through suicide, but to anyone who seeks a deeper understanding of the all-embracing mercy of God. It's in many ways a "how to" book: how to move beyond judgment and unforgiveness; how to release feelings of anxiety, hopelessness, and guilt; how to cope with grief and loss; and perhaps most importantly, how to live in the reality that it's never too late to pray — that since God is not limited by time, we can pray *now* for His grace *then*.

— **VINNY FLYNN, author of** *7 Secrets of Divine Mercy* **and** *Mercy's Gaze*

This is a much-needed presentation of a topic too often avoided, but you have wisely ventured to shed light from a Catholic perspective on this critical issue facing Western society today. Many thanks for your great insights, which will bring solace and support to many!

— MOST REVEREND ROBERT J. BAKER, Bishop of
Birmingham, Alabama

Death by suicide is a topic that is clouded with misinformation and fear. In *After Suicide*, Fr. Chris Alar and Jason Lewis offer a beacon of light to those who are left behind to grieve. A tribute to a deeply loved grandmother, this heart-felt book shows that the mysterious ways of God can always provide us with hope of Divine Mercy. If you or some-one you love has been touched by the pain of a self-inflicted death, this resource can help bring peace and comfort, and above all ... hope.

— SUSAN TASSONE, author of *Day by Day with Saint Faustina: 365 Reflections*

My heart goes out to all who tragically lose a loved one. Those raised in the Catholic faith will find great solace and comfort within these pages. All readers searching for healing will be invited to an abundant and much needed offering of mercy, wisdom, and hope.

— DR. MOLLIE MARTI, founder,
National Resilience Institute

Father Alar, Jason Lewis, and *After Suicide* have provided those of us who are suicide bereaved and have faith with the kind of hope we've craved ever since our devastating loss. No other book exists to help those who are struggling with their experience of loss — or, perhaps, struggled with suicidal thoughts and feelings — within the context of their faith. It is a majestic effort of love to all who have lost a loved one to suicide and a tribute to Fr. Alar's grandmother.

— DR. MELINDA MOORE, clinical division director,
American Association of Suicidology and co-lead,
Faith Communities Task Force, National Action Alliance

AFTER SUICIDE

There's Hope for Them and for You

By Fr. Chris Alar, MIC
and Jason Lewis, MIC

MARIAN PRESS
STOCKBRIDGE MA 01263

Available from:
Marian Helpers Center
Stockbridge, MA 01263

Prayerline: 1-800-804-3823
Orderline: 1-800-462-7426
Websites: TheDivineMercy.org
marian.org

Library of Congress Catalog Number: 2019945415
ISBN: 978-1-59614-434-7

Publisher: Marian Press
Publication date: September 1, 2019
First edition, 3rd printing (July 2021)

† IMPRIMATUR †
Most Rev. Mitchell T. Rozanski
Bishop of Springfield, Massachusetts
September 6, 2019

Nihil Obstat
Rev. Mark S. Stelzer, STD
Censor Librorum
September 6, 2019

Imprimi Potest
Very Rev. Kazimierz Chwalek, MIC
Provincial Superior
The Blessed Virgin Mary, Mother of Mercy Province
July 29, 2019

Nihil Obstat
Dr. Robert A. Stackpole, STD
Censor Deputatus
July 29, 2019

For
Grandma
&
Clare

CONTENTS

~ PREFACE ~

The main title of this book, *After Suicide*, connotes a topic that is both daunting and unsettling. Dealing with the aftermath of a suicide is difficult, to say the least. It is for this very reason that the authors of this book hope to encourage in you an "epiphany of hope." At first glance, the words "epiphany" and "hope" instill in us a sense of mystery and expectation.

An *epiphany* is a revelation of something that was formerly unknown. In Christianity, the Feast of the Epiphany is the celebration of the revelation of the Incarnate Word, of Jesus coming into the world as its Savior. The Magi see a bright star in the coal-black night and follow it. They are on a quest to find something to satisfy their restless hearts. They seek happiness and peace as they travel through the uncertainty of night to arrive at the crib of the baby Jesus, the true Light of the World. They traveled far through the dark of night to find the revelation of hope: Jesus, the Savior.

Hope is also a mysterious word. Defined as the combination of the desire for something and the expectation of receiving it, it is often understood in our everyday language as a mere wish that we would like to see realized.[1] But hope in its truest sense is much more than a mere wish. It's a God-given gift, a virtue that offers answers, happiness, and peace amidst the uncertainties and darkness that often penetrate our personal worlds. Christ has promised a better world to come; therefore, hope, rooted in faith, can sustain us through the trials of life, human difficulties, or tragedies that may otherwise seem overwhelming. Described as "a sure and steadfast anchor of the soul" in the Epistle to the Hebrews (6:19; RSVCE),[2] hope is the virtue that will be ultimately fulfilled in Heaven.

Epiphany and hope really do go together. Epiphanies are those "ah-ha" or "eureka" moments of illumination, often breaking through the thick clouds of darkness and confusion to reveal something that gives us hope. In writing this book, its authors have had numerous epiphany moments. The book was initially the inspiration of Fr. Chris Alar, MIC. As a priest and pastor of souls, after the suicide of his grandmother, he felt drawn to share his own epiphany of hope with those who have lost a loved one by such tragic means. He recognized the uncertainty and grief that suicide brings in several families in the course of his ministry, so he set out to address the tremendous rise in suicide that is occurring across the world today. Along the way, he reconnected with a long-time friend and religious brother, Jason Lewis, who had also walked through the darkness of pain, grief, and loss to find the light of hope.

Part One, "There Really Is Hope *for Them*" (hope for the salvation of those who have died), shows how our prayers today, even for those who died years ago, can aid their salvation at the moment of their death. Part Two, "There Really Is Hope *for You*" (hope for those left behind), expands the focus to offer the epiphany of hope and healing to anyone who has suffered the loss of someone close to them, particularly a suicide, because there is hope in the fact that communion with a loved one is still possible in this life; and there is hope in the possibility of reuniting with that same loved one after death.

It is the prayer of these authors that this book brings you to your own personal epiphany of hope, even in the midst of your unique pain and loss. They have been praying for you and your lost loved one already, offering monthly Mass for all who will read this book. While the focus herein is suicide, the points made throughout, such as the power of our prayers to transcend time and the hope of salvation for your loved one, do not apply just to those who have died by suicide, but by other ways, such as natural causes, accidents, violence, or an overdose.

Through the theological and pastoral reflections and insights presented here, the goal of this book is to offer hope to the families of the thousands and hundreds of thousands — if not *millions* — of souls who have died sacramentally unprepared to meet the Lord and whom they fear may be separated from Him. While it is important that one is never presumptuous of God's mercy, believing the soul of their deceased loved one could never be anywhere but in Heaven, it is equally important that one does not despair of their eternal fate, as well. Thus, the intention of this book is to show how these souls may be saved and enter into eternal life through our intercessory prayers for them.

This may seem a bold and presumptuous claim. Bold, *yes*! Presumptuous, *no*! A confident prayer filled with hope in the infinite power of Christ's Divine Mercy, *absolutely*!

Just as the Magi did in their quest for a newfound hope, let us set out together on this journey, to discover that "the people living in darkness have seen a great light; on those living in the land of the shadow of death a light has dawned" (Mt 4:16; NIV).

~ INTRODUCTION ~

I Found Hope and So Can You

My name is Fr. Chris Alar. I am a survivor of a loved one's suicide. Her name is Mary Alar, and she is my grandmother.

She died on Father's Day, June 20, 1993. She left no note.

If you're reading this book, you too may have experienced, or know someone who has experienced, the searing loss of a loved one, especially to suicide. If that's the case, let me assure you: There is hope.

Right now, it may not seem like there's much hope. You may doubt or barely believe that your loved one could possibly enjoy the peace of God in Heaven. Or maybe you're wondering if it's possible that your own suffering, and perhaps your feelings of guilt, will ever allow you peace.

Well, let me say it again: There is hope. Real hope.

Not only is there hope of salvation for your deceased family member or friend, but there's hope of relief and peace for you. Trust me — I know.

The impact of my grandmother's suicide was earth-shaking, and it had a painful effect on me and my entire family. When I first heard the news, I not only despaired of her ever entering into Heaven — because of what I had always been taught about those who "commit suicide" — but I also felt a crushing weight of soul-numbing guilt for years to come.

Then I found hope.

This book is about the hope that I found, a hope I now feel called to share with you. As a priest who speaks at parishes and conferences across the country, I've met hundreds of people who have experienced the loss of someone to suicide. Each time I hear their stories, my heart breaks for them. I want to scoop them up in my arms, hold them tight, and let them know they are not alone. I want to give them the same hope and consolation that I myself have received since learning about Divine Mercy, especially as it relates to those who have taken their own life.

That's what this book is about: hope after the loss of someone we love. Of course, the pain of losing someone will never completely disappear, but there is hope for them and hope of consolation for your grief-weary soul in the aftermath of such tragedy.

In this book, my co-author Jason Lewis and I will examine what the Church really teaches about suicide and present the theology behind this hope. Later, we will suggest three basic spiritual principles that will help you navigate through the painful waters of grief from a loss that may have pierced deep into your soul. We will show how you can find hope and consolation in your grieving process, particularly through certain components of the Divine Mercy message and spirituality, so that you can begin to live your life again.

Although Jason and I are not licensed mental health professionals, we are not without knowledge on this subject. We both have advanced degrees in philosophy and theology and have received several years of pastoral training in the seminary, which has now been complemented by years of practical experience in the vineyard of the Lord. Moreover, both of us have lost loved ones who were very close to us. So, in what follows, we'll be drawing not only from the training that's offered through priestly formation and pastoral ministry, but on our own personal experience.

In one sense, this book is not intended to be one of *prevention*, offering medical help and counseling to those considering suicide. (For these instances, please seek medical help immediately and call the National Suicide Hotline at 800-273-8255 [TALK] or 800-SUICIDE.) But in another sense, it can be considered *preventative* because, according to psychologist Dr. Melinda Moore, "one suicide prevention strategy is to target the persons who are impacted by suicide because they may be more at risk of suicide themselves. There is now compelling evidence that people exposed to suicide, particularly those who are emotionally close or biologically related to the deceased, are at elevated risk for suicide themselves."[3] Thus, in its *postvention*[4] character, this book is also preventative in that it strives to help those who are trying to cope after the loss of a loved one and prevent them from becoming the next victim of a suicide.

In the course of our research, we were quite surprised to learn that even the Church does not treat the topic of suicide at great length. However, we can draw out several implicit points from her rich teaching, as we intend to do throughout these pages. Other than liturgical prayers for "One who died by suicide" and a few specific articles contained in the *Catechism of the Catholic Church*, there aren't many teachings or pastoral programs designed specifically to address this critical issue. That is why we felt it our calling to begin a much-needed ministry of education about suicide. We saw it as our duty, myself as a priest and Jason as a fellow member of the Marians, to share our experience and findings with others. We have both suffered the loss of someone close to us, and we believe we can help those who have also been involved, either directly or indirectly, with such a tragic loss.

We understand this may be a difficult topic to reflect upon, and we understand there may be many different reasons leading you to pick up this book. That's why we are asking you right now to make the journey of reading this book steeped in prayer. God's loving mercy will not fail you. Together we will look at areas of hope that will lead us to the heart of His mercy, for your departed loved one in Part One, and for you in Part Two. If at any moment the next two chapters become a little heavy, whether due to the sensitivity of the subject matter or because the theological content becomes too deep, don't worry. We are leading you to "The Bridge of Trust," which leads to the "shore of hope" of recovery in grief that is offered *for you* in Part Two.

So thank you for joining us on this difficult, yet inspiring journey. And may the power of Divine Mercy console your heart and strengthen your hope — even after the loss of a loved one — as it did for us.

~ PART ONE ~

There Really Is Hope for Them

I know well the plans I have in mind for you
says the Lord, plans for your welfare and not
for woe so as to give you a future of hope.

— Jer 29:11

As a priest, in saying that there's hope for those who have taken their own lives, I want to emphasize that suicide is never the answer. In this life, it's a permanent response to temporary problems. Furthermore, it hurts the people who are left behind, causing all sorts of heartache and harm in ways the deceased would never have imagined.

I also want to emphasize that while what I'm about to explain reveals that there certainly is hope after suicide, there is no guarantee of salvation for anyone. There is often great cost to the souls of those who die in this way. It's more than likely that they will have to at least suffer great pains in Purgatory, including remorse over having cut their own lives short and the knowledge that they've hurt those who love them. As we'll soon see, however, there's something you and I can do that's very effective for shortening, or even eliminating, that suffering.

And so the hope remains.

Here in the five chapters of Part One, we'll cover the topic of hope for those who have died, particularly by their own hand. In Chapter One, I will tell you who my grandmother was and briefly recount her tragic death and how it greatly affected my life. In Chapter Two, we'll cover the Church's hope-filled teaching on suicide. In Chapter Three, I'll tell my own story of experiencing what I call my "epiphany of hope." In Chapter Four, we'll look more closely at the consoling theology behind the epiphany of hope. Finally, in Chapter Five, we'll see the reason for hope at the end of our lives.

Now, let's begin our journey of hope.

CHAPTER ONE
My Grandmother and Suicide

*M*Y GRANDMOTHER'S LIFE. My grandmother on my father's side is named Mary (Domansky) Alar. As mentioned previously, she took her own life on Father's Day, June 20, 1993. But before I recount the events of that excruciating day and its aftermath, I first want to tell you about who my grandmother was. Why is that important? Because my grandmother was so much more than just "someone who committed suicide." *Much* more.

Born in 1916, Mary was the daughter of Slovak immigrants who met and married in the United States. My great-grandmother often regaled her young children with stories about the "Old Country," and in 1923, she decided it was time for them to see it for themselves. With the permission of her husband, who stayed behind to work, she and the kids headed off to Slovakia.

The visit was wonderful; however, as the family tried to return to America, they had problems getting a visa and ended up stranded in Europe for nearly three years. My poor great-grandfather ended up spending every penny he had to bring them back home. Not surprisingly, that was the last time any family member of my grandparents' generation ever went back to Slovakia. On a positive note, my grandmother learned to speak Slovak and got to know the country of her ancestors. Still, with the family's savings eroded, their financial situation became dire.

In fact, the family became so poor that by the time my grandmother was 12, she was forced to quit school to help support her family. She went to work as a cook and housekeeper for the wealthy and prominent McIntyre family of Monroe, Michigan, who are known for inventing the Monroe auto shock absorber. Growing up, I clearly remember hearing stories from my father about how my grandma labored "tirelessly" (pun intended) for the McIntyre family over the years. Moreover, seeing the abundant wealth of this family only highlighted what Mary and her family did not have. It eventually got to the point where my grandmother disliked working for them, but she had no other choice.

Eventually, things started to improve for Mary when, at the age of 20, she got engaged to a man who had a good job in Detroit, working in the automotive industry. Unfortunately, he died tragically in a car accident just three days before their wedding day in 1937. My grandmother always held a special place in her heart for that man, but he obviously was not my grandfather. Mary met my grandfather, Joseph "Joe" Alar, a few years later, and it certainly wasn't your typical introduction.

It happened at William C. Sterling State Park in Monroe, where my grandmother loved to spend time on her only day off each week. In addition to being enamored with the beauty of the surroundings, the price of admission was just about right: It was free. The country was still in the midst of the Great Depression, and going to that park for recreation brought her a little peace and joy while allowing her to save every penny she earned.

Unfortunately, the situation for my future grandfather was even more difficult, as he was out of work and didn't have a single cent to his name. The able-bodied young man came to Michigan from northern Minnesota, looking for work after hearing rumors of jobs available with the Civilian Conservation Corps. At that point, however, he was unsuccessful in his job search and basically homeless. Coming across my kind-looking grandmother in the state park, he told her he was hungry, since he hadn't eaten in three days. He asked if she could spare any food, which is not typically your best pickup line!

She replied, "I'm sorry, I don't have anything to eat." But, feeling pity for the starving man, she invited him to come secretly to the McIntyres' home that evening, since she would be working. Specifically, she instructed him to hide outside the main kitchen window until she could find a way to help him. Joe did as he was told, and as my grandmother cooked fried chicken for the family dinner, she discreetly threw a few pieces out the window, where my grandfather waited in the bushes. Not surprisingly, he devoured the fried chicken as if he hadn't eaten in ... well ... three days! Because he hadn't eaten in so long, the chicken was too much for his poor stomach, and he vomited it all up right in the McIntyres' bushes, leaving quite a surprise for their unfortunate family gardener. What a way to meet your future spouse!

But the vile scene did not repel Mary or reduce her compassion for Joe. Being a wise man, my grandfather recognized Mary's goodness, and he began to court her. Eventually his efforts paid off, and my grandmother agreed to marry him. (I guess you could say any couple named *Mary and Joseph* would be bound to receive God's graces!) They would later have three children, one of whom was my father, Charles, the middle child and eldest boy.

Both of my grandparents worked hard to support the family — my grandfather as an industrial millwright, and my grandmother as an industrial sewer, fabricating leather seats for cars in the automotive manufacturing industry. It was a hard life for them, but they had a happy family. While they certainly didn't have a lot of money, they saved and sacrificed enough to send their children to Catholic school. My outdoorsman dad even contributed by putting food on the table that came from his hunting and fishing adventures.

As the kids grew and my grandmother aged, she suffered one physical ailment after another. More than likely, many of her health problems — nagging arthritis, for instance — came from years of hard manual labor. As often happens to many struggling people today, my grandmother drifted away from her Catholic faith, and her sad life history didn't help. Through all the work and pain she endured, she didn't always maintain her faith in a good and loving God. Again, she'd been raised poor, her family remained poor, and she had to keep on working despite tremendous physical pain. With such an arduous life, she wondered aloud where God's good will was for her and her family.

Still, my grandmother soldiered on. Now, I can't say she was uncomplaining. In fact, her main way to "vent" was to do just that: complain. But even though she bemoaned her situation frequently, she kept on going, working and cooking for her family — and do I miss her cooking! That was one job she didn't mind so much, and she was great at it. She especially liked to cook old family recipes handed down across generations.

Moreover, while my grandmother enjoyed cooking, she absolutely *loved* the music of her ethnic roots. Every day at 1 o'clock, she'd have my grandfather turn on her beloved program of traditional Czech music, including polkas. And both of my grandparents would go to Czech dances. In fact, it's because my grandparents coerced my father into attending a polka dance that he met my mother; so you might say that I'm a proud product of polka music!

While my grandmother certainly wasn't perfect, she was a very loving and unique person. Even though she stopped practicing the faith by not always receiving the Sacraments, in another sense she never stopped practicing it. Here's what I mean: She had a lively awareness of the beauty of creation, deeply loved her family, and took great care of us all. You might also say she was benevolent toward the poor to a fault. In other words, the same generosity that led her to feed my grandfather when he was hungry and out of work led her to give away some of the best things the family possessed to those in greatest need. Of course, that would annoy my grandfather to no end, especially when she was giving away his new coat or shoes to those who went without. To my dad and me, my grandma's charity was of the same sort you read about in the lives of saints, like Sts. John Paul II or Mother Teresa of Calcutta. And yet such generosity was an ordinary part of my grandmother's life. Yes, she complained, but she also loved her neighbor. So can I really say that she'd completely lost her faith? Maybe not completely.

In this sense, my grandmother reminds me of many faithful men and women in Sacred Scripture who became vexed with God. Yes, it happens, and it's all right. If you don't believe me, simply turn to the psalms of complaint, found throughout the Book of Psalms. Or think of how Moses cried out to God again and again in frustration as he struggled to lead the Israelites to the Promised Land. Or recall the complaints of the suffering protagonist in the Book of Job as he endured one tragedy after another.

After learning of all her disappointments in life — the loss of her fiancé, never having anything significant to possess, and constantly suffering from years of hard labor and physical ailments — one could better understand why my grandmother had a hard time believing in God's goodness. I'm sure many of you have some family and friends who fall into the same category.

Was my grandmother angry with God because she still believed and still trusted, but felt betrayed by One whom — perhaps — she still loved? I don't know the answer to that question. But I do know our faith teaches that *love* is the greatest virtue and, as I mentioned, Mary Alar certainly *loved*. I also know that when we take the time to get to know another person's story, there's always more to them than we initially perceive. Once we truly get to know another's heart, it's hard not to be moved by the difficult circumstances and burdens they have faced. It's hard not to feel sympathy for them, and it becomes easier to see the flashes of gold in them that others often overlook.

I'm sure you could tell similar stories about those you love. And I'm certain that God sees even greater nuggets of gold in them than you do.

*M*Y GRANDMOTHER'S SUICIDE. My grandmother took her life on Father's Day, June 20, 1993. I know this is the third time I have mentioned that date, but it is a date indelibly etched into my memory.

We were following our annual tradition of having the whole family gather together for a picnic at my aunt's house. That particular year, I was in between college and my first professional engineering job, so I happened to be home for a short weekend visit. Not seeing my grandmother at the family party, I was told she was feeling too ill to attend — or so she said. At some point that afternoon my grandma took her own life. As with anyone's choice to do such an action, I will never know exactly what factored into that dreadful decision.

Using a small handgun that was kept in the house for protection, my grandmother shot herself in the bathroom and lay in a pool of blood for what authorities estimated to have been about two hours. Leaving the picnic to go visit her, my father found her in that lifeless state. I cannot even imagine the shock that must have overwhelmed him when he came upon that tragic scene. In some ways, it's obvious: The suicide of someone close to us is an extremely painful experience for all family and friends. I remember how shaken my father was by finding his mother dead by her own hand — on Father's Day, no less.

My dad is a tough guy. As a Marine who served in Vietnam, he's always been strong. But finding his mother like that must have been beyond difficult. He didn't say much about it; he wouldn't — he didn't have to. Losing your mom is hard enough on its own, but losing her to suicide and being the one to find her? There are no words to describe such an experience. Even though all of us who have grieved a suicide have something in common with other bereaved people, there's still something uniquely devastating about grieving a suicide.

As for me, I'll never forget that day, and for years afterward I lived with guilt and regret from it. The reason was because I blamed myself for being "too busy" to visit my grandma with my father that day, since I had left the party to go see my girlfriend instead. When I returned home, my distraught mother told me the news. I was stunned. I couldn't even grasp the reality of what had just happened. My grandmother was gone. I couldn't believe this was the end to such an amazing life — a life filled with suffering, but also a life filled with so much love, tenderness, and care.

After reading about these events, one could ask, "Father Chris, where did you find any hope for her soul? How did you cope with such a loss?" At this point, I am going to ask you to be patient. I promise we will answer these questions in a very thorough way in the next chapter, where I will explain what I learned years later in North Carolina regarding Divine Mercy for those who succumb to suicide. We will also answer these questions in Part Two, where we offer hope to those survivors left behind — hope to get you through the next day. But for now, I will discuss the period following my grandmother's death.

As the years went by, and as difficult as it was, I attempted to deal with my loss as best I could. I started to realize it was something that I could never change. In the meantime, I still had my own life to live, and I knew I needed to remain focused and put my energies into building a successful career and life for myself.

This was easier said than done, however. For many years, I continued to grapple with recurring thoughts about my grandmother's death. Whenever her passing would come to mind, I would try to block it out, suppressing any feelings that emerged. This is a natural reaction, because those memories were forcing me to face unresolved questions and emotions that I did not *want* to deal with — that I didn't know *how* to deal with. Despite a great amount of prayer and healing, one particular question haunted me: "How could my grandma, a woman of 77 years of age, arrive at the determination to take her own life by suicide? And by means of a handgun!"

Continuing into my priesthood, the more I heard the stories of other lives rocked by such an unnatural means of dying, the more I sought to understand the "why" of someone ending their own life. Here, my "inner engineer" met my "inner pastor." I began to research suicide and was soon startled by what I discovered. I learned that those who have endured a painful loss to suicide are hardly alone. Sadly, suicide is more prevalent today than ever before, and it tears apart the family — the very fabric by which our society is held together. To get a better understanding of just how common this devastating affliction has become, let's take a deeper look at certain facts about suicide and its nature.

STAGGERING STATISTICS. Before researching the nature and causes of death by suicide, I hadn't realized what a chronic problem it has become in our country and around the world.

I hadn't realized that an estimated 50 percent of people in the U.S. personally know someone who has died by means of suicide.[5]

I hadn't realized that "since 1999, the suicide rate in the U.S. has gone up across all racial and ethnic groups, in both men and women, in both cities and rural areas, and across most all age groups,"[6] and from 1999 to 2017, the rate of suicide in the U.S. increased by 33 percent.[7]

I hadn't realized that from 2008 to 2015, rates doubled among children who were hospitalized for suicidal thoughts or activity.[8]

I hadn't realized that in recent years, nearly 800,000 people worldwide take their own lives every year. That's more deaths per year than occur annually from "conflicts, wars, and natural disasters combined."[9] Speaking of wars, about 20 U.S. military veterans take their lives every day.[10]

I hadn't realized that for every suicide, there are 25 suicide attempts, which is one every 27 seconds,[11] and a 2015 study suggested "that for each death by suicide 147 people are *exposed* (6.9 million annually)."[12]

And I most certainly hadn't realized that the number of people who reported having suicidal thoughts during the period from 2017 to 2018 is roughly the combined population of Boston, Chicago, Washington, Los Angeles, Miami, and Seattle.[13] And this fact doesn't even take into consideration that many suicides, and instances of people having suicidal thoughts, go unreported.[14] (For additional statistics on death by suicide in the U.S., please see Appendix B.)

CULTURAL PROLIFERATION. These facts and statistics on the prevalence of suicide in our culture are astonishing, to say the least. It's clear that this phenomenon reaches far beyond isolated incidents involving a few troubled individuals (which is a common misconception), and that stories like my grandmother's were much more widespread than I ever imagined. (For this reason, the Centers for Disease Control and Prevention [CDC] released a specific package on suicide prevention in 2017. Please see Appendix D for details.)

In fact, the problem of suicide has become so far-reaching that many professionals have tended to categorize it as an *epidemic.* In medical terms, an epidemic is a widespread outbreak of a disease or plague, limited to a geographic region or population for a limited period of time. Thinking about this caused me to wonder if the current high frequency of suicide could even be labeled a *pandemic*. I pose this question because a pandemic is understood to be an outbreak of a widespread disease or plague that grows beyond a specific region with no definitive end in sight; containment or isolation of its proliferation is unforeseen, and it poses imminent danger to vast numbers of people.

Some may argue that suicide is not considered a pandemic because it is not "contagious." However, I would respond that suicide can be "spiritually contagious," as we see from the so-called Werther effect, which occurs when suicides that are made public encourage others to imitate them.[15] Even if suicide is not officially categorized as a pandemic, it certainly seems as though it should be.

Consider also the widespread acceptance of the occurrence of suicide in mainstream culture. We have almost grown numb to its many manifestations, which have taken the form of physician-assisted suicide; post-traumatic stress disorder (PTSD) leading to suicide; drug overdoses; homicides followed by suicide; and even a subtle glamorization of death by suicide in popular media. These manifestations are too numerous to cite and treat individually, but let's look at just a few examples.

First, let's consider an example of an unhelpful portrayal of suicide in popular media, namely the hit Netflix show "13 Reasons Why," an adaptation of the young-adult pop novel by Jay Asher. Producers behind the show claim to mean well by educating teens and the public on teen behaviors that can lead to suicide, such as bullying, sexual harassment, and rape. However, many school counselors and psychologists have serious concerns over the show's potential effects.[16]

The basic premise is that a high school girl named Hannah Baker chooses to end her life by suicide, but before "the final act," she records 13 cassette tapes. On each tape, she gives one of the reasons why she "committed suicide." The story follows the survivors of Hannah's death as they decide what to do with the tapes, their contents, and Hannah's death.

Statistical data indicate that following the show's release, the number of cumulative Internet searches for suicide-related terms increased by 19 percent. Searches for the phrase "how to commit suicide" went up 26 percent,[17] and "there was nearly a 30 percent increase in the overall suicide rate among U.S. youths ages 10 to 17 in the month following the show's release."[18]

Thus, although the show and the book are hugely popular among teens,[19] it is highly questionable whether they are "contributing to the conversation" on suicide and other teen issues in a healthy or truly helpful way. In fact, they go against the best practices laid out in the widely accepted "Recommendations for Reporting on Suicide."[20] According to multiple experts, the story shines the spotlight on real tragedy in a way that may lead to imitation, not aversion; to more tragedy, not more healing.

Another risk of such a series is that it seems to subtly depict suicide as a solution to one's problems and a way to gain a hearing from those who hadn't been paying attention. It appears to send the wrong message that ending one's own life will have a greater impact than living will. It also poses a real risk of modeling the behavior imitated in copycat suicides. And "13 Reasons Why" is just one expression of the proliferation of suicide in our culture today.[21]

*A*DDICTION. Now let's consider another factor contributing to suicide in our modern society: addiction. Manifested in alcoholism, drug abuse, and the current opioid crisis, substance addiction is ravaging our nation and the souls of its people. We see it reported every day in the media. We see it in our neighborhoods and streets. We see it in our homes and families. I hear of its tragic consequences every day in the confessional and in spiritual direction. So many people are deeply affected when their family and friends fall into the throes of addiction.

Addiction may be a great mystery to those who have never been touched by its allure. But addiction may be just as great of a mystery to the alcoholic or drug addict. Nobody sets out to become dependent upon an enslaving substance. For some people, once they've consumed alcohol or certain other substances, a chain reaction seems to follow. Immediately, a powerful sense of euphoria and heightened well-being almost "incarnates" itself in the user, blocking out — albeit temporarily — feelings of depression, darkness, pain, and anxiety. The user may even be tempted to call it a spiritual experience.

We know, however, that this feeling of ecstasy is merely a *pseudo*-spiritual experience, a fleeting imitation of an authentic spiritual experience. Yet the effect of an encounter with a particular substance can be so powerful that it triggers a mental obsession in the brain, generating a desire to return to the source of the perceived well-being and the pseudo peace that it obtained before. When this behavior is repeated over and over, physical dependency can follow.

With substance abusers, alcohol and drugs seem to incite reactions in the deeper spheres of the person that are psychological and spiritual. As we will later see, God Himself created the human person with a strong desire and instinct to strive for *Him* as *the* source of fulfillment. So when an "appetite" for alcohol and drugs becomes a substitute for our natural desire for spiritual fulfillment in God, it gains a certain kind of strength. It grips the mind of the addict, and an obsession to seek more of the substance takes over his entire thinking, compelling him to seek more of the source of the *pseudo* spiritual experience.

Of course, repeated "union" with certain substances can even result in life-threatening physical addictions as well. Regardless of whether their addiction is physical, psychological, or both, addicts lose the power of free will in choosing to consume a given substance or not. The substance becomes a necessity, and it may require more and more of it to produce the desired effect of euphoria.

At some point, however, the substance ceases to work. The euphoric effect devolves into an elusive, unobtainable end that the addict can never recapture. Yet his mind recalls this state of pseudo-well-being and insists that it is still attainable. The more he seeks, the less he finds, leaving him in the death grip of addiction. This state of being eventually becomes a hellish prison in which the addict feels inescapably trapped. The magic solution that once liberated the user from his pain, anxiety, depression, and fear now amplifies these negative emotions. A feeling of hopelessness sets into the soul, and severe depression and despondency become the person's constant companions.

This apparently hopeless situation can lead to another problem difficult to recognize, but a real one, nonetheless: *indirect suicide*. This form of suicide is different than most kinds of suicide. Many times, when we talk about suicide, we're referring to a specific incident. Indirect suicide happens when a person doesn't obviously "commit suicide," but their negligence or refusal to set aside life-threatening behaviors ultimately leads to their death. It is as if the person says, "I know these drugs and alcohol will eventually kill me, but I don't care. I can't stop!" And they don't, which often results in tragic consequences, including death.

One prevalent example is opioid addiction. As many of you know, opioid addiction is a huge and growing national problem. People fall ill, are prescribed pain medication, and then become addicted to it. Sometimes, if pregnant women take opioids during their pregnancies, their unborn babies also acquire an addiction.[22] The CDC determined that as a result of the "opioid crisis," a public health emergency exists nationwide.[23] How bad is this crisis? According to the CDC, "Every day, more than 130 people in the United States die after overdosing on opioids."[24] The U.S. comprises only five percent of the world's population but consumes nearly 70 percent of the total global opioid supply,[25] creating an epidemic that has resulted in tens of thousands of deaths each year.

Of course, when speaking of deaths resulting from these types of dependencies, we must realize that, as mentioned previously, addictions go hand in hand with a certain amount of enslavement to the drug of choice. After a while, use of the drug isn't a matter of free choice anymore. As we will soon discuss, that factor mitigates culpability; it means that a person may be less than fully responsible for their actions (see *CCC*, 1859-1860), although there may still be some culpability based on how they entered into the addiction in the first place. Whatever the case may be, addicts persist in unhealthy, or even downright dangerous behavior, and that's not consistent with proper self-love and good stewardship of one's life.

Although this all sounds overwhelmingly depressing, even here there is *hope*, as we will soon see. But many users are unable to find, or even imagine finding, a way out of this seemingly hopeless state. Haunted interiorly by intense confusion and distress, they may feel that death is the only way out — the only solution to alleviating the extremity of such darkness. Many users have sought escape from this horrid state of mind by making the wrong decision of ending their lives. Now, let's try to better understand how to respond in such situations.

SUICIDE PREVENTION. In the introduction, we specified that our focus in this book is more *postvention* than *prevention*; hence the title of the book: *After Suicide*. We also stressed that our approach primarily is spiritual-pastoral rather than medical-clinical. However, given the proliferation of suicide today and the many factors that may lead to it, we felt it imperative to briefly touch upon some preventative guidelines currently embraced by the medical community.

Most research suggests that — oftentimes, but not always — a person inclined toward suicide will exhibit certain warning signs. (Please see Appendix A for a list.) If you detect such signs, certain actions may prove helpful.

For example, although it may seem counterintuitive and even uncomfortable to broach the subject of suicide, mental health professionals encourage dialogue with those who struggle with suicidal ideation (suicidal thoughts). One guide on suicide prevention states:

> A suicidal person may not ask for help, but that doesn't mean that help isn't wanted. Even the most severely depressed person has mixed feelings about death, wavering until the very last moment between wanting to live and wanting to die. Most suicidal people do not want death; they want the pain to stop. Suicide prevention starts with ... the warning signs and taking them seriously. If you think a friend or family member is considering suicide, you might be afraid to bring up the subject. But talking openly about suicidal thoughts and feelings can save a life.[26]

The National Alliance on Mental Illness (NAMI) agrees that dialogue is crucial:

> There is a widespread stigma associated with suicide and as a result, many people are afraid to speak about it. Talking about suicide not only reduces the stigma, but also allows individuals to seek help, rethink their opinions and share their story with others. We all need to talk more about suicide.[27]

An example of this is Kevin Hines, one of the few people to ever survive jumping off of the Golden Gate Bridge. He later recounted that he "paced the bridge for an hour, crying, hoping and praying that one person would ask him what was wrong. He said he would have told them everything."[28]

Likewise, the effectiveness of open dialogue implies the importance of empathetic listening. In the article "How to Help Those Considering Suicide" on a commonly-used psychology website, it states:

Perhaps the simplest, most effective way to help a suicidal friend is to simply listen, empathize with their struggles, and ask questions. If a friend says *anything* that indicates they might be struggling in general, don't let the conversation stop there. Ask them to elaborate a little further, and listen attentively. Express compassion, grace, and sympathy toward them.[29]

Your compassionate presence can offer a ray of hope, a sense of comfort and security, to someone struggling in the midst of darkness. That might be all they need to take the necessary and courageous initial steps toward a better future.

Most often, people who vocalize these battles are seeking help in a roundabout way, but ultimately they *can* be helped. Most suicide survivors note that with help and hindsight, they cannot believe they ever found themselves in a momentary position of such intense feelings of hopelessness.[30]

What is important to stress — indeed, what makes suicide itself such a tragic choice — is that feelings of insurmountable hopelessness are typically *temporary*. Simply talking through such feelings can dramatically minimize the perception of inescapable doom. NAMI's professional research further supports the possibility of a brighter tomorrow. Its September 2018 blog post notes the following:

The act of suicide is often an attempt to control deep, painful emotions and thoughts an individual is experiencing. Once these thoughts dissipate, so will the suicidal ideation. While suicidal thoughts can return, they are not permanent. An individual with suicidal thoughts and attempts can live a long, successful life.[31]

Take courage — real hope remains for those who struggle with thoughts of ending their own lives.

Another resource for assisting someone with suicidal thoughts could be this very book. Once you familiarize yourself with the three spiritual principles and spiritual aids in Part Two, you can easily apply these tools in your discussions with someone experiencing suicidal ideation. These principles and aids have proven highly effective for people suffering in the darkness of addiction, grief, and other struggles. Clinical psychologist Dr. Melinda Moore, after reading an early draft of this book, said these principles may indeed help prevent further suicides, because those who suffer the intense aftermath of a lost loved one to suicide are often at the highest risk of potentially taking their own lives.

If someone you know shows signs of suicidal ideation, contact a professional as soon as possible. Hospitalization may be the best immediate option to ensure their safety. Additionally, the local pastor may be a great resource as well to help those in need of emotional and spiritual assistance.

Again, take courage. Trust in God's grace, and assure those having suicidal thoughts that you are present and committed to help them in their troubled time.

Let's now take a deeper look into some of the underlying reasons that contribute to the alarming increase in the suicide epidemic.

CAUSES OF SUICIDE. Although Appendix A lists several risk factors for suicide, suicide is rarely caused by one single factor, and the reasons for it are not always apparent. Surprisingly, researchers have found that "more than half of people who died by suicide did *not* have a known diagnosed mental health condition at the time of death."[32] My grandmother did not show outward signs of any mental illness, which is why her death was such a shock to our family. So how could she, and so many others, feel compelled to do such a thing? Among the many reasons contributing to increased risk for suicide are relationship problems or loss; substance misuse; physical health problems; an array of mental disabilities; and job, money, legal, or housing stress.[33]

Recent research has even shown that there are "new" reasons for suicides that have extended beyond the aforementioned "traditional" reasons:

Many studies now point to the internet as a new and significant risk factor in the increased suicide rate. Instead of traditional depression and obvious risk factors like financial or relational distress, social media allows normally functioning people to feel inferior or isolated relative to a curated set of "peers." This in turn creates deep-set changes in self-worth without any actual changes in lifestyle, relationships, or economic standing. In fact, a person can now browse Instagram while sitting at a job they genuinely enjoy and feel woefully inadequate or alone, even if they have a healthy friend group and different types of relationships.[34]

Sometimes life becomes so difficult that people feel undervalued or disrespected. They may be totally overwhelmed, feeling helpless and unable to accomplish anything. They may be marginalized or treated as outcasts for many different reasons. Their pain is real, and they may lose sight of the fact that their life is a gift from God.

For me, that last statement, that suicidal people fail to see *life as a gift from God*, seems to hold the key. As I looked into some of the specific and varied reasons for the suicide problem today, they all seemed to underscore Pope St. John Paul II's spot-on diagnosis that we are living in "a culture of death," a phrase from his papal encyclical *Evangelium Vitae* (*The Gospel of Life*).[35] I was troubled when I reflected on this reality. Does Christ not bring us the "Gospel of Life"? Has He not conquered sin and death and set the human spirit free for abundant life?

Again, my "inner engineer" and my "inner pastor" were driven to ask questions: How did we arrive at this point? What is the root cause of this culture of death and one of its most acutely distressing expressions, the dramatic increase in suicide rates?

After much thought and prayer, I came to the conclusion that there is one fundamental root cause of our modern suicide crisis: a lack of faith in God. Coupled with this primary cause, there are also secondary factors that contribute to the lack of faith in our individual and communal lives — namely, a disordered attachment to "the world" and the influence of the demonic. Let's look at these now.

A LACK OF FAITH IN GOD. We live in a world that increasingly gives no time or space to God. The secularism that started with the French Enlightenment of the 17th and 18th centuries has spread around the globe, significantly reducing the opportunities to learn about, experience, and practice religious belief in many spheres. When society reduces its openness to grace, the supernatural consequences become dire. We leave our souls barren and vulnerable to corruption.

Think about it: This life is difficult enough, even with all the graces that come through active communion with God. But when people live without God and His grace, it can destroy them. In fact, it *does* destroy them.

The world today has become more secularized than at any point in human history. When secularism takes extreme forms, aiming to remove God from every facet of our lives, our society is doomed to unhappiness and discontentment. In essence, we publicly "commit suicide" on virtually every social and communal level. With the elimination of the Holy Spirit, the "Lord and Giver of Life,"[36] and therefore of life-giving vitality from our environment, would it not follow that some individuals living in barren communal circles might be seriously affected, fall into depression, and develop a certain predisposition toward taking their own lives?

As my friend Gene Zannetti, who has a master's degree in clinical psychology, points out, suicide is often directly related to depression. He finds it interesting to note, however, that the effects and the causes of suicidal depression are different from one another. For example, anxiety, suicidal ideation (suicidal thoughts), and substance abuse are likely *effects* of depression, whereas purposelessness and hopelessness are often *causes* of depression. Purposelessness and hopelessness can follow quite naturally from a society entrenched in relativism and atheism, because a life without purpose or meaning is a life without hope.

A related problem is that the Church and God are becoming less and less important in today's culture. Many people, especially our impressionable youth, become victims of this Godless society. They don't have God in their lives because there is no supporting culture that fosters a living and active faith. As a result, they wallow in a sea of hopelessness, clutching at false gods and trying desperately to fill the void in their lives. Often through no fault of their own, they innocently go down the wrong path in their quest to end their agony of emptiness.

The answer to this hopelessness is something that is sadly disappearing from our society today: attending faith-based services. Some have drawn connections between attending religious observances and suicide prevention. Even the *Wall Street Journal* has published an opinion piece acknowledging this relationship. In her article "Is God the Answer to the Suicide Epidemic?" Ericka Andersen writes:

A 2016 study published in JAMA Psychiatry found that American women who attended a religious service at least once a week were five times less likely to commit suicide. The findings ... are consistent with 2019 Pew Research findings that regular participation in religious community is clearly linked to higher levels of happiness. ... [T]here's strong evidence that people who attend church or synagogue regularly are less inclined to take their own lives.[37]

The human person is created for deep communion with God. As the *Baltimore Catechism* states, we are created "to know God, to love Him, and to serve Him in this world, and to be happy with Him forever in the next."[38] And what is ultimate happiness? Happiness is the fulfillment of all of one's desires. So only in God will man find the truth and happiness — that fulfillment of desire — for which he unceasingly longs and searches. Given this inner longing for something greater than ourselves, St. Augustine observes that "our heart is restless until it rests in [God]."[39] The fact is that our loving Father and Creator desires our happiness and fulfillment even more than we do!

The elimination of God from our communal circles, from our culture and society, is nothing short of evil. But as St. Thomas Aquinas and many other theologians and philosophers have taught, evil is not an "actual thing"; rather, it is a *privation* of the good. That means that evil doesn't exist on its own as a created thing because God is Goodness itself, and He creates only things that are naturally good.

Evil becomes present when intelligent creatures, such as Satan and his demonic forces or we human beings, reject God, His love, and His commandments. We oust Him from our society — from our courts, schools, work environments, and even our families — and in doing this, we remove Goodness itself from our lives. What is left behind is a gaping void that is "evil," a privation of the good. Is it any wonder that we see so many school shootings in our country today? We've eliminated the very thing that makes anyone or anything *good*. We've gotten rid of God, the source of love, of justice, of life. That's not going to help society get any closer to joy or contentment; instead, it has the opposite effect.

I remember seeing a T-shirt on a woman in an airport a few years ago. It said, "Columbine, Sandy Hook ... God, how can you let this happen in our schools?" The line below was God's response: "I'm not

allowed in your schools!" As this reminds us, without God, even institutions that are solid centers of learning and order can become places
of chaos and turmoil.

Furthermore, ridding society of God rids society of peace. I once
heard the evangelist Fr. Mitch Pacwa, SJ, say on one of his EWTN
shows, "The reason for so many suicides today is a lack of peace. And
without God, we don't have peace." As Jesus said to the humble
Polish nun St. Maria Faustina Kowalska in the 1930s, **"Mankind will
not have peace until it turns with trust to My mercy"** (*Diary of
Saint Maria Faustina Kowalska*, 300).

Peace comes with love of God and neighbor, and with the
indwelling of the Trinity in the soul. Peace comes through the Sacraments and a life of love, not from the removal of God, because God
is love itself. Our faith suggests that, if we welcome the One who is
Goodness and Love itself, then peace will follow.

As mentioned, some professionals have even correlated nonreligious affiliation with suicide rates and found that nonreligious
affiliation was the strongest contributing factor to an increase in
suicide. One study concluded: "Religiously unaffiliated subjects had
significantly more lifetime suicide attempts and more first-degree relatives who committed suicide than subjects who endorsed a religious
affiliation."[40]

Of course, sometimes depression, mental illness, or the tragedies
of life can impede or steal our peace. Even people of faith can become
overwhelmed by sorrow and the troubles of this valley of tears, and
die by their own hand. I'm certainly not intending to cast doubt on
anyone's faith or morality. People of all sorts struggle with depression
or mental illness, whether they have faith or not. Nevertheless, I can't
help but think that these large numbers of suicides would be substan-
tially reduced if we allowed God His rightful place in our lives and in
our society.

I am not alone in my assessment. Saint Teresa of Calcutta spoke
often about the great material poverty in the East where she served;
yet she insisted that the spiritual poverty of the West is far greater. She
spoke of the smiles, the love, and the patience in suffering she found
among the materially poor. She contrasted that to the emptiness she
saw in the faces of "the spiritually poor" in affluent countries of the
West — no doubt caused by the addictions, violence, destruction, and
joylessness that can afflict those with all the material comforts of the

world.[41] Mother Teresa saw the problem with secularism and knew it would spread like a spiritual disease at an epidemic level.

*T*HE *ALLURE OF THE WORLD AND ITS "GODS."* Mother Teresa told us again and again about the problems she saw in the West, but have we listened? Have we responded to her powerful words, her prophetic insights, and her example of a life given to God? The answer to this question is "not really." This is the reason why faith is so important. Christianity shows us how we can put God first in our lives and refuse to be bound by the false "gods" of this world.

I haven't been a priest for long, but I've heard hundreds, if not thousands, of confessions. Yet not a single person has ever confessed to me that they broke the First Commandment. We assume that because we don't actively worship the gods of other religions, we are not guilty of this sin. However, I am sure that all of us have broken the First Commandment at one time or another. You see, sometimes we supplant God as the King of our hearts and replace Him with things such as sex, power, or money. In fact, we can call these three things the "gods of this world."

Sexual activity outside of marriage offers us merely an illusory path to joy. It enables us to use another as an object of our personal pleasure, rather than reinforcing a bond of commitment to another in an inseparable union of marriage. Outside of marriage, sex is a false imitation of the union between Christ and His Church.

Power can make us feel as if we are accountable to no one. As we accumulate earthly power, it becomes all too easy to believe that we are becoming more like God (note the sin of Adam and Eve [see Gen 3:5]) and maybe that we are even becoming "God."

Love of money is another form of idolatry. As we focus our attention on limited, earthly goods, we can fall into a false sense of security that we have no need for God. Yet as the *Catechism* teaches us, "He who loves money never has money enough" (2536).[42] The love of money blinds us and diverts our focus from our ultimate destiny, which is God Himself. If we find our "rest" and security in money, our hearts become filled with temporal, disposable "junk" that never satisfies our transcendent, eternal desires. Only in God do our hearts find rest, fulfillment, and peace. As Jesus Himself revealed to us, "You cannot serve God and mammon" (Mt 6:24).

These false gods offer us apparent joy, a temporary state of peace to relieve our stress and anxiety. As Thomas Aquinas states, we cannot live without joy, so if we don't have spiritual joy, we will seek joy in carnal pleasures.[43] But eventually, all of these idols reveal themselves to be purveyors of a counterfeit joy, a lesser joy than the unending, eternal bliss for which we were made: union with God.

Old age and frailty reveal the falsehood of the god of sex as well as the limits of earthly power. And every twist and turn of the stock market, every boom and bust, reveals the limits of the power of money. This is why religious priests (such as myself) and consecrated brothers and sisters take the three vows of poverty, chastity, and obedience, which give us the grace to overcome the temptations of money (poverty), sex (chastity), and power (obedience).

When we put all our hope and confidence in one or all of these false gods (or any other "gods" you can think of), eventually we will come crashing down. In our society, we see this everywhere. The brutal reality of facing the world after such a fall often results in a complete inability to handle everyday life. Tragedy and even suicide often ensue.

But there's more to our struggles with temptation than just fighting the world and the flesh. We are fighting the devil as well, in a spiritual battle for our very souls.

DEMONIC INFLUENCES. Many people don't want to talk about the devil today. Many don't even believe in him, characterizing him as a primitive attempt to explain human evil and sin, or repudiating all belief in him as mere superstition. There are those who want to believe he's just a figment of our imaginations, a "bogeyman" who haunts the nightmares of children and the childish.

That's unfortunate. I say that because our faith tells us clearly about Satan's existence, his (limited) power, and his schemes. Indeed, part of the liturgical rite of Baptism and the renewal of our baptismal vows explicitly asks us to reject Satan and "all his works" and "empty promises." If he doesn't exist or is just a figment of our imagination, then what's the point of rejecting him?

This failure to believe in him is one of the devil's greatest weapons, because it allows him to catch us unprepared in his efforts to snare our souls. Church tradition tells us that one-third of the angels of Heaven fell, becoming the demons of hell (see Rev 9:1; 12:4). Given the role of the devil and his fallen angels in attempting to destroy humanity, I can certainly believe that the devil has been whispering in the ears of many, tempting them to commit crimes or even take their own lives. For example, after a horrible school shooting in Florida, investigators questioned the shooter as to his motive. He replied that he was simply following the instructions of the voices in his head as he went through the school on a rampage.[44]

Certainly, the experience of hearing voices can be caused solely by mental illness, but we must not be too quick to dismiss the possibility that this was the work of demonic forces. That is why it is so important to have God in our lives and as the foundation of our society. Since He is the all-powerful God who created all things, the devil has no power over Him, and consequently, no power over us if we don't give it to him. When we turn to God, His grace can protect us against any assault from the evil one and his minions.

Like St. Faustina, the Polish mystic who received Christ's Divine Mercy revelations in the 1930s, we have immediate recourse to the power of God. Once, while she was interceding for the salvation of souls, Satan tried to impede Faustina's efforts, but she persisted in prayer without fear or concern. She recounts:

> Paying no attention to Satan, I continued to pray with redoubled fervor for sinners. The Evil Spirit howled with fury, "Oh, if I had power over you!" and disappeared. I saw that my suffering and prayer shackled Satan and snatched many souls from his clutches (*Diary*, 1465).

*P*REPARING FOR *H*OPE. We have seen the statistics on suicide and its worldwide impact, some effective preventative tips, the disturbing examples of some of the causes of suicide in our society, and the reasons that our culture has been thrown into such disarray. The one significant point worth reemphasizing is that if you are reading this book after having lost someone to suicide, or you know someone in such a situation, you are by no means alone. Needless to say, that doesn't make the pain any less acute. The trauma and suffering you are experiencing may be so extreme that it could take years, if not decades, to begin to return to a life of normalcy.

As you probably know, there's really no shock like the shock of hearing that someone you love has taken his or her own life. And it's made even worse for many Christians by a very real fear for the state of their loved one's soul. After I found out about my grandmother's suicide, I couldn't say much. All I could think about was the way her life ended, with no chance for her to repent, and concerns about her eternal destiny flooded my mind. After all, doesn't the Church teach that taking one's own life guarantees that one automatically goes straight to hell? No, it doesn't.

Why? Because in this case there is something greater at work than our fear of God's punishment, and that is Divine Mercy. And what is Divine Mercy? In the words of Fr. Seraphim Michalenko, MIC, "Divine Mercy is when God loves the unlovable and forgives the unforgivable." When God's love encounters our misery and suffering, it takes action to alleviate it. This is mercy and is truly the answer to our suffering. It should give us the ultimate hope for those we have lost.

Now, I'll share with you the hope-filled reasons for their salvation, and later in Part Two, the means to hope for your healing.

CHAPTER TWO

The Church's Hope-Filled Teaching

GRAVE SIN, GREAT MERCY. Over the course of previous decades and even centuries, there has been considerable confusion over the Church's teaching, understanding, and practice regarding the eternal fate of one who has died by suicide. For example, as I asked at the end of Chapter One, doesn't the Church teach that people who kill themselves are automatically damned to hell? No.

Let's unpack this for a moment, beginning first with why suicide is so serious. In the Gospel of Mark, we read:

And one of the scribes came up and heard them disputing with one another, and seeing that he answered them well, asked him, "Which commandment is the first of all?" Jesus answered, "The first is, 'Hear, O Israel: The Lord our God, the Lord is one; and you shall love the Lord your God with all your heart, and with all your soul, and with all your mind, and with all your strength.' The second is this, 'You shall love your neighbor as yourself.' There is no other commandment greater than these" (Mk 12:28-31).

The problem is that sin, especially suicide, violates these commandments of loving God and neighbor. That is why the Ten Commandments prohibit us from doing such things. Sins against the first three commandments are violations against the love of God, and sins against the remaining seven commandments are violations against the love of neighbor.

So herein lies the issue: Suicide is immoral. Yes, it's a serious sin. Yes, it has the possibility to cause eternal separation from God, which is hell. Why? First, it is a violation of the love we are to have for God. Many times we fail to fully recognize that God is God, and we are not. We often choose to do our will, not His. He is the master of life, and we human beings are not. "We are stewards, not owners, of the life God has entrusted to us. It is not ours to dispose of" (*CCC*, 2280).

Second, suicide hurts our neighbor, which is a sin against the virtue of charity. All of us who have endured the loss of someone to suicide know the sort of trauma, pain, and grief that it causes for those left behind. I don't blame my grandmother for the trauma her suicide brought to our family. After all, she'd lived with horrible pain for such a long time that it's amazing she was able to endure it as long as she did. Still, her suicide deeply wounded those who loved her. I cannot help but feel hurt by the pain she brought to my family, especially to my father. Provoking so much agony in the lives of those a person loves is something very serious.

Third, suicide contradicts love of self (see *CCC*, 2281). Some people may respond, "Huh? Love of self? But isn't Christianity all about self-*less* love?" Yes, but that doesn't mean we shouldn't have a *right* love of self. In fact, we *should* have a proper love for ourselves. Has God not created us? Are we not lovable to Him? Some may have a hard time believing that God loves them, but if they understand that God created them out of love, and they remain in existence because God loves them, they may begin to believe it. God sustains all things in existence solely out of love, because His nature is to love. Once He has first loved us into existence, God *will always* love us because it is impossible for God to hate what He created — that would go against His very nature.

The question then is, should we not love that which God Himself loves? What sort of love of neighbor would the Golden Rule ("Do unto others as you would have them do unto you") be commanding if we didn't love ourselves at all? Clearly, then, suicide violates the basic duty of self-care, self-love, and stewardship of the body — a temple of the Holy Spirit — that was entrusted to us. The second of Christ's two great commandments is to "love your neighbor *as yourself*," not to love your neighbor "*instead of yourself*."

In light of these points, using the classic language of Catholic moral theology, we say that suicide is "grave matter." It is a violation of the Fifth Commandment: "Thou shalt not kill." Although it's understandable that a person undergoing great pain, whether physical, mental, emotional, or spiritual, may want to end that pain, suicide should never be thought of as a means to achieve that end. The desire to end pain is actually morally acceptable and even desirable, but the means we choose to end that pain may not be. Suicide, or other acts such as euthanasia, are examples where the end does not justify the means.

In light of the seriousness of suicide, it is correct that this sin is labeled as "objectively" grave matter. When looking at the act of suicide itself, we must understand that this sin may cause the loss of one's soul. However, in order to determine if the sin is also "subjectively" grave matter — definitively causing the loss of one's soul — more factors need to be taken into consideration. And all of these factors are known not to us, but to God alone. Thus, while suicide is objectively grave matter, it may or may not be subjectively grave matter.

That brings us to the central question of this chapter: If suicide (and assisting anyone in suicide) is a serious sin and should never be considered the answer to any problematic situation,[45] why isn't it necessarily damnable? Expanding on the idea above, there's a difference between committing a wrong act and being fully culpable, or *guilty*, of that wrong act.

Just think of the difference between a small child who throws a temper tantrum in the middle of the store and a grown man who starts punching people because they don't have the product he wants. They're both shouting, hitting people, and generally raising a fracas. But the grown man can cause a lot more damage and is a lot more culpable, or responsible, than the small child.

Why? Because he has *full knowledge* that what he's doing is wrong. Moreover, he has a strong, free, informed *will* that could and should restrain him from such bad behavior. Again, both the child and the man are objectively behaving badly. But the man is probably far guiltier than the child, unless impelled by some inexplicable reason to act in such a way. If that is the case, "subjectively" both the man and the boy may not be fully responsible for their actions — the boy because of his young age and the man because of some extenuating circumstance, such as mental illness. As mentioned, many times only God knows all the factors that are present when persons make the decisions that they do.

What this means is that there's a difference between a "mortal" and a "venial" sin, between a sin that has the capacity to damn because it *kills* grace in the soul and a sin that only *wounds* grace in the soul. As Scripture tells us, some sins are deadly and some sins are not (see 1 Jn 5:16-17).

We are saved by the presence of sanctifying grace in our souls, and by sharing in the divine life and love of God through that grace. We are damned if we knowingly commit mortal sin, which kills divine life and love in our hearts, and refuse to repent. But, as you may already know, God sends *no one* to hell. Those who go to hell, choose hell. Thus, there is only one way someone will go to hell, and that is to die in an unrepentant state of mortal sin. The *Catechism* states:

> To die in mortal sin without repenting and accepting God's merciful love means remaining separated from him forever by our own free choice. This state of definitive self-exclusion from communion with God and the blessed is called "hell" (1033).

It is also important to keep in mind that the Church teaches that three conditions must be present for a sin to be *mortal*:

1. There must be *grave* matter — the sin committed must be truly serious, such as sin against love of God or neighbor (adultery, for example);

2. The person must have *full* knowledge of the gravity of the sin;

3. And the person must commit the sin with full freedom of the will (one freely chooses it) [see *CCC*, 1857].

Likewise, the Church teaches that "although we can judge that an act is in itself a grave offense, we must entrust judgment of persons to the justice and mercy of God" (*CCC*, 1861). In other words, we can know that an act such as suicide is objectively grave and *may be* a mortal sin; however, we cannot know that it is *definitively* a mortal sin. This is because we don't know exactly what someone knew or didn't know about the seriousness of the act, or if their will was entirely free when committing it.[46]

When we consider the particular case of my own grandmother — and by extension, of the many who have died by their own hand — we must keep a few things in mind regarding whether or not her sin is "damnable": (1) We know that the act of suicide is objectively grave matter and a truly serious offense against love of God, neighbor, and self. (2) She may *or may not* have had *full knowledge* of the gravity of her action. (There is no way for us to know for certain.) But (3) did she really commit the act with full freedom of her will? Did she really *want* to take her own life apart from any undue influence and burden? I believe not. If this is the case, her sin was not damnable — and the same points apply to anyone else who has completed suicide.

The *Catechism* addresses this question directly, saying, "Grave psychological disturbances, anguish, or grave fear of hardship, suffering, or torture can diminish the responsibility of the one committing suicide" (2282). Read that again. Please, read and reread this declaration of Mother Church. Let it sink into your heart, as if coming from the lips of a tender, loving, and understanding mother. Our beloved's culpability, the responsibility for their action, may be reduced if they experienced "grave psychological disturbances, anguish, or grave fear of hardship, suffering, or torture." In the case of suicide, one could even argue that "torture" could apply to mental, not just physical, duress.

I believe that most suicides happen as a result of one or more of those conditions. It seems that my grandmother's did. She was in a prodigious amount of pain and had been for decades. She was depressed as a result of all that hardship. She had a well-founded reason to fear further suffering, because nothing was relieving her agony. In a way, you could say that she was both physically tortured (by her body, racked in pain) and mentally tortured by depression and the mental trauma resulting from estranged family relationships. Thus, I doubt if her suicide was done with full freedom of the will and that she really *wanted* to complete such a desperate act.

Maybe that is why the 20th-century Austrian visionary Maria Simma, when asked during an interview, *"What happens to [the souls of]* people *who have committed suicide? Have you ever been visited by these people?"* answered this way:

> Up to now, I have never encountered the case of a suicide who was lost — this doesn't mean, of course, that that doesn't exist — but often, the souls tell me that the most guilty were those around them, when they were negligent or spread calumny. ... These souls do regret their act because, as they see things in the light of God, they understand instantly all the graces that were in store for them during the time remaining for them to live ... In the end, what hurts them most is to see the good that they could have done but didn't, because they shortened their lives. But when the cause is illness, the Lord takes this into account, of course.[47]

Illness may often play a part in lessening the guilt of suicide, since many suicides are associated with some form of "mood disorder," such as clinical depression, which can lead to feelings of despair.[48] Depression can destroy a person's capacity to reason clearly, thus affecting their free will. Some sufferers have described their depression as like living in a thick, dark forest from which they felt helpless to ever find a way out. Undoubtedly, depression can so severely impair sound judgment that a person may be liable to do things they never would have considered otherwise.[49]

As we can see from the example of my own grandma, it's often the case that those who take their lives are suffering from an illness of some kind, be it emotional, physical, or spiritual. Their action is not necessarily a consequence of their character or how they are living their life. Suicide is often the final act of someone trying to end extreme pain or torturous anxiety. Someone trying to cope with suicidal feelings, or one who has succumbed to them, has usually been enduring some form of extreme depression, misery, or pain.[50]

When we have a pain in our back or foot, we almost always use that as an indicator that it is time to see a doctor, and we go. But people who have a pain in their mind and are depressed often ignore it and reason that they'll feel better tomorrow. Left untreated, depression can end up manifesting in tragic ways; if we take this point to the extreme, many cases can therefore be considered "death by depression" rather than "death by suicide." Those who attempt suicide are often unable to think clearly and rationally through their pain, despite the best efforts of loved ones and professionals to support them in their suffering.[51]

As mentioned previously, the inability to reason clearly affects a person's free will and has a bearing on whether or not their suicide can even be *considered* a mortal sin.

SUICIDE MAY NOT BE WHAT YOU THINK. To say that *suicide may not be what you think* is a surprising statement. In many places in this book, I use the word "despair" to describe why some people turn to suicide. Perhaps this is where a common misunderstanding about Church teaching on suicide comes into play — the belief that it is unforgivable because it results from despair. I believe this misunderstanding prevails due to confusion regarding the meaning of the word *despair*.

The popular understanding of despair is to "give up all hope." Regarding those who end up taking their lives, this may well be the case. They don't believe they can continue to endure the daily, torturous agony. They believe there is no "hope" for the end of their suffering or that it will be diminished in the slightest way.

My grandmother was an example of this kind of tormented person. After a herculean effort to deal with her trauma, anxiety, depression, and pain, she finally succumbed and gave up the fight. People in this type of situation have nothing left to give to the battle. They are completely spent. In a sense, they give up hope; they have *despaired*. Unfortunately, many of them have surrendered and ended their lives as a result. What we need to keep in mind is that this action should never be viewed as the solution to the problems we face in this lifetime.

This kind of despair, however, is most likely *not* the same kind of despair that the Church defines as the *sin of despair*. That sin, per se, is extremely serious and can jeopardize one's salvation. The *Catechism* informs us that the First Commandment is concerned with sins against hope, namely, despair and presumption:

> By *despair*, man ceases to hope for his personal salvation from God, for help in attaining it or for the forgiveness of his sins. Despair is contrary to God's goodness, to his justice — for the Lord is faithful to his promises — and to his mercy (2091).

Is this the same kind of despair that causes most suicides to take their own lives? I don't believe so. I don't believe my grandmother ceased completely to hope for her salvation from God — she simply wanted the pain to end. She wanted to be with God in Heaven, where there would be no more pain or suffering. Unfortunately, her means to reach that goal was the incorrect means.

Therefore, it seems that one can possibly "despair" in the commonly understood sense and still be saved. What, then, is the only *unforgivable sin*? Actually, it is the final impenitence that can come from despair — but from despair as the Church defines it, not despair as it is usually understood. The only unforgivable sin is refusing to repent and ask for God's mercy and forgiveness; it is adamantly refusing to allow any love into your heart, and basically refusing to love or allowing yourself to be loved in return. Thus, the essence of the only unforgiveable sin is not the emotional state of depression or despair that leads to that sin; what leads to that sin is simply an unrepentant heart so hardened that nothing can crack it.[52]

This is different from the type of despair experienced by my grandma and many others like her. For them, there is often a flicker of hope. There is hope that the pain will end and that God will have mercy on their souls for being unable to continue the struggles of their earthly journey. Most of these people are not choosing suicide as some damnable repudiation of God. Again, I don't think most suicides are making such a rejection. As we will see in the next chapter, even if they set out initially with no consideration of God's will, the Merciful Savior may touch their hearts with His grace in the last moment of their lives, and if they accept that grace, they may still be saved.

As Fr. Ron Rolheiser, OMI, states regarding those who have succumbed to suicide:

> We can be overpowered, and some people are, but that's not despair ... Beyond mental illness we can be defeated in life by many other things. Tragedy, heartbreaking loss, unrequited obsession, and crippling shame can at times break a heart, crush a will, kill a spirit, and bring death to a body. And our judgment on this should reflect our understanding of God: What all-loving, merciful God would condemn someone because he or she ... could not weather the storm? Does God side with our own narrow notions where salvation is mostly reserved for the strong? Not if Jesus is to be believed.
>
> Notice when Jesus points out sin he doesn't point to where we are weak and defeated; rather he points to where we are strong, arrogant, indifferent, and judgmental. Search the Gospels and ask this question: On whom is Jesus hardest? The answer is clear: Jesus is hardest on those who are strong, judgmental, and have no feeling for those who are enduring the storm. Notice what he says about the rich man who ignores the poor man at his doorstep, what he says about the priest and scribe who ignore the man beaten in a ditch, and how critical he is of the scribes and Pharisees who are quick to define who falls under God's judgment and who doesn't.

Only a [faulty] understanding of God can underwrite
the unfortunate notion that being crushed in life constitutes
despair.[53]

This should underscore the point that no one can judge a person
whose choice we cannot fathom. Because we now better understand the
mitigating circumstances surrounding suicide, the Church has recently
turned to a more personalist view in discerning the path of pastoral
care in these situations. The Church and society as a whole have begun
to see suicide more often as an act of desperation, of surrender to a
human condition that has made living unbearable, than as a cowardly,
purely selfish act, or as the sin of despair that is a total rejection of God.

As a result, the Church now tends to look upon those who
have taken their own lives with *compassion, not condemnation,* and
with *mercy, not judgment.* Masses and prayers are now offered for the
deceased, and they are often given full burial rites. This was not always
the case. In past times, it was commonly assumed that those who chose
to take their own lives were acting freely, and psychological duress was
not always taken fully into account. Those who had taken their own
lives were often denied Christian burial.[54]

Today, those mitigating factors are generally taken into account.
Therefore, the *Catechism* now teaches the following:

We should not despair of the eternal salvation of persons
who have taken their own lives. By ways known to him
alone, God can provide the opportunity for salutary repentance. The Church prays for persons who have taken their
own lives (2283).

This teaching will become an extremely important part of the
story that I will tell in the next chapter, so please make a mental note
of it. And to repeat the Church's teaching on sin: "although we can
judge that an act is in itself a grave offense, we must entrust judgment
of persons to the justice and mercy of God" (*CCC*, 1861).

Wow! This should give us some serious hope! Now, let's look at
the graces and the hope that the Church currently affords those who
have taken their own lives.

THE EXAMPLE OF CHRISTIAN BURIAL. The Church's stance on suicide didn't always seem to be so "hope-filled." But that perception wasn't actually due to her *teaching*; rather, it was due to her *practice* or *discipline.* One specific example is Christian burial. But how could this be?

Sometimes people are incorrectly scandalized that Church discipline has changed. For example, I can't tell you how many times I've met older, fallen-away Catholics who have said, "The Church began to lose me when they changed the rule of not eating meat on Fridays." But that's no more scandalous than the father of a family who changes rules for his kids as they grow older. For instance, when I was 7, I had to be in bed by 8 p.m. When I was 13, I could stay up until 11 p.m.

Church practices or disciplines, like family rules, can change. However, Church doctrine (or teaching) is a different matter. While Church discipline can change, Church doctrine *develops.* For instance, the Church's teaching on conscience and religious freedom developed with the Second Vatican Council as she pondered more deeply the dignity of the human person. This developed teaching, which was an advancement and not a break from previous teaching, changed the Church's practice regarding how she relates to people of other world religions and how she exercises Church discipline.

Consider again the example of not eating meat on Fridays. The Church's discipline still holds that there should be some penance every Friday, but now it is left to the personal conscience of each believer as to what specific penance is to be undertaken, which is more in keeping with the Church's developed teaching on the exalted role of one's conscience in the moral life.

Something similar happened to the Church's practice regarding who was allowed to have a Christian burial. As the Church pondered more deeply the findings of modern psychology and gained a deeper understanding of the human person, she made her *discipline* on this topic more lenient. As mentioned earlier, in the past, people who had died by suicide were many times not allowed to have a Christian funeral and were prohibited from being buried in the consecrated ground of a churchyard.

Why? Because, as discussed above, suicide was equated with the sin of despair and considered self-murder in almost every case, with the person who perpetrated the murder having no opportunity to repent.

(Still, even in the days when the laws were more stringent, the Church did take a person's mental state into account before actually prohibiting a funeral and burial.)[55] Thankfully, the *Code of Canon Law* no longer specifically mentions suicide as an impediment to funeral rites or church burial.[56]

So Catholic funerals are now permitted for people who have died by their own hand. Again, that is a change from past practice, and that's really important to emphasize. *Practice* has changed. A *discipline* has changed. But Church *teaching* (or doctrine) regarding faith or morals has not changed. Rather, it's developed as new insights and information have come to light. Thankfully, the Church's growth in understanding of the human person has affected her practice regarding who may be admitted to Christian burial.[57]

As such, the Church has formulated prayers designated for "One who has died by suicide" in the official book of rites, called the *Order of Christian Funerals*. These prayers reflect the Church's true belief in the possibility of salvation for those who take their own lives and will be treated in a later chapter in the section "The Christian Funeral: A Wake of Hope."

Now that we have seen how the Church views victims of suicide in a new light, it is time for us, too, to view them in a new light — the light of hope.

CHAPTER THREE

The Epiphany of Hope

OPPRESSED BY GUILT. Many who have lost someone to suicide often feel guilt, shame, or embarrassment. You may feel this way when coworkers and friends ask what happened to your loved one — I know I did. In fact, after my grandmother's suicide, I went so far as to request my parents not mention in her obituary that she "committed suicide," because I didn't want people judging our family.

Ironically, I am now embarrassed that I was so embarrassed back then. The reason is because feelings pass and change over time. Mine sure have. Feelings are temporary, which is why St. Ignatius of Loyola instructed us to never make major decisions in times of extreme consolation or desolation. During those times, we are usually motivated primarily by feelings that are only temporary. When we are mourning the loss of someone who has taken their life, these fleeting feelings may sometimes take over, causing us to blame ourselves for the death of our family member or friend. However, it's important to keep in mind that when these feelings arise, you should not put all the burden on your own shoulders.

In my grandmother's case, and in most suicides, when it comes to responsibility the only thing we can know for certain is this: Although some guilt may reside with us because of our neglect, the person ultimately "responsible" for a suicide (but perhaps not fully culpable, as we explained) is the person who died by suicide. We can't expect that we can always stop a person determined to end their own life. No matter what you did or didn't do, no matter what you said or didn't say, ultimately, the decision was in their hands, and they made it.[58]

Some of you who are reading this may realize that you had a strained relationship with the person you have lost, or that you said or did something that was at best unhelpful, and at worst, very hurtful. Conversely, others may know intellectually that you did the best you could, that you didn't cause your loved one to kill themselves, that you aren't to blame — and yet, you can't shake feelings of guilt or leave behind the "what ifs."[59]

During my high school years, I lived in the same town as my grandmother, so I knew very well that she was suffering. I knew she was in pain and depressed in her home. After her death, I often asked myself, "Did I visit her as often as I could have? Did I fail to do something that could have helped ease her pain? Could I have said or done something differently that could have changed the outcome?" These "what if" questions can unfairly haunt us for a lifetime if we let them.

Yes, it is true that I was very busy in high school and college. I was active in sports, worked hard at my studies, was socially active, and had a great girlfriend. In other words, I was a typical teenager immersed in numerous activities. So at the time it seemed there was really nothing more I could have done about my grandmother's pain. Thus I thought that I should not carry an extreme burden of unnecessary guilt.

Following her death, however, a cycle of guilt began to torment me. I started to think that I should have been more active in helping her through prayer and intercession. I began to feel remorseful, wishing I had been more present to her in small ways that took no time at all, such as giving her a kind word or a quick telephone call to let her know I was thinking about her. Many of you may share those same feelings, regretting how present you might have been to those you loved before they died. This cycle is vicious and, in many ways, can control us unless we place it in God's hands.

A great way to begin letting go of this burden is through the Sacrament of Confession. For some of you, it's the place where you can safely confess real sins and real guilt — even the worst sins, and where you can be given a penance in reparation, and receive absolution. For others, it's the place where you can take those guilty feelings and share them with a priest. You can tell someone honestly and confidentially how you are feeling. Whether or not there's anything to absolve, the priest can truly help you to unburden yourself. If there is something to absolve, you will then be objectively forgiven of your sins, regardless of how you may feel.

No matter what you did or didn't do; no matter what you said or didn't say; no matter what, God can and will forgive you. If the priest gives you absolution, there is no wondering, "Am I forgiven?" When the priest says you are forgiven, you are guaranteed forgiveness! Christ's words to His apostles tell us that the authority to forgive sins is given to the priest, so when he absolves you from your sins, you are absolved in Heaven (see Mt 18:18; Jn 20:21-23).[60] What an incredible grace God has given us through the Church!

So, if you're angry with someone who died by suicide, bring it to the confessional. If you're having a hard time forgiving them for leaving you this way, bring it to the confessional. If you're in shock that someone who was such an important part of your life is gone, and you're frantically trying to figure out how to carry on without them, bring that fear to the confessional.

You can be totally open and honest — it's all right. Whatever you say in Confession won't leave the confessional. That is a guarantee. That's part of the reason why my General Confession (which I will explain shortly) mattered so much to me, and led me to the next stage in the healing process of lamenting my grandmother's suicide. In order to get to that stage, I had to face my past.

One of the most difficult parts of my past, however, was accepting the fact that I could not change it. In fact, speaking of Confession, I have a confession to make: I don't even remember my grandmother's funeral. I know I was there physically, but I have no recollection of any specific details. I blocked it out, in a sense — a response that isn't uncommon for survivors in similar situations. Some of us may even feel guilty if we didn't shed tears at our loved one's funeral. In such a state of shock, this too is not uncommon. As we will see in Part Two, the grieving process takes time, and nobody handles the immediate impact of suicide in the same way. There is no "textbook answer" for how a survivor should respond.

The bigger problem for me, I believe, was that I don't think I even prayed for my grandma at her funeral, which really bothered me later on. In time, I would discover this was the root cause of most of my guilt. In fact, it gnawed at my conscience for a long time until it manifested in my life 10 years later. Thank God that I found healing for this guilt through an aspect of God's mercy that I never knew before — something that was so revolutionary that it changed my entire life and ultimately led me to the priesthood. Before I get to that, however, I should share a little about those 10 intervening years.

JESUS TOOK THE WHEEL. After my grandmother's death, I began the attempt to move forward with my life. Having earned my bachelor of science degree in industrial engineering, I began work in the automotive industry; later, I became an engineering manager at a Fortune 500 auto supplier in Detroit. It was a great job and I was making excellent money, but something still seemed to be missing in my life.

In 1997, I completed my master's degree in business administration (MBA) at the University of Michigan, thinking that would help me climb the corporate ladder and bring "happiness" to my life. Yet still, something was *missing*. What I didn't realize is that there's a difference between *earthly happiness* and *ultimate happiness*.

Happiness in one sense can come from this world. For instance, I was extremely "happy" when the Detroit Red Wings hockey team won four Stanley Cup championships in 11 years. And I was "happy" that I had nice material things and could pay all my bills. However, *ultimate happiness*, the fulfillment of all desires that I mentioned earlier, is something only God can provide — and that had eluded me. This ultimate happiness will only occur when we are united with God, and we can only do that when we fully love Him. And we can only love God if we come to know Him, because we cannot love what we do not know. So until I was able to start knowing God and loving Him, I continued to search in vain for true happiness in all the wrong earthly places.

The ancient Greek philosopher Aristotle talked about something called *telos* (pronounced "tell-os"), which is the purpose or "end" for which something is created. For example, when an acorn becomes an oak tree or a kitten becomes a cat (I am one of the few guys I know who actually likes cats), they have achieved their telos. So what is our *telos*? What is our purpose in life?

To understand our true purpose and end as human beings, it is helpful to turn to the Church's understanding of happiness. Remember, the *Baltimore Catechism* teaches that the purpose for which we are created is "to know Him [God], to love Him, and to serve Him in this world, and to be happy with Him forever in the next."[61] God always loves us, but it is only when we can come to know and love Him in return that we will be "ultimately happy." The *Catechism of the Catholic Church* defines happiness as "joy and beatitude over receiving the fulfillment of our vocation as creatures: a sharing in the divine nature and vision of God ... [Who] put us into the world to know, love and serve him, and so come to the happiness of paradise."[62]

Not understanding this at the time, and still seeking fulfillment from worldly sources, I resigned from my job, struck out on my own, and went to North Carolina to start my own business. I thought being my own boss and having unlimited earning potential while living in a beautiful location was perhaps the answer to finding true, or *ultimate*, happiness.

For a while, the move appeared to be very fruitful. After a few years of hard effort and a lot of stress, things started going very well for me, materially speaking. I had a home on beautiful Lake Norman near Charlotte, with my office building located on the other side of the same lake. Some days I even drove my boat to work. I was making more money than I ever had in my life, and I had plans to marry the prettiest girl in North Carolina. On paper, I had everything a young man could ask for, yet something was still missing — or rather, "Someone" was missing. Thankfully, that *Someone* decided to mercifully intervene in my life. It happened while I was driving home from work late one night.

During my commutes to and from my office, I'd noticed a church under construction in a rapidly growing suburb of Charlotte called Huntersville. When I would pass by, however, I would try to ignore the church. In fact, I would look in the other direction or turn on the radio to distract myself. I did whatever I had to do to avoid paying attention to that church. Why? Because I wasn't practicing my faith, and my conscience was beginning to bother me.

What was my response? My first response was to keep ignoring it, but something inexplicable kept pulling me toward that church.

Then, late one night in the early 2000s, as I was returning home from work, I again passed by this church, named St. Mark Catholic Church. Suddenly, it felt like I had lost my power steering. The wheel literally turned hard to the right, and my car rolled into the driveway leading to the parking lot. At the time, the church itself had not yet been built, and there was only a worship center standing on the grounds. I remember it was a bitterly cold night, pitch black outside, with no visible signs of life other than a few cars in the parking lot.

I sat for a moment and tried to assess the situation. However, I quickly became more preoccupied with my surroundings, feeling drawn to the building in front of me. I recall asking myself, "Why am I here?" I felt compelled to find out. Following my impulse, I exited the vehicle and went to each door of the worship center. It was a long, rectangular building. I tried to get inside — again, not knowing exactly why. All the doors I tried were locked.

Foiled in my plans to get in, I decided to leave. However, as I was walking back to my car, something kept nagging at me — there was one more door. It was on the far side, on the opposite end of the building, but something kept telling me to go check that door. Initially, I didn't heed the inspiration, and I started back in the direction of my vehicle. I got back into the car and placed the key into the ignition. I hesitated for about three seconds before starting it. Those three seconds, along with what I am about to explain in the next section, changed my life forever.

That last door kept pricking at my conscience. Finally, I couldn't stand it any longer. In the dark, I made my way back to the far door on the opposite end of the building. I tried the door. It was unlocked. I opened it and walked right into perpetual Eucharistic Adoration.

Now, it's a sad commentary on my Catholic formation that this was the first time I had ever been to Eucharistic Adoration in my entire life, even though I was born and raised a Catholic. It was on that night, standing before the Eucharistic Lord, that God poured His grace upon me. In an instant, I suddenly knew that Jesus Christ was present in the Eucharist: Body, Blood, Soul, and Divinity. In an instant, everything changed. In an instant, I started to return to God. But to get there, God had to literally pull me into that church parking lot. I've been amazed at that ever since.

Why? Because I worked in the automotive industry; my father worked in the automotive industry; my grandparents both worked in the automotive industry; and God got me to come back to Him by means of an automobile ... now that's divine humor for you!

"*PRAY THE CHAPLET FOR HER.*" After that experience in Adoration, I kept going back for more. I seemed "to catch fire," and I even started going to a Bible study, something I would have never contemplated prior to that time. A fire for the faith began to grow in my heart. But I knew there was one thing keeping that fire from becoming a blazing inferno: my sins. As I've mentioned, I had been living a rather worldly life up to that point, and I decided I needed to do a deep cleansing of my soul. So I discerned that I needed to make what is called in popular usage a *General Confession*.

Normally, in Confession we just confess the sins we've committed since our last Confession, and perhaps any grave sins we remember that we hadn't confessed before. In a General Confession, on the other hand, we mentally walk through our entire life, from our earliest recollection, confessing our sins as we go. We don't have to treat it as if we've never been to Confession before. It's just that a General Confession is a good spiritual practice to help us see our whole life in the light of God's grace and to recall and confess sins we may never have identified before. After all, time and maturity give us a new perspective on our past that we may not have had at the time we committed certain sins. In fact, we might not even have realized that they were sins at the time.

Bringing this clearer perspective into the confessional can make a huge difference in our walk with God. Like a good *particular examen* (a daily prayer practice designed by St. Ignatius of Loyola, guiding us to discern where and whether we've cooperated with God's grace during our day), a General Confession helps us to see all the times God's grace was actively working in our lives.

So in 2003 in North Carolina, I made an appointment and met with a priest for a General Confession. (Please don't do this kind of Confession unannounced with 15 people behind you in line on Saturday afternoon, because it can take a while!) My Confession helped me tremendously as I recalled and confessed sins from grade school up through my professional career. I began to feel the burdens lifted off my shoulders as I spoke. I continued to progress through my life until I got to the year 1993. It was then that I told the priest, "What happened in 1993 still bothers me."

"What bothers you?" he asked.

"My grandmother's death," I replied.

I told my confessor that I was not there for her and that I barely remember being physically present at her funeral. Even more disappointingly, I felt emotionally and spiritually absent from the whole event. I reiterated to him that I was so concerned about my college degree, my job, my new home, and my girlfriend that I don't even remember praying for her. I told him that this bothered me now because my grandmother had already been judged by God, and I'd missed my opportunity to pray for her 10 years ago, when she was sick and passed away. But what I really feared most arose from something I'd heard long ago about Church teaching — that if you die by suicide, you automatically go to hell — and at the time I still believed this to be true.

When I said this to the priest, he bluntly replied, "That's not what the Church teaches."

Like many people, I had always thought it was Church teaching, so the priest's words were a revelation for me — a revelation of sudden *hope*.

Then the priest said something that changed my life. He said, "Go home tonight and pray the Chaplet of Divine Mercy for the salvation of your grandmother's soul [see Appendix C for how to pray this prayer]. It's an incredibly powerful prayer, and when you pray it tonight, God can offer those graces from your prayers to assist her at the moment of her death and judgment. Your prayers now can help her to say 'yes' to God's offer of mercy back at that moment!"

I had never heard this concept before, so before I could even ask what the "Chaplet" was, I said, "Huh? Father, she's already been judged, so it's too late. She died 10 years ago! She's either in Heaven or hell now for all eternity, so there's nothing I can do for her at this point. At best, my prayers might relieve some of her time in Purgatory, if she even made it that far, but her eternal fate was already determined years ago. There's nothing my prayers can do about that now."

He said, "Look, God is outside of time. There is no *past* for God. There is no *future* for God. There is only one big 'eternal now' for God. Scripture tells us that 'with the Lord one day is as a thousand years, and a thousand years as one day' (2 Pet 3:8). Or as St. Augustine said, 'The eternity of God is exempt from the relation of time.'[63] In other words, God sees everything at one instant. From the beginning of time to the end of the world, He sees it all instantaneously, without compromising our free will. How do you think that the Virgin Mary was immaculately conceived?"

I responded, "By the Passion, Death, and Resurrection of Jesus Christ."

He said, "Yes, but how could Mary be immaculately conceived by those merits of Jesus' life and death when Jesus hadn't even been born yet? She was conceived 48 years before the Passion, Death, and Resurrection of Jesus! The answer is because God is outside of time."

He continued, "Regarding our prayers, God is *omniscient* (meaning all-knowing), so He knows every single prayer we will ever make, whether they are in the past, present, or future. And He is *omnipotent* (meaning all-powerful), so He can take all those prayers into account and apply them to any point in time, even to the past."

Grandma
1916-1993

My grandma holding me alongside my mother, Rosalie, and sister, Pamela.

My grandma with me, my sister, and my mother at a dinosaur park in Vernal, Utah, in 1974.

Back row from left: My dad, Charles; Aunt Susan; Mom; and Grandma. Front row from left: me on my cousin Mary's shoulders, Pam, and my cousin Joey.

Clare Emily Wood
Oct. 7, 1996-Aug. 10, 2014

Sammie Wood at her daughter's memorial.

Father Chris and Jason
signing books at the
Catholic Marketing
Network conference.

On the "EWTN
Live" set with Fr.
Mitch Pacwa, SJ.
Broadcast date:
July 17, 2019.

Answering viewers' questions regarding suicide.

EWTN LIVE | 1-800-273-8255
National Suicide Hotline
1-800-221-9460   205-271-2980

On pilgrimage up Apparition Hill in Medjugorje, 2019.

Jason's family – left to right: Chad (brother), Larry (Dad), Joyce (Mom), and Jason on a family pilgrimage in Medjugorje.

Charlie Bear — the furry companion of Jason's "circle of trust."

Jason, Fr. Seraphim, and Jason's parents, Joyce and Larry, at St. James Church in Medjugorje.

*M*Y *EPIPHANY OF HOPE.* This concept, that God is outside of time, was something I guess I had always known, but had never really thought much about. And I certainly had not known that it meant we could assist our loved ones at the moment of their death years ago with our prayers today. How could this be? I thought my grandmother had been judged and there was nothing I could do to help her now. Basically, I thought her eternal destiny had been sealed and my prayers were powerless to change that. Because I did not know the Church's real teaching on suicide (see Chapter Two), I was afraid that her eternal fate was dire because of what she did at the end of her life. What the priest explained to me next changed my whole understanding in an incredible way.

As my General Confession continued, my confessor kept emphasizing the importance of praying for my grandmother and how my prayers for her today can make a difference in her eternal fate, even though she died 10 years prior. He said, "You see, suicide is a grave sin, and your grandma will need all the help she can get. So, with God's grace, through your prayers, she may be better able to say 'yes' to God when He comes to her at the moment of her death."

The priest then began to explain why we can have this hope. He said, "In the *Diary of Saint Maria Faustina Kowalska*, she records that Jesus visited a despairing soul three times, giving the soul three opportunities to accept Him and to save it from hell (*Diary*, 1486). So we can infer that the souls of those we love have a similar chance to repent, to say 'yes' to Jesus and be saved, even if they appear to be in despair!"

At this point I knew nothing of St. Faustina or her *Diary*. Saint Faustina records the incident the priest related to me as a "Conversation of the Merciful God with a Despairing Soul." Here's an excerpt from that conversation (the full text is in Appendix E):

Jesus: **O soul steeped in darkness, do not despair. All is not yet lost. Come and confide in your God, who is love and mercy.**

— But the soul, deaf even to this appeal, wraps itself in darkness.

Jesus calls out again [a second time]: **My child, listen to the voice of your merciful Father.**

— In the soul arises this reply: "For me there is no mercy," and it falls into greater darkness, a despair which is a foretaste of hell and makes it unable to draw near to God.

Jesus calls to the soul a third time, but the soul remains deaf and blind, hardened and despairing. Then the mercy of God begins to exert itself, and, without any co-operation from the soul, God grants it final grace. If this too is spurned, God will leave the soul in this self-chosen disposition for eternity. This grace emerges from the merciful Heart of Jesus and gives the soul a special light by means of which the soul begins to understand God's effort; but conversion depends on its own will. The soul knows that this, for her, is final grace and, should it show even a flicker of good will, the mercy of God will accomplish the rest.

My omnipotent mercy is active here. Happy the soul that takes advantage of this grace (*Diary*, 1486).

So let's break this down a bit. In this encounter, Jesus is reaching out to a despairing soul.[64] Clearly, this is taking place at the moment of death, or else the grace He is offering would not be called "final" grace. That must mean that at this point, there are still opportunities for God's grace to lead one to conversion and repentance. Remember, the Church defines *death* as the moment of separation of the soul from the body at the end of one's life, not when all vital signs indicate someone has physically died.[65] Because the former may possibly come hours after the latter, one can better understand that during this "time," God can work miracles if He so chooses.

Here we have evidence in the writings of a canonized saint that God comes to the soul three times at the moment of death because He desires that all may be saved and none lost (see 1 Tim 2:4; see also 2 Pet 3:9). We can infer, therefore, that God comes to each and every person in their final moments (not *only* to those who have taken their own life, but to anyone who has died) and offers His saving mercy.

When the priest told me of that occurrence, I thought it was absolutely beautiful. But was it true?

The idea that Jesus comes to a soul three times at the moment of death, giving an opportunity for repentance no matter what the person has done, went contrary to what I had ever learned as a Catholic.

However, the priest assured me that this is what it said in St. Faustina's *Diary*, written by the first saint canonized by Pope John Paul II in the third millennium. He then added that if I had any doubts, I could verify that Church teaching also confirms it. As the *Catechism* teaches: "We should not despair of the eternal salvation of persons who have taken their own lives. By ways known to him alone, God can provide the opportunity for salutary repentance" (2283).

I replied, "Father, then we're good here, because there's no way my grandmother will not say 'yes' to Jesus when He comes to her and offers her the chance to repent. This is awesome! Thank you, Father, I think we are done here!"

He stopped me: "Hold on, there's a problem. You said your grandmother had fallen away from the Church. Do you know if she received the Sacraments before she died?"

"I don't know," I replied.

"The problem," he said, "is that your grandmother, for whatever reason, may have turned away from God in her life, not necessarily a conscious rejection, but one of not seeking Him. If this is the case, she may not recognize Jesus when He comes. That's what sin does. It puts a veil up between our soul and God's grace such that, although His grace and love continue to be showered upon us, we are not able to receive it. Our vision of God is blurred in a way."

The priest went on, "Your prayers can help to lift that veil so your grandmother may see God more clearly, and then she'll have a much better chance of recognizing God for who He is. Remember, she has to say 'yes'; you cannot say 'yes' for her. But you can certainly help. This is the whole point of intercessory prayer, no matter when it is made."

"Oh, man," I said. "I thought all was good, but now I am worried that she could be lost because she might not recognize Jesus when He comes. Because she wasn't seeking Him, especially at the end of her life, she may be unable to say 'yes' to Him at the moment of her death!"

"You didn't let me finish," he said. "She may not recognize Him *without* your intercessory prayers. But *with* your prayers, she'll be given more grace, grace allowed by the mercy of God. That is why Mary said at Fatima that there are many souls lost to hell — because there is nobody to pray for them!"[66]

"You mean I can get her out of hell?" I exclaimed. "I don't think that is what the Church teaches."

"No, I am not saying that at all! Hell is permanent, and *once* someone goes there, it cannot be undone. The grace of your prayers can assist her before that is ultimately determined, as if God is allowing them to be factored into the equation before her final fate is sealed."

He continued, "You see, your prayers are like a squadron of dive bombers coming in from now [2003] to aid in the war being fought for her soul back in 1993. They are coming in on the hands of Mary, back to your grandmother at the moment of her death but before her particular judgment (again, because God is outside of time). The graces from these Chaplets you pray for her tonight just may be enough grace for her to turn around and say 'yes' to God before her judgment, when otherwise she would not have."

I was hanging on his every word as his sentences pierced my soul.

"Your grandmother is like a wounded soldier who cannot help herself as she lies on the battlefield, in danger of [spiritual] death. Through your prayers, you come in like a fellow soldier, putting her on your shoulders and taking her to safety. Left alone like a wounded soldier in the field, she would die. Remember, she still has to cooperate and let you assist her, and she needs to choose to accept God's love as St. Faustina explained in her *Diary*. That choice is hers and hers alone. But your prayers, Chris, can offer your grandma the help she needs at that crucial time to choose to welcome God's saving grace."

He told me that God will always do His part, but we should also do our part (meaning praying for our loved ones). And what he had explained as "my part" made perfect sense. Then he finished by explaining what "God's part" is.

Again, he referred to St. Faustina's *Diary*. There, she tells us that Jesus comes to the soul who seems past all hope, who seems to be beyond the reach of God's grace:

God's mercy sometimes touches the sinner at the last moment in a wondrous and mysterious way. Outwardly, it seems as if everything were lost, but it is not so. The soul, illumined by a ray of God's powerful final grace, turns to God in the last moment with such a power of love that, in an instant, it receives from God forgiveness of sin and punishment, while outwardly it shows no sign either of repentance or of contrition, because souls [at that stage] no longer react to external things. Oh, how beyond comprehension is God's mercy! Although a person is at the point of death, the merciful God gives the soul that interior vivid moment, so that if the soul is willing, it has the possibility of returning to God (1698).

I said, "Father, this is absolutely amazing. What a grace! You mean to tell me that we have a God so loving, so merciful, that He will allow someone like me, who selfishly missed the chance to pray for his own grandmother at the time of her death, to help her now to possibly be saved, even though it is 10 years later?"

"Yes!" he exclaimed.

I was in awe at this discovery. All I kept saying was, "Wow!" Then and there, I truly had an *epiphany of hope* — an *epiphany of Divine Mercy!* Overwhelmed with joy, I cried out, "Father, all I know is that I need to spend the rest of my life spreading this message of God's mercy!"

At the end of this life-changing conversation, my confessor handed me a prayer card that explained how to pray the Chaplet of Divine Mercy. I had never heard of it prior to that day. Guess where that card was printed? It was from the National Shrine of The Divine Mercy in Stockbridge, Massachusetts, my future home as a priest. At the time, I didn't know that the Marian Fathers were *the* Divine Mercy priests. And now I am one of them! I have truly never been happier in my entire life. God knew what He was doing when He had me make that General Confession — He was bringing a greater good out of an objective evil. He even used my grandmother's suicide as a means of helping me discover my own vocation, where I would become an instrument of Christ's Divine Mercy to touch and heal other suffering souls.

But at the time, I only knew that I had to pray for my grandma. I knew what I was going to do. I went home that night, prayed the Chaplet of Divine Mercy for her, and suddenly I felt something. I felt that my prayer made a difference for her — a big difference. Maybe that Chaplet allowed her to enter Heaven, even though she had taken her own life years earlier, even though it had seemed there was no hope. Thanks be to God, I believe the Lord allowed His grace to flow through me to help my grandmother that night.

My encounter with the priest blew my mind, and still does to this day. It truly was my "epiphany of hope." If you've lost someone to suicide or in any other manner, it can be for you as well. The beautiful revelation here is that the grace the priest described to me is available to anyone who has died by any means, not just by suicide. This means that we can offer help and have hope for all of our deceased loved ones — through the grace and mercy of God, which can flow through our prayers. I pray this story gives *you* hope. Even though we may not have met personally, I assure you, you and your lost loved ones are in my prayers, my Mass intentions, and my heart.

Nevertheless, although this story may be inspiring to some, it may raise many questions for others. It is always good to answer such questions, so now let's look at a few of them; these are questions that I have been asked since I started telling this story.

IS THERE REALLY TIME? It is a fact that we humans tend to "anthropomorphize" God; that is, to project human qualities or behaviors upon a divine being. This is good when it helps us to better understand Him in ways we can relate to, because we are, in fact, human. There is a limitation to this way of thinking, however, because it may cause us to place human limitations on God, tempting us to believe that He is powerless in certain areas.

For example, I often hear people say, "But Father, in cases like suicide, there isn't time for God to make any such offer of mercy at the moment of death. If the person died quickly — if your grandmother shot herself — how was there time between pulling the trigger and her dying of the gunshot wound for God to make three visits to her soul? How did she even have time to repent, which is a requirement for salvation?"

To answer such questions, I point out that God can do more in a split second than you or I can do in a lifetime. He sustains all of creation in existence from moment to moment. And yet compared to the full extent of His power and might, that's nothing.

Incredible as it sounds, then, God could have communicated with my grandmother, or with your deceased family member, in the instant between their attempting suicide and their actual death. As we learned from the testimony of St. Faustina, He can have entire conversations with the soul at the moment of death, and as many have testified, He can show someone their entire life in an instant. As people often describe such experiences, "My entire life flashed before my eyes." Also, just think about your dreams at night. Upon awakening, it may seem like you saw events unfold in great detail over an extended length of time. But such dreams often last only a few seconds or minutes in real time.

When I am questioned about God's ability to communicate with a soul in an instant, I often ask, "Do you not think that in the time it took that bullet to travel three inches, causing my grandma's death, God couldn't perform a miracle?" Of course He could have! For that is the critical time during which we hope these souls have repented. In fact, they may have more time to repent than we realize, because we do not know when the soul actually separates from the body — it may be as long as a few hours after death. Remember, the *Catechism* states that "by ways known to Him alone, God can provide the opportunity for salutary repentance" for souls who fell victim to suicide (2283).

I found an example of another saint who bore witness to just such a final act of repentance in the case of a suicide, so I would like to quickly share it here.

Saint John Vianney (1786-1859) was a priest at a small country church in the town of Ars, France. He transformed it from a place devastated by Enlightenment ideas and local hedonism to a great center of piety and devotion, helping to restore Catholicism in the wake of the French Revolution. Vianney helped foster all of this through endless hours in the confessional, a life fraught with suffering but marked by miracles, and tremendous love of Our Lady.

In 1856, a woman came to Ars. She had just lost her Godless husband and was despairing because she thought he must be in hell. As St. John Vianney was walking from his 11 o'clock catechism class toward the church to hear confessions, he stopped next to the lady and said to her, "He is saved!"

The lady was visibly shocked. The holy priest repeated it twice more and then explained to her, "He is in Purgatory and you must pray for him. Between the parapet of the bridge and the water he made an act of contrition." Vianney told her that the Virgin Mary had secured that grace for him because he sometimes joined in his wife's devotions to the Blessed Virgin Mary.

The woman later explained to another priest who had accompanied her on pilgrimage to Ars:

> I was in black despair because of the tragic death of my husband. He was an unbeliever, and my one object in life was to bring him to God. I did not get the time. He com-

mitted suicide by drowning himself. I could only think of him as lost. Oh! Were we never again to meet? Now you heard what the Curé d'Ars told me more than once: "He is saved!" So I shall see him again in Heaven![67]

It really is possible that someone who *chose* to end their own life can also *choose* to repent and accept God's mercy. There's real hope. It should also be pointed out that the man in this instance was an unbeliever, yet he was saved in an instant in part by the faith and devotion of his wife. Thus, we can do the same for those we love. However, please don't come to the conclusion that, because you are suffering and God is merciful, taking your life is the answer. This may be the sin of presumption and can possibly lead to eternal separation from God. Please don't ever take that risk!

CAN I MAKE A DIFFERENCE? Yes. The perfect example of this is the Gospel story where Jesus heals the paralyzed man (see Mt 9:1-8; Mk 2:1-12). Four men wanted to bring their friend to the feet of Jesus because they believed He could heal the man. The crowds in the house, however, were too large to permit them to reach Him. Undeterred, they lowered the sick man on his bed through the roof down to the feet of Jesus.

They had faith, and with faith, Jesus says we can move mountains. When they got the man to Jesus, He immediately healed him. But what did Jesus say? Did He credit the paralytic's faith as the reason for his healing? No. Scripture says, "And behold, they brought to him a paralytic, lying on his bed; and when Jesus saw *their* faith, He said to the paralytic, 'Take heart, my son; your sins are forgiven'" (Mt 9:2; emphasis added). It was because of the faith of the four men that Jesus was able to work this miracle. So *your* faith can help those God places on your heart who are in need of healing and even salvation. Jesus wants to bless every person in every way possible, even if it is through someone else! **But we need to believe.**

God doesn't automatically bring a greater good out of evil. In fact, evil usually just breeds more evil. Think, for instance, of the fact that people who are bullied often become bullies themselves. Or think of the evil we're dealing with in this book, the evil of suicide. Studies show that such an act often leaves other evils in its wake: more acts of suicide, broken marriages, alcohol or drug abuse, loss of faith.

In short, evil often leads to an ongoing cycle of evil.

Here's one thing, however, that can break that cycle of evil: Divine Mercy. As we've learned, God has the power to bring greater good out of evil, and that power is called Divine Mercy.

But again, the power of Divine Mercy to bring good out of evil is not automatic. It requires something on our part, something that unleashes its power.

What is it?

It's called our faith, also known as *trust*.

Here's how one of my fellow Marian priests reflects on the idea that faith and trust unleash the power of Divine Mercy:

> Why couldn't Jesus work many miracles in his hometown of Nazareth? (See Mk 6:5.) Remember that? All he could do was small miracles, like maybe healing somebody's ingrown toenail. But why couldn't he work the big ones? It was because of *people's lack of faith*. Think of it! The all-powerful God-man, the one who walks on water, casts out demons, and heals the deaf and the blind — *that great man*, in a certain sense, is *powerless* when we don't give him our faith! But it's faith, it's *trust*, that unleashes the power of his mercy. That's why St. Thérèse so emphasized trust. That's why Jesus asked St. Faustina to paint an image of Divine Mercy with the signature, "Jesus, I trust in you."[68]

So why does Jesus want us to trust in Him? Why does He want us to have faith? So He can have mercy on us. It's so His mercy can bring not just good out of the evil in our lives, but an even greater good.

But will we let Him? Will we give Him our trust?

Those are key questions.

Of course, a tragedy as terrible as suicide can test our faith and make it difficult to trust in God. So if we are struggling with unbelief, what do we do? Again, we can turn to Scripture. In Chapter 9 of the Gospel of Mark, the father of a boy troubled with an unclean spirit cried out to Jesus, "Lord, help my unbelief!" (Mk 9:24). Why did he bother to do this? Because he had *hope*, an expectation, that Jesus would help him — help him to believe. That is the power of hope. Hope is the key to help us deal with the life-altering tragedies we are forced to endure.

*H*OW IS THIS POSSIBLE? How then can we make this claim that our prayers are effective, regardless of when they are offered? As the priest in North Carolina told me, one reason is because God is *omniscient*, meaning He is "all-knowing" and has knowledge of every prayer we will ever pray before we pray it. The *Catechism* states, "To God, all moments of time are present in their immediacy. When therefore he establishes his eternal plan of 'predestination,' he includes in it each person's free response to his grace" (600). Or, as well-known philosopher and author Peter Kreeft states, "All time is simultaneously present [to God] in eternity, as all the events in the novel are present in the mind of its author."[69]

The other reason is because God is *omnipotent*, meaning He has the power to take those prayers into account and apply them to the past, present, or future. For example, Jesus said it was the prayers of St. Faustina, which she made 1,900 years later, that helped Him to endure His bitter Passion (see *Diary*, 1212; 1214; 1224). These instances show that our prayers can transcend time. Our prayers for someone even after their death can make a difference in their salvation, not just shortening their time in Purgatory, because God doesn't receive our prayers "after" that person dies. For Him, my grandmother's suicide didn't happen over a decade ago; everything is present to Him instantaneously.

It certainly doesn't seem fitting that our God, who is all-loving and all-merciful, would render our heartfelt prayers ineffective simply because of the date that we offered them. When my grandma took her own life, I was not actively practicing my faith, nor was I even slightly aware of the full impact of God's love and mercy. Later, when I returned to God and the Church, I prayed for her with a disposition that was far more sincere than it would have been had I prayed 10 years earlier. Maybe that is why God allowed it to happen that way. Based on my experience, I find it entirely plausible and totally commensurate with His benevolence that God would accept my prayers for her salvation regardless of when they were made.

Great figures of the Church, such as Padre Pio and Dorothy Day, have stated that our prayers reach "outside of time." Great Christian writers such as C.S. Lewis and modern-day theologians and philosophers such as Fr. Robert Spitzer, SJ, Jimmy Akin, and Peter Kreeft have all reiterated this belief. (For a detailed explanation, please see "Theological Underpinnings: Eternity, Time, and Power" on page 179.)

Therefore, at this point we will continue our discussion presuming this point to be true. As we will explain more thoroughly in the "Theological Underpinnings" section, although it is not appropriate to pray for certain things in the past, other things are entirely appropriate.

For now, I want to share one more story about how the Lord convinced me that this amazing hope is not too good to be true. I hope it will convince you, as well.

*T*OO GOOD TO BE TRUE? Even after I found peace with my grandmother's death, became a priest, and started to share my story with others who were grieving, I had some doubts. I was tempted to think that such hope was "too good to be true." But then, once again, God stepped in.

It happened when I was conducting a parish mission, which is an event where a priest or other speaker about the Christian faith comes to a church to speak about God to the lay faithful. During that particular mission, I began to experience fear and doubt about whether or not my grandmother was really helped by the Chaplet of Divine Mercy I had prayed so many years after her death. Thinking my actions could make a difference in her eternal fate began to sound like pride to me, and like St. Faustina, I was challenged by the evil one.

In fact, my doubts became so strong that I decided I was no longer going to share the story at any of my talks at parishes or conferences. I said to myself, "Maybe I imagined the feeling that she was okay after all, and maybe she didn't even make it to Heaven." And then I prayed, "Lord, if this is real, and You want me to speak about it, then You'll have to show me." I don't encourage anyone to ever challenge God like that, but the good Lord knew I was struggling, and He does allow us to question Him. It didn't take long for Him to answer.

On that very same day I decided not tell my story, I was walking from the rectory to the church to give the final talk of that three-day parish mission when something astounding happened. As I was crossing the parking lot, a young woman was getting out of her car, and our eyes made contact. I smiled, but I could see that she was thinking as she looked at me, as if she couldn't determine whether she knew me or not. Then she asked, "Are you Fr. Joseph?"

I answered, "Well, sort of. That is an honorary title given to the director of the Association of Marian Helpers, and I currently serve in that role. My name is Fr. Chris Alar."

She then asked, "Are you the priest who made a CD and talked about his grandmother committing suicide?"

Surprised she would bring that up after I had just decided not to tell my grandmother's story, I answered, "Yes, I am."

She asked, "Do you have a moment? I really need to speak with you."

I agreed, and she began to tell me an amazing story. She said, "Father, like you, I lost someone close to me who took their own life. It was my uncle four years ago, and like you, I was struggling greatly because I didn't pray for him at all before he died. I figured it was too late to do anything about it when later I realized my grave lack of charity."

I responded, "Please don't beat yourself up. Those things happen when sometimes we are trying to get our own lives back in order."

"No," she said. "You see, I was just selfish and didn't pray for him. And like you did with your grandma, I thought he went to hell and that it was partly my fault. Then I heard your talk, and I immediately began to pray for him. I prayed many Divine Mercy Chaplets, hoping it would help."

"That's wonderful." I said.

"Well, this is what I wanted to tell you. A few months ago, I went to a priest for Confession. He is known to be a mystic and perhaps can even read souls. I'm not sure. Well, anyway, I finished the Confession and as I was getting ready to leave, he said to me, 'By the way, your Chaplets worked.'"

"'Excuse me?' I replied. He said, 'Didn't you have an uncle who took his own life four years ago?' I immediately responded, 'Father, how did you know that? I never mentioned that.' He answered, 'Well, he is now in Heaven.' Trying to hold back my shock, I questioned him, 'Father, how do you know?' He replied, 'I just saw it.'"

I was completely blown away by her story. After all, just a few hours earlier I was greatly doubting my own story. And just a few minutes before, I'd determined not to tell it again unless God showed me a sign that it was true, that my grandma and other souls can be helped at the moment of death through prayer, even if our prayers come years later. Well, here was the astonishingly clear confirmation. God is good! God is *merciful!*

Now at this point, you may be saying, "That's great for you, Fr. Chris, but I don't have that assurance for my loved one." And maybe you're not in a place to feel very much hope. Maybe you're wondering if there even is a God, just like my grandmother may have wondered in the midst of all her pain and trials.

If that is your situation, please know God is real and He is always calling out to you and me. The hope for me came when I finally answered Him, wondering how I could possibly doubt His mercy after so many experiences of His goodness in my life. I found consolation in the mystical experiences of St. Faustina, who also experienced doubt in God's goodness, even though she was having *visions* of Him! She relates her own doubts, saying, "I have wasted so many of God's graces because I was always afraid of being deluded" (*Diary*, 143).

It is not uncommon for us to question and even doubt God's infinite mercy. One reason for that is because it's humanly impossible to comprehend the "breadth, length, height and depth" of Christ's divine love that "surpasses knowledge" (Eph 3:16-20). But Jesus wants to give us every assurance imaginable that we can *trust* in Him. Trust is the key to unlocking the floodgates of His mercy. As He communicated to St. Faustina (emphasis added):

> **My daughter, speak to priests about this inconceivable mercy of Mine. The flames of mercy are *burning* me — *clamoring* to be spent; I *want* to keep pouring them out on souls; *souls just don't want to believe in My goodness*** (*Diary*, 177).

We doubt because it is difficult to comprehend that God's goodness can be so extraordinary. In fact, His mercy is so great that often we find it *unbelievable*. Indeed, His love for poor sinners is so great as to be inconceivable. He tells St. Faustina, **"The flames of mercy are burning Me — clamoring to be spent"** (*Diary*, 50). He *wants* to pour out mercy upon us and those we love more than we can even believe.

But we need to believe. We *can* believe, because God is truth and He cannot lie. He is Mercy itself. That is why we call Him "Jesus, the Divine Mercy." Let us receive these clamoring flames of Divine Mercy by saying, "Yes, Jesus, I believe. I *trust* in You! Pour out Your mercy all through my loved one's soul! Have mercy on them. Have mercy on us and on the whole world!"

CHAPTER FOUR

The Spiritual Theology of St. Faustina
— A Theology of Hope

Now I want to share with you some basic, yet very interesting and relevant theology behind this "epiphany of hope" — theology that's well worth your consideration. According to the priest I met during my General Confession, because God is outside of time, we can still pray now for those we care about to receive grace at the very hour of their death and judgment to aid them in their salvation. (Again, for a much deeper explanation of this theology of the eternity of God, please see the section titled, "Theological Underpinnings: Eternity, Time, and Power," on page 179.)

Although this is an amazing concept, another question you may be asking is this: "Why, then, do we need to pray for people if Jesus comes to each person with an offer of mercy at the hour of their death?"

That's a hugely important question. As we've discussed, the priest gave the answer, "So we can assist them, that they may be better able to say 'yes' to Jesus through the grace of our intercessory prayers." While this is certainly true, it may be helpful to dig a bit deeper into the teaching of St. Faustina, who also discloses to us an "epiphany of hope." Her teaching will enrich us with even more hope for those we miss so dearly. In this chapter, we will explore Faustina's spiritual theology, a "theology of hope" for those who have died suddenly or tragically by any means.

A WITNESS TO HOPE. Perhaps the greatest biography ever written on Pope St. John Paul II is *Witness to Hope* by George Weigel. And I believe it may not only be the greatest biography, but the best title for that pope, because at his core, he really was a *witness to hope*.

And why was St. John Paul II such a witness to hope? I believe that St. Faustina had something to do with it. Like St. John Paul II, St. Faustina was Polish, and from a worldly perspective, both lived in the wrong place at the wrong time. But from God's perspective, they were exactly where He wanted them to be at the right time. The Poland of John Paul and Faustina's day suffered the highest percentage of casualties during the worst war in human history, World War II. Amidst that terrible darkness, however, Jesus gave a light to the world, a powerful message of hope.

It began with Faustina. Just before the war, Jesus appeared to this Polish nun and gave her not a new Gospel, but a message that accentuates the heart of the Gospel: God's merciful love, the understanding that God does not abandon us in our suffering and darkness but pours even greater mercy into our hearts and lives if we accept it. I believe the heart of this hope-filled message is best captured in the Image of Divine Mercy (the painting based on St. Faustina's vision of Jesus, included on the inside back cover of this book), which depicts our Risen Savior stepping into our darkness while inviting us to pray, "Jesus, I trust in You." That's Divine Mercy: God coming toward us, meeting us in our suffering, and acting to do something about it.

John Paul II loved the message and devotion of Divine Mercy. In fact, he went so far as to say, "The Message of Divine Mercy has always been near and dear to me. ... [My personal experience of Divine Mercy] I took with me to the See of Peter and which in a sense forms the image of this Pontificate."[70]

If the Divine Mercy message *forms the image* of John Paul's Pontificate, as depicted by his very own words, then this magnanimous contemporary figure cannot be understood apart from the message of Divine Mercy. John Paul saw it as a special gift of God for our time; thus he promoted the message to the whole Church, and people throughout the world have fallen in love with it because of the hope that it brings. And it's especially hope-filled for people like us, people who have lost someone dear to us. Let's now look at it more closely as a spiritual theology of hope, one that depends on prayer and relies on Divine Mercy.

*T*HE NECESSITY OF PRAYER. Earlier, I cited a passage from St. Faustina's *Diary* that demonstrates the incredible power of intercessory prayer. The passage is so vital in giving us hope for the salvation of those we've lost that it is worth reading again:

> I often attend upon the dying and through entreaties obtain
> for them trust in God's mercy, and I implore God for an

abundance of divine grace, which is always victorious. God's mercy sometimes touches the sinner at the last moment in a wondrous and mysterious way. Outwardly, it seems as if everything were lost, but it is not so. The soul, illumined by a ray of God's powerful final grace, turns to God in the last moment with such a power of love that, in an instant, it receives from God forgiveness of sin and punishment, while outwardly it shows no sign either of repentance or of contrition, because souls [at that stage] no longer react to external things. Oh, how beyond comprehension is God's mercy! ... Although a person is at the point of death, the merciful God gives the soul that interior vivid moment, so that if the soul is willing, it has the possibility of returning to God (1698).

Let's look also at another passage where Faustina is communicating with a dying soul to obtain Divine Mercy for them:

I often communicate with persons who are dying and obtain the divine mercy for them. Oh, how great is the goodness of God, greater than we can understand. There are moments and there are mysteries of the divine mercy over which the heavens are astounded. Let our judgment of souls cease, for God's mercy upon them is extraordinary (1684).

Let's now consider these two passages together. The context of these passages is that Faustina was *praying* to obtain Divine Mercy for dying souls. She sees how incredible God's mercy and goodness is — far beyond our comprehension. It is literally "greater than we can understand." So great and unfathomable is God's goodness and mercy that "the heavens are astounded." Think about that. Angels and saints, principalities and powers, all of the heavens are *astounded* by the greatness of God's "extraordinary" mercy. This should give us great consolation and unquestionable hope. God's mercy is not only "greater than we can understand," but it is also beyond the comprehension of *all the heavens.*

Looking further at the passages together, Faustina insists that we cannot possibly judge a dying soul even when it may appear "as if everything were lost." The soul cannot show reactions externally in this moment of dying, but interiorly, "God's mercy upon them is extraordinary." However, we can and must *pray* to obtain this incomprehensible mercy for dying souls for the instant of their death. That is part of our intercessory role as members of the Body of Christ.

Now let us add yet one more powerful *Diary* passage related to obtaining mercy for dying souls at the moment of death, given by Jesus Himself as He pleads with Faustina:

> **Pray as much as you can for the dying. By your entreaties obtain for them trust in My mercy, because they have most need of trust, and have it the least. Be assured that the grace of eternal salvation for certain souls in their final moment depends on your prayer** (1777).

Jesus asks Faustina to "pray as much as [she] can for the dying" and explains that *trust* is the key that unlocks His unfathomable mercy. He also discloses to Faustina that dying souls often lack trust in His infinite goodness, and that her prayers hold the key to unlocking the trust necessary for them. Wow!

Now let's look at all three power-packed passages together. Faustina sees that her "entreaties" on behalf of the dying open the floodgates of Jesus' Divine Mercy to such a degree that His grace is "always victorious" when she intercedes for them. (Note: Although our intercession is no guarantee of another's salvation, we will later explain why we have this hope.) Our intercession can be so powerful that "the soul, illumined by the ray of God's powerful final grace, [can] turn to God in the last moment with such a power of love that, '*in an instant*,' it receives from God forgiveness of sin and punishment."

This illumination of God's final grace in "that interior vivid moment" is so compelling that the soul responds with "*a power of love*" that completely purifies it of both sin and any punishment due for sin. It is as if the soul were just reborn anew in an *instant* to new life, as in Baptism or when we receive the graces promised through observing the Feast of Divine Mercy Sunday.[71] *This* is inconceivable goodness. *This* is grace beyond comprehension. *This* is unfathomable Divine Mercy!

Thus, we can make the claim that the soul turns to God in part because of our prayers. That is why Jesus commanded Faustina to pray for the dying, saying, "**[E]ternal salvation for certain souls in their**

final moment depends on your prayer" (*Diary*, 1777). God's goodness is so great that He is begging us to assist these souls. We can trust in the power of our prayers to help release the graces from God that the dying need for salvation. We can unlock these graces so that the souls of our loved ones can be cleansed. We can make a difference!

Why? Because our prayer is both an *act of love* for our neighbor (the second greatest commandment) and an *act of trust* in God (an expression of the first and greatest commandment). God sees our love for our neighbor and our love for Him and takes that as an open door, the giving of our consent to all the graces He wants to pour out upon us, and especially upon a soul at the last hours of his or her life. As an Anglican preacher once put it, "Our prayers do not persuade God to help us, they permit Him to." His response, mercy, is a response of His love for us. God is justice, and His justice demands an appeal to His mercy for the sins of every person, yet His mercy is so great that He is moved by *our* love on the dying person's behalf! It is then up to that soul to accept the graces that come from God as a result of our appeal.

By way of example, I believe in my heart that my grandmother most certainly accepted those graces when they were offered to her. God saw the love in my heart for her and was moved by this love. He sees the love we have for both our loved one and for Him and, in His inherent Fatherly goodness, is moved to "shower graces" upon them, which (along with their acceptance of those graces) also satisfies all justice required for their sins, including the sin of suicide. For as St. Peter teaches us, "love covers a multitude of sins" (1 Pet 4:8).

So, for some souls, the reception of God's final grace in their final moments really does depend on our prayers, as Jesus said, because it depends on love. And as St. Faustina did in answer to Christ's request, we should pray for them as much as we can. However, if you're like me, this may tempt you to scrupulosity. In other words, you may feel a pressure to overdo it, pray too hard, and feel guilty if you're not praying all the time.

Wait. Did I just say pray "too hard?" Is that even possible?

Yes, it is. According to Jesus' words to St. Faustina, we actually *can* pray too hard and overdo it:

After Holy Communion today, I spoke at length to the Lord Jesus about people who are special to me. Then I heard these words: **My daughter, don't be exerting yourself so**

much with words. Those whom you love in a special way, I too love in a special way, and for your sake, I shower My graces upon them. I am pleased when you tell Me about them, but don't be doing so with such excessive effort (*Diary*, 739).

Pondering this amazing passage, we should be struck again with the immensity of Jesus' love and mercy. Here, He expresses His love for those whom Faustina loves and showers His graces upon them for her sake, showing how much He loves Faustina. We, too, should find hope and be consoled about the fate of those we love and have lost. Jesus loves those whom *we* love, and how much more? Remember the Gospel story of the four men and the paralytic (see Mt 9:1-8; Mk 2:1-12). That is why, if you have faith, even if the level of faith of your loved one is unknown, there is still hope!

Let's pray for those whom we have lost, then, but let's do so with peace, knowing that those we love in a special way are also loved by Jesus in a special way. We don't need to exert ourselves so much, causing ourselves anxiety and stress, wondering if we've said enough prayers for them or if our prayers were long enough. God steps in, and *He* provides the grace for those souls, even when we are tired and fatigued and sometimes unable to pray any more for them.

It's important to emphasize that the grace comes from God, not us, but that He uses us and our prayers in His work of salvation. How does that happen? The Catholic faith teaches that it is through the Sacraments that we are incorporated into Christ's Mystical Body. In a certain sense, as we will explain later, when we pray, Jesus prays. He is the mediator between God and man (see 1 Tim 2:5). In the Sacraments, we are closely joined to Him. We can see this in Jesus' words to Saul of Tarsus (the future St. Paul) when he was hunting down and killing Christians. Jesus said to him, "Why do you persecute *me*?" not, "Why are you persecuting *my followers*?" (see Acts 9:4; emphasis added).

Hopefully these concepts now make sense, and we now understand that our prayers *can* be very efficacious no matter when they are made. But *what* should we pray?

WHAT TO PRAY? The concept of God's "timelessness" and the help that prayer offers our loved ones is especially applicable to the Mass. In his book *Spirit of the Liturgy*, Cardinal Joseph Ratzinger (the future Pope Benedict XVI) states that at the Mass, the roof of the Church opens up in a way, and Heaven and earth are connected as at no other time. The angels and saints ascend and descend, and "sacred time" (God's time) is united with "physical time" (our time). At Mass, you are spiritually present at Calvary when the one sacrifice of Christ for the salvation of mankind is actually occurring.[72] Although you are physically present in a church pew in the 21ˢᵗ century, you are spiritually present at an event that occurred almost 2,000 years ago!

Ratzinger continues by stating:

> Now if past and present penetrate one another in this way, if the essence of the past is not simply a thing of the past but the far-reaching power of what follows in the present, then the future, too, is present in what happens in the liturgy ... Past, present, and future interpenetrate and touch upon eternity.[73]

Since the Mass is the most powerful form of prayer, it's a great practice to have a Mass, or even several Masses, said for your deceased family and friends. It's also good to attend Mass and pray for the salvation and repose of the souls of those God places on your heart. You can do this especially during what one of my friends, Fr. Michael Gaitley, MIC, calls the "supercharged moment" of the Mass.[74] What moment is that? It's the *concluding doxology*, when the priest at the altar takes the Body and Blood of Christ into his hands and offers it up to the Father with these words:

> Through him, and with him, and in him, O God, almighty Father, in the unity of the Holy Spirit, all glory and honor is yours forever and ever. Amen.

This moment is supercharged because, at the Mass, Jesus is giving Himself — Body, Blood, Soul, and Divinity — into our hands: literally into the hands of the priest and spiritually into the hands of all the lay faithful who are uniting their own sacrifices to the offering of the priest at the altar. Together, each in our own way, we offer Jesus' infinite sacrifice of love on our behalf to the Father. That's the power of the Mass. It's Jesus' own sacrifice of love in our hands, held up to the Father, and the Father cannot resist such a perfect offering.

United with Christ and in Christ, we are inserted into the life of the Most Holy Trinity — a communion of triune love!

The Mass really is the most perfect form of prayer in all its tenderness and intimacy. Prayer is nothing but communion with God, and the prayer of the Mass is perfect communion with God, because it is the prayer and sacrifice of the Son to the Father, by the power of the Holy Spirit with us in union with God. That is why Fr. Edmund McCaffrey, former abbot of Belmont Abbey in Charlotte, North Carolina, used to describe the Mass as "God offering God to God." It is God the Holy Spirit, offering the sacrifice of God the Son, to God the Father, in atonement for our sins and the sins of the whole world. This is why the Mass has infinite value and provides the most fruitful opportunity to pray for our deceased loved ones.

Masses and perpetual enrollments in a spiritual benefit society such as the Association of Marian Helpers are some of the most effective means of interceding for our loved ones, both living and deceased. Such enrollments allow us to share in the graces of other association members' prayers and good works. (For more on this, see Appendix G.)

*T*HE CHRISTIAN FUNERAL: *A WAKE OF HOPE.* Liturgical theology contains a principle referred to in Latin as *lex orandi, lex credendi,* that is, "the law of prayer [is] the law of belief." In other words, the way we pray affects what we believe; likewise, what we believe affects the way that we pray.[75] The Church's official liturgical book of prayer for those who have died is called the *Order of Christian Funerals,* which is used for the vigil (wake), the funeral (with or without Mass), and the committal (burial) of the deceased. The opening and closing prayers of these rites provide two options for "One who died by suicide." They reveal a great deal about the Church's hope for the deceased and for those who mourn their death. Let's consider each of these prayers and then unpack their significance.

One who died by suicide

God, lover of souls,
you hold dear what you have made
and spare all things, for they are yours.
Look gently on your servant N.,   [*Hope for them*]

and by the blood of the cross forgive his/her sins and failings.
Remember the faith of those who mourn   [*Hope for you*]
and satisfy their longing for that day
when all will be made new again
in Christ, our risen Lord,
who lives and reigns with you for ever and ever.
Amen.[76]

OR

Almighty God and Father of all,
you strengthen us by the mystery of the cross
and with the sacrament of your Son's resurrection.
Have mercy on our brother/sister N.   [*Hope for them*]
Forgive all his/her sins and grant him/her peace.
May we who mourn this sudden death be comforted
and consoled by your power and protection.   [*Hope for you*]

We ask this through Christ our Lord.
Amen.[77]

First, let's consider the structure of these liturgical prayers. They are addressed to Almighty God, who is the "lover of souls" and "Father of all." The first prayer expresses that He "hold[s] dear" what He has made and "spare[s] all things" because they are His very own. Both prayers exemplify the Church's belief that God is a loving Father who desires eternal life for all His children. The prayers then offer petition on behalf of two entities: the one who has died by suicide and those who mourn. (Notice that the structure of this book parallels the structure of the Church's prayer — hope *for them* and *for you*.) Finally, the Church makes its petition through Christ with confident hope and trust in the merits of His Cross.

Now let's consider some essential content in these prayers. First, they ask for the forgiveness of (all) the sins of the one who died by suicide. We might not give much thought to the significance of this petition at first glance, since we have grown accustomed to pray for God's forgiveness. However, these prayers seek the Father's forgiveness of sins for one who is already dead, presumably for three days or more if it's a funeral Mass, at which time the soul is already separated from the body. The Church holds that a soul undergoes personal judgment immediately upon death. As the *Catechism* states:

Each man receives his eternal retribution in his immortal soul *at the very moment of his death*, in a particular judgment that refers his life to Christ: either entrance into the blessedness of heaven — through a purification or immediately — or immediate and everlasting damnation (1022; emphasis added).

According to the Church's understanding, the soul would have received its particular judgment at the moment of bodily death, therefore already determining its eternal fate — Heaven (whether by way of Purgatory or not) or hell. But with these funeral prayers, the Church is interceding for the soul post-death and post-judgment. The prayer of the Church cannot "change God's mind" regarding the particular judgment of a soul. The key point to emphasize is this: The Church's prayer for one who died by suicide can only be effective — or even make sense — *if God is eternal and outside of time, and our prayers can make a difference applied at the moment of death*. If the salvation of our loved one who died by suicide is not a possibility, then this prayer is pointless and essentially invalid, since it is offered post-judgment.

Another significant point to note about these prayers is that they can be effective in obtaining forgiveness because of the mystery of the Cross of Christ. The Cross is the means by which we can have hope in the Father's mercy upon those who died by suicide. The Cross makes atonement for all sin and merits the infinite mercy of the Father and lover of all souls. It offers the hope of eternal life with the loved one for those who mourn, to "satisfy their longing for that day when all will be made new again in Christ, our risen Lord." For this reason, Mass(es) offered for those who have died by suicide offer incalculable hope for their salvation and are particularly appropriate and effective when celebrated in the funeral rites for their repose.

The hope provided through the Church's intercession for the deceased in their final moments is not limited only to souls who die by suicide; it is offered to *all* who die *by any means*. As we have already established, the Church (we) can offer intercessory prayer back in time to avail a soul of the graces necessary to recognize God's final act of mercy in its passage through "the gates of death." Let's consider the "General" option offered in the Liturgy that can be used for the opening and closing prayer at a funeral Liturgy for anyone who has died.

> Holy Lord, almighty and eternal God,
> hear our prayer for your servant N.,
> whom you have summoned out of this world.
> Forgive his/her sins and failings
> and grant him/her a place of refreshment, light, and peace.
> Let him/her pass unharmed through the gates of death
> to dwell with the blessed in light.[78]

In this prayer in particular, three points stand out: 1) God is addressed as "almighty and eternal," demonstrating the Church's faith that He is omnipotent and timeless; 2) the soul has already been "summoned out of this world" by God, meaning that it no longer exists in its former earthly state; and 3) the Church petitions the almighty and eternal God to "forgive his/her sins and failings" and to "let him/her pass unharmed through the gates of death to dwell with the blessed in light." This third point demonstrates that the Church petitions God for forgiveness of "sins and failings" *prior* to the soul's passage into eternity. But again, note that the person is already dead when the Church makes this prayer on their behalf.

Given these three points from prayer option 3 in the rite, we can firmly conclude that the Church's liturgical prayer applies to the soul at the moment of death. In this way, sins can still be forgiven and the soul can gain eternal life "with the blessed in light." The Church's intercessory prayer in a funeral Liturgy offers an epiphany of confident hope to all who have lost a loved one — by any means — and confirms the intercessory power of our prayers back in time for their salvation.

*P*RAY *WITHOUT CEASING.* Saint Paul exhorts us to "pray constantly" (1 Thess 5:17). But let's face it: We can't be attending Mass 24-7. However, we can have our hearts disposed in an attitude of prayer throughout the day, striving to be in continual communion with God. And there is another way in which we can connect with the Liturgy by way of what I call a sort of "extension" of the Mass. It involves the Rosary and the Chaplet of Divine Mercy, both of which are a form of participation in the Paschal Mystery of Christ that we celebrate in every single Liturgy. Let me explain.

The Mass is divided into two parts: The Liturgy of the Word and the Liturgy of the Eucharist. What is the nature of the Liturgy of the Word? It is a meditation on Scripture. And what is the Rosary? It, too, is a meditation on the life of Christ in Scripture (not a "bunch of Hail Marys," as is commonly thought). For this reason, I recommend praying the Rosary as an extension of the Mass.

After the Liturgy of the Word, the Mass enters into the Liturgy of the Eucharist. This is when the priest offers *sacrifice*. Now think about what the Chaplet of Divine Mercy does. It allows you to exercise your common priesthood, bestowed on you in Baptism, in an offering of sacrifice (see *CCC*, 1546-1547). Remember, through your Baptism, you share in the three offices of Christ: priest, prophet, and king. And a priest offers sacrifice.

I've seen the power of the Divine Mercy Chaplet. I've heard the testimonies. Do you know who it's especially powerful for? The dying. In a rare communication from God the Father to St. Faustina, He said:

When this chaplet is said by the bedside of a dying person … unfathomable mercy envelops the soul, and the very depths of My tender mercy are moved for the sake of the sorrowful Passion of My Son (*Diary*, 811).[79]

Does this mean that prayers *not* said by the bedside of a dying person have no merit in God's eyes? I wasn't there "by the bedside" of my grandmother when she died. While it is extremely powerful and grace-filled to be physically present and praying as someone is dying, I don't believe our Lord meant to say that any prayers not uttered in the immediate presence of the dying are without merit. Remember, God is pure spirit, and by His nature He is outside of space, not just outside of time. He is present everywhere simultaneously, and therefore, the same concept regarding time can apply to space, meaning we can make those prayers from anywhere. As St. Faustina said:

It sometimes happens that the dying person is in the second or third building away, yet for the spirit, space does not exist. It sometimes happens that I know about a death occurring several hundred kilometers away. This has happened several times with regard to my family and relatives and also sisters in religion, and even souls whom I have not known during their lifetime (*Diary*, 835).

I wasn't physically present praying for my grandmother when she shot herself, but since God is outside of space as well as time, in some way I *can* be there, praying for her and obtaining the grace for her to accept God's mercy. You can be there for your loved one, too, no matter how, where, or when they died.

Now I would like to make one last point about Faustina's spiritual theology of hope through prayer.

OFFER IT UP. When I was young, if I started to complain about something, my mother was quick to tell me to "offer it up." I used to think it simply meant I was not going to get what I wanted, and so I learned to really dislike that comment, especially when it meant that I didn't get to go fishing! But what she really meant to tell me was, "Don't just stand there and complain; you can actually put your suffering to good use!"

What use? The salvation of others! You see, just as our prayers can assist those who have died, so too can our sufferings. It's a teaching of our faith that we can make atonement for our sins and the sins of others. (Remember the words of the Divine Mercy Chaplet, which we pray "in atonement for our sins and those of the whole world.") We see this at Fatima, for instance. Mary encouraged the shepherd children to pray and offer sacrifices for others, telling them, "Pray, pray very much. Make sacrifices for sinners. Many souls go to hell, because no one is willing to help them with sacrifice."[80]

We've already covered the supercharged moment of the Mass and the Chaplet of Divine Mercy, so it should now be clear where and how we can offer up our prayers. But we can also unite our *sufferings* to the suffering of Christ who sacrificed Himself on the Cross for the salvation of mankind. That is what the Mass is all about — we are spiritually present at Calvary while Christ is on the Cross paying the debt for every person's sin. (Remember, one of the reasons Christ had to die on the Cross is because the penalty, or wage, for sin is death [see Rom 6:23]. When we sin, we deserve to die; but when we accept the saving grace offered by Christ, He pays the debt of sin for us, dying for our sins so that we may live. It is neither a re-enactment, nor do we actually re-crucify Christ. He made that sacrifice on the Cross once and for all on Golgotha.)

Because the sacrifice of Calvary is mystically made present at every Mass throughout the world, and is offered up to the Father by the priest, we can also offer up our sufferings, uniting them to that moment of offering at Mass or when we pray the Chaplet. This is an incredible gift given to each of us. Jesus empowers us to participate in His own work of salvation, actively helping Him to save others through our own prayers and suffering.

In their book *Now is the Time for Mercy*, Fr. George Kosicki, CSB, and Vinny Flynn explain the great importance of our participation in Jesus' mission:

> [T]he saving work of Jesus is not finished. He "needs" us to cooperate with His work of redemption and bring His mercy to this generation. This kind of partnership involves a sharing in His sufferings in order to share in the saving work of mercy. This is the meaning of the cross of suffering. It is salvific; it is precious. Don't waste it![81]

By offering our prayers and sufferings for others, we can be partners in Jesus' redemption — we can be "co-redeemers" in our own limited way. This is confirmed in Jesus' words to St. Faustina, recorded in her *Diary*:

> **I thirst. I thirst for the salvation of souls. Help me, My daughter, to save souls. Join your sufferings to my Passion and offer them to the heavenly Father for sinners (1032).**

So why does God allow such pain and suffering in the world? It is because suffering is redemptive and God wants to bring a greater good out of it, namely the salvation of souls. As St. Paul said, "Now I rejoice in my sufferings for your sake, and in my flesh I complete what is lacking in Christ's afflictions for the sake of his body, that is, the church" (Col 1:24).

You might ask, "What could possibly be lacking in the sufferings of Christ?" The answer is, "Your sufferings!"

Everyone is suffering in one way or another. You may be carrying the unfathomable weight of the loss of someone very close to you. That's an incredibly painful, yet powerful suffering to offer up for their benefit — not only for their salvation, but for their release from Purgatory. Isn't it amazing how our sorrow for them can actually be useful to them through our prayers when we offer it up?

According to many saints, suffering can have as much or even more spiritual power than some other forms of prayer. According to words popularly attributed to St. Teresa of Avila:

> One must not think that a person who is suffering is not praying. He is offering up his suffering to God, and many a time he is praying much more truly than one who goes away by himself and meditates his head off, and, if he has squeezed out a few tears, thinks that is prayer.

It's extremely important to realize this point. When we are in the midst of suffering, everything may feel very dark; thus, we may not have the capacity nor the awareness to offer up our suffering as prayer at that exact moment. Suffering often blurs our vision and weakens our will. But when we gain clarity, we can consciously will to apply, or *reapply*, that suffering for the needs of others.

It is not my intent to detract from the redemptive power of our suffering in the present moment, as that is when it can be most powerful. However, following our earlier point about God's eternal omniscience and omnipotence, we can conclude that He also has the knowledge and power to apply the merits of our suffering to any moment in time. If we are nearly incapacitated during extreme moments of pain and suffering and not even thinking about consciously offering it up, I don't believe that our loving God will refuse to accept our offer of suffering at a later time when we are more consciously aware and physically able to do so.

This all stems from the mercy of God. In essence, what we bring to the table is our trust that He can in fact do this, and even this trust itself is a grace from God. For example, if you had horrible headaches when you were younger before they were finally cured by a doctor, you can still offer them up now for the conversion and salvation of your children (especially if your children were the ones giving you the headaches!). Perhaps you didn't understand the concept of "offer it up" when you were 25, when you had the headaches, but now you do. Do you think those offered sufferings have no value in the eyes of God today? I believe they most definitely do. From the writings of St. Paul, we know that absolutely nothing of value is lost on God, for, "We know that in everything God works for good with those who love him, who are called according to his purpose" (Rom 8:28).

At one point, Jesus said to St. Faustina, **"You are not living for yourself but for souls, and other souls will profit from your sufferings. Your prolonged suffering will give them light and strength to accept my will"** (*Diary*, 67). It is staggering to think that we can offer our suffering to assist our loved ones, even at the moment of their death, in the same way we can offer our prayers — and we all have a lot of suffering to offer!

Unfortunately, it seems that few people see any value in their suffering and miss opportunities to receive many graces because they may disdain suffering, rather than offering it up. Some even believe their sufferings are vindictive punishments from God. Certainly our sufferings are a consequence of the sins of mankind, but the last thing God wants to do is punish us for them. Instead, He wants to bring a greater good out of them.

When I go to visit certain nursing homes, it often breaks my heart, primarily because of the suffering of the residents, but even more so because few of them seem to see any value in their suffering. Many of them seem to believe they are simply a burden to society and their families (nothing could be further from the truth), and consequently they often lose all will to live. Unfortunately, they are missing out on a great opportunity — their suffering can be redemptive, and is extremely powerful when offered up to God for the salvation of souls.

That is why St. Faustina wrote: "If the angels were capable of envy, they would envy us for two things: one is the receiving of Holy Communion, and the other is suffering" (*Diary*, 1804). This is incredible! However, most people are apathetic about Holy Communion, and most people want nothing to do with suffering. Yet these two things are exactly what the angels would envy us for, firstly because they are spirits and can't receive the Eucharist, and secondly, because they have no bodies, they cannot suffer like our Lord did. Both of these graces unite human persons most intimately with Jesus — in a way that the angels cannot be united to Him.

*W*E NEED TO DO OUR PART. That doesn't mean we are supposed to happily endure all suffering, or that we are never supposed to seek relief or the alleviation of pain. Not at all! Jesus Himself asked for the cup of suffering to be taken away during His Agony in the Garden. (Remember, however, that He asked that this be according to the Father's will, not His will.) Jesus also accepted help on the way to

Calvary and experienced moments of relief as well. He did not endure His Passion as a superman, but rather as a man, as someone with a family and friends, as someone who needed help, who needed other people along the way.

Therefore, the Church has been proactive in establishing hospitals and innumerable works of mercy, all in order to help people recover from pain and illness, to meet their physical needs and alleviate their suffering. Catholics are in fact called to avail themselves of the right and proper natural and supernatural means to relieve suffering. All of these are manifestations of the Holy Spirit as the "Comforter." His comfort gives strength to the one suffering. Sometimes, such comfort will take away suffering; other times, as it did for Jesus, that comfort will strengthen one to suffer in peace.

So when you're ill or in pain, talk to your doctor. When you're feeling emotionally or spiritually barren, talk to a counselor,[82] priest, or spiritual director. Seek professional assistance in your grief if you or those whom you trust think it would be helpful. Seek the help you need, when you need it. Christianity isn't stoicism; we are not called to simply suffer silently, never uttering a peep when something's wrong. No, we are meant to be members of the family of God, and family members take care of each other.

Another point to remember is that you don't have to wait for help — it is available immediately. Local Outreach to Suicide Support (LOSS) Teams "now exist across the United States and internationally and act as models of what can be created within a faith community when a suicide death occurs. Lay ministers and faith leaders may be activated to compassionately and nonjudgmentally appear on the site of the suicide to provide information and resources, as well as show love and support to the newly bereaved. What better way to demonstrate the love of God in those moments of intense pain and isolation."[83]

Have you ever wondered why certain tragedies seem to have such radically different effects on different families? Why do such life-changing events bring some people closer together, but tear others apart? I believe the answer is that many people are afraid to seek help. This fear must be overcome. To try to "go it alone" is contrary to our communal nature and often leads to an inability to function socially in the same way after a tragedy as before it.

Organizations such as churches, support groups, and other social groups can be of tremendous help to us. Look at how Jesus Himself sought help during His life. It was not by living in isolation, but rather surrounding Himself with a "support" team of men and women. God often uses others to help us in our suffering, and He encourages us to seek such support. To quote opinion writer Ericka Andersen from the *Wall Street Journal* once again concerning the role of religious practice in suicide prevention:

> The Bible says that "the dwelling place of God is with man." Put another way, churches are nothing but people meeting together for spiritual communion. The setup might look simple, but a house of worship is a transcendental doctor's office offering preventive care, support group therapy and a healing hope.[84]

Now that we've considered these points about the value of suffering — and also our need for help and healing from suffering — let's consider another point. Why is suffering so misunderstood in our culture today? A major reason is that many in the modern world don't even believe there's life after death, so suffering has no eternal value to them.

But there is life after death. Death, judgment, Heaven, and hell — known as *the Four Last Things* — are for real.

CHAPTER FIVE

The Hope of Life after Death – The Four Last Things

People in our day are hungry for hope. That may explain the smashing success of *Heaven is for Real*, a book about a boy who purportedly had an experience of Heaven and came back to tell the tale.[85]

Now, the title of the book gets it right. Heaven is for real, and knowing that it's real is a source of our hope for those we have lost in this lifetime. Because, for Christians, the afterlife involves more than just Heaven, we should also cover all of what are traditionally called "the Four Last Things" — death, judgment, Heaven, and hell — because they're all very real.

*D*EATH. Death is spiritually defined as the separation of the soul from the body at the end of our physical life. It is a topic that many of us want to avoid, even for those with faith. It means the "end of the world" as we know it — that is, the mode of being that is familiar to us. It is a step into the unfamiliar, a realm that we have yet to experience. As human persons, we often fear the unknown, so we avoid it. We commonly joke that there are only two certainties in life, death and taxes; however, most of us probably spend much more time thinking about our taxes than we do our inevitable death. But let's face it: While some may evade taxes, *no one* evades death. Should we not spend a little more time thinking about what death actually means for us in the big picture?

We are all going to die. Period. This reality of death should beg the question, "What does my *life* mean?" What is the purpose of my existence, the purpose of my *be-ing*? This is the most fundamental question we can ask ourselves — one we should all take seriously. After all, it is a matter of *eternal* life and death!

Remember, God's intended purpose in creating us is so we can enter into a communion of love with Him and with one another. This communion entails the gift of oneself to God and to others in relation, in imitation of the three Persons of the Trinity. Disordered self-love, or selfishness, brings a lack of harmony into our relations. This is why St. Paul tells us that "the wages of sin" is death (Rom 6:23). Adam and Eve fell into original sin, and with that descent into spiritual death came physical death as well, when mankind turned from love and trust in God toward love and trust in self instead.

Yet, in many ways this "punishment" is a gift of mercy from God. Why? Because death reorients us to consider the reality of our finite existence. We are mortal beings, incapable of surviving death on our own. The reality of death reorients us to the reality of our relation with God and with others. Just as importantly, it accentuates our need for God in restoring order and harmony in our lives and our world. It cuts to our core as human persons and directs us toward our eternal purpose and the fulfillment of our deepest longings and desires.

Death, however, is not what God had intended for us from the beginning.

"But how can that be?" you may well wonder. "Isn't everything that happens under the providence of God? In other words, if it's not *willed* by God, the all-powerful sustainer of everything that exists, how could it happen?"

Good questions indeed. And they have a fascinating answer. Let's begin by making a quick distinction: There's a difference between God's *ordained* will and His *permissive* will. His ordained will is for the good — it's what He wants to happen and what He intended for us from the beginning. It did not include suffering and death as we know it, as the result of sin. However, that ordained will includes the choice for His creatures to have free will, and with that comes the possibility of sin and its consequences of suffering and death. That means God, despite His power, chooses not to directly control our every action out of love.

He wills the good, but He also wants His creatures to be able to choose freely. He wants us to love from our own free will. Thus, in His permissive will, He allows us to make our own decisions, good or bad, and He allows the consequences that come as a result of those decisions. Therefore, in a sense, He *has* to permit the existence of evil. It's not what He intended, but it's the price He paid for our freedom, for our ability to love Him as free creatures rather than simply to obey Him as robots or slaves.

It was once said that God took the greatest risk of all in giving us free will out of love, because with that came the chance that we would sin, hurt others, and choose not to love Him in return. Human freedom, then, holds the answer to one of the most common questions in the world: *Why does a good and loving God allow evil in the world?* The answer given above may be hard to understand at first, but it makes sense if you take the time to really contemplate it.

God did not will that physical death be the end of any of us; it is a consequence of our sin. However, He will use the consequences of our sin (evil) as the occasion to bring a greater good out of it. In fact, the prayers of the Mass underscore this point, where it states in the *Roman Missal*: "... for your faithful, Lord, life is changed not ended, and, when this earthly dwelling turns to dust, an eternal dwelling is made ready for them in heaven."[86]

Indeed, God made us for life, not for death. He made us for communion and for love, not for separation from our loved ones. Death is thus rightly called an "enemy" in Scripture, the last enemy to be overcome (see 1 Cor 15:26). However, as a result of Christ's victory over death, Christians believe in the resurrection of the dead and the life of the world to come. This belief gives us hope for the future — if we can somehow see beyond our present pain, which oftentimes we do not. That earthly pain reaches its zenith when we lose someone to death and we are left behind. That is when our faith and perseverance is tested; we have to go on in this valley of tears, enduring loss after loss until finally we ourselves are called home by the Lord of Life.

Therefore, Christians are not forbidden from grieving the death of our loved ones. We are not bound to some fake happiness, to some smiling denial of the sorrow tearing at our hearts. Jesus Himself wept over the loss of Lazarus (see Jn 11:35) and mourned over Jerusalem, which was so blessed and yet so often unfaithful (see Mt 23:37-39). Grief over death is a part of life.

As we will discuss in Part Two, we can and should grieve the dead. When we do, it's not a lack of faith or a betrayal of their memory. Rather, it's a normal part of our human condition. Sometimes, our sorrow is magnified by the fact that those close to us may have died tragically and suddenly, as is the case with most suicides. Many people do not have the grace of a happy death. My grandmother did not.

So where's the hope for them?

Their hope is in the Crucified and Risen Jesus. Our hope is in a God who loved us so much that He sent His Only Begotten Son to live as one of us, to suffer alongside us, and to die for us to pay our penalty for sin — meriting for us eternal life. He rose to life, defeating death, and continues to come to us through the Church and her Sacraments. He can also come in a more direct way to souls at the moment of their death, as we saw in St. Faustina's *Diary* (see 1486 and 1698).

Reading the words of Jesus to Faustina about the depths of His mercy for the souls of the dying, we can come to one conclusion: There's hope. No matter how someone died, no matter how far beyond hope they seem to be now or at the hour of their death, there's still hope for their salvation. Death is simply the door to that new life.

*J*UDGMENT. We believe that God is the perfect, omniscient judge. As mentioned earlier in this chapter, we further believe that He made us all to have free will, and having free will means that our actions have real consequences. So when we die, we undergo what's called the "particular judgment." God judges us each individually, and we enter into the state of eternity that our choices on earth merit: Heaven, hell, or Purgatory (see *CCC*, 1021).

It may sound strange to say it, but I find hope in God's judgment.

Why? First of all, because God, who is perfect justice, will take *everything* into account. Think back to Chapter Two, where we discussed the conditions for mortal sin. It's not enough for someone to have committed a gravely wrong action for them to be damned. That act must have been performed with *full knowledge* and *full free-dom* of the will for it to be damnable.

God is a just judge. He knows everything and sees everything. Nothing is hidden from Him, so He has perfect knowledge of my grandmother's pain. He was present to her through every agonizing night and every dark day. As I stated earlier, I doubt that the just and loving God whom I serve is likely to say that my grandmother made her fatal decision with full freedom of the will in the sense that she *wanted* to commit the act.

I may be wrong, as nobody knows for certain other than God and my grandmother herself, but I believe her depression and pain drove her to take her life, and that God's justice did take that into account when she came before Him for judgment. Yes, God is the judge, but He also defends the soul against the devil, the accuser of us all (see Rev 12:10).

In that role, the devil will bring up anything that he can against us to condemn us. However, pious tradition tells us that at the time of our judgment, Satan can only bring up unconfessed sins. Confession not only cleanses us of our sins in the eyes of God, but it removes us from the hands of the devil through the power and merits of the Precious Blood of Jesus Christ. Indeed, Scripture says, "As far as the east is from the west, so far has he removed our sins from us" (Ps 103:12; NABRE). So if all your sins are forgiven in the confessional, there is nothing the devil can justly accuse you of at the time of your judgment!

But that's not the last of my reasons for hope. I've got one more, one great, crowning reason for my hope, and that's our Blessed Mother, Mary Immaculate. She is the Spouse of the Holy Spirit, who descended upon her, and she welcomed Him so completely that she was with child by the Holy Spirit. Your mother and mine is the Spouse of the Paraclete, the same God who desires us to be with Him forever in eternal bliss.

Also, Mary is the Queen of Heaven by right of being Mother of Christ the King, the Son of David. Do you know what the role of the queen mother was in the Davidic royal family, the line from which Jesus came? The role of the queen was to serve as an advocate on behalf of the people, including the poor peasants, and this is exactly who we are when we stand before the throne of God. She was the voice of mercy in the court of the king. That is why, when we offer prayers or sufferings for our loved ones, we should place them into the hands of Mary and ask her to take them to Jesus. Since she is the Mother of the King, and an advocate on behalf of the poor (us), we can know with confidence that she joins her prayers with ours, enriching them with her merits, so that our prayers become hers also.

It doesn't stop there. When Mary said *yes* to being the Mother of Jesus Christ, she also said *yes* to becoming the Mother of the Church. We are all members of the Mystical Body of Christ, and the Mother of "Jesus the Head" must also be the Mother of the Body, as well.

In the previous chapter, we spoke of the efficacy of our prayers on behalf of one another, particularly at the moment of death. We pointed out that God sees the love that we have in our hearts when we pray for our neighbor, and He responds to this love by bestowing graces upon those for whom we pray. Love responds with love. God, the great lover of souls, allows His grace to flow through our love for our neighbor to impart the particular graces they need, including the grace of a willing disposition to receive His grace. In a way, God makes Himself dependent upon our faith and trust in Him to open the floodgates of His mercy.

Mary is the Mother of Mercy. Who loved Jesus as much as she did? And what heart trusted in His word more than hers? Sometimes we lack the necessary trust in God to allow His grace to become effective in us. But Mary *never* lacked trust. Consider the Visitation, when Mary went out to meet Elizabeth, her cousin, who was pregnant with John the Baptist. Upon hearing the voice of Mary, Elizabeth was filled with the Holy Spirit. The babe leapt in her womb, and she exclaimed, "Blessed are you among women, and blessed is the fruit of your womb! ... And blessed is she who *believed* that there would be a fulfillment of what was spoken to her from the Lord" (Lk 1:41-45; emphasis added).

Also consider that once when Jesus was preaching, a woman from the crowd "raised her voice" and exclaimed, "Blessed is the womb that bore you, and the breasts that you sucked!" (Lk 11:27). Yes, Mary was indeed blessed as the chosen vessel to bear and nurse our Lord, but Jesus emphasized that the even greater cause of her blessedness was her faith and trust, proclaiming, "Blessed rather are those who hear the word of God and keep it!" (Lk 11:28). Mary always believed God's Word, even when it seemed incomprehensible that she would bear the Son of God as a virgin.

So we can be assured that when we come before God for our particular judgment, we will have a mother who is present with a Heart full of trust in His mercy. When we lack the necessary trust in God's unfathomable love and mercy for us, Mary intercedes for us with the love and trust of her own Heart. As our mother, she supplies the trust that we lack to help us at the hour of our death. Our loving, perfect, most tender mother is part of our "defense team," interceding for us before the throne of God.

Maybe now you'll see why I have so much hope in the judgment of God: I have His mother on my side. We all do. If we've shown her the slightest sign of love or devotion, or if someone has asked her to help us, then we've got the most powerful intercessor in the created world on our side, asking God for mercy on our behalf.

Knowing that this is true, we who mourn should pray the Rosary for those God puts on our heart, asking Mary's intercession for them. (To learn more about the power of the Rosary, see Fr. Donald

Calloway's book *Champions of the Rosary: The History and Heroes of a Spiritual Weapon.*)[87]

Finally, I have hope in the judgment of God because His justice is always conditioned by His merciful love, and His justice serves His mercy. In fact, Jesus told St. Faustina, **"The greater the sinner, the greater the right he has to My mercy"** (*Diary*, 723). Since that's the case, we need not fear an "unfair" or harsh judgment from God, because even with a multitude of sins on our soul, God's mercy will be abundantly poured out if we are truly sorry for them. In such a case, God's mercy certainly trumps His justice![88] Then we will make it to Heaven, even if it is by way of Purgatory.

*H*EAVEN *(SOMETIMES VIA* PURGATORY*)*. As the *Baltimore Catechism* states, we're meant for Heaven. We're meant to be saved. So what will Heaven be like? We do have Scripture, Tradition, and the teachings of the Magisterium, philosophers, and theologians over the centuries to help us better understand it. The Church offers us a glimpse of what Heaven will be like: "Those who die in God's grace and friendship and are perfectly purified [whether in this life, or in the next life in Purgatory] live forever with Christ. They are like God forever, for they 'see him as he is,' face to face" (*CCC*, 1023).

What does it mean to see God "face to face?" Doesn't the Bible say that no man has seen the face of God? Yes, but the Bible also says we *will* see God, as Scripture points out in Revelation 22:4. Tim Staples, former Southern Baptist and convert to the Catholic faith, explains this apparent contradiction. He says that this doesn't mean we will see God with our physical eyes, as He is pure spirit, but rather with our intellectual minds:

> In other words, man cannot see God in any sense with his natural powers. The saints and all of the blessed can be said to have "seen" and that they do "see" the divine essence with a directly intuited, intellectual vision.[89]

This is what we call the *beatific vision*, seeing God as He is once we behold Him in Heaven. As Staples explains, "[T]he Church teaches Heaven to be primarily a state rather than a place," so the beatific vision cannot be understood as people looking at God and then looking away from Him. "The blessed will be in a *state* of [contemplation] of God that is constant."[90] Staples continues:

Heaven is principally a state of utter and absolute fulfillment. In the possession of God in the beatific vision the
blessed will experience what cannot be put into words; a
radical union with God that transcends anything we could
envisage. And it is precisely because of that radical union
with God in Christ, the blessed will also experience a union
with the other members of the Body of Christ that transcends our ability to imagine as well.[91]

But this point leads to another question I often hear: "Father, I
will never be happy in Heaven if all of my children are not there." In
response, I would say that here on earth, we have only a dim sense of
what Heaven will be like (see 1 Cor 2:9; 13:12), and so it is difficult for
us to understand how we will experience things after death. But we are
promised in Revelation 21:4 that God "will wipe away every tear from
their eyes, and death shall be no more, neither shall there be mourning
nor crying nor pain any more, for the former things have passed away."

Since missing our loved ones would fall under the category of
pain or mourning, God promises that He will wipe even that away.
In Heaven, all will be well. We will be past the point of any kind of
mourning. How? Hopefully we'll find out someday, when we're there.
Therefore, our focus should be on bringing our living loved ones to
Christ and praying for our deceased loved ones — so that they *will* be
there, rather than worrying about how we can be happy if they aren't.

Our hope is that, through the mercy of God and our prayers, our
loved ones will accept God in their last moments, pass swiftly through
Purgatory with our intercession, and be waiting for us in Heaven.

We also have the testimony of the saints, who have a lot to say
about Heaven. To get one "first-hand account" of what Heaven is
like, let's turn again to St. Faustina, who was given a glimpse of this
incredible reality:

Today I was in Heaven, in spirit, and I saw its inconceivable
beauties and the happiness that awaits us after death. I saw
how all creatures give ceaseless praise and glory to God. I
saw how great is happiness in God, which spreads to all creatures, making them happy; and then all the glory and praise
which springs from this happiness returns to its source; and
they enter into the depths of God, contemplating the inner

life of God, the Father, the Son, and the Holy Spirit, whom they will never comprehend or fathom.

This source of happiness is unchanging in its essence, but it is always new, gushing forth happiness for all creatures. Now I understand Saint Paul, who said, "Eye has not seen, nor has ear heard, nor has it entered into the heart of man what God has prepared for those who love Him" (*Diary*, 777).

[A] vivid presence of God suddenly swept over me, and I was caught up in spirit before the majesty of God. I saw how the Angels and the Saints of the Lord give glory to God. The glory of God is so great that I dare not try to describe it, because I would not be able to do so, and souls might think that what I have written is all there is ... all that has come forth from God returns to Him in the same way and gives Him perfect glory (*Diary*, 1604).

God created us to be in communion with Him as His adopted sons and daughters. We are meant to be members of the *Communion of Saints*, all gathered together in Heaven for all eternity in joyful bliss. But to do this, to live in complete harmony with others, is demanding. To be in Heaven is to share in the life of God Himself, and the life of God is absolute, self-giving love. So even the slightest sin (self-love) gets in the way of that total self-gift. That's why no one imperfect in love will enter Heaven.

But that doesn't mean that all flawed people go to hell, either. (We are all flawed.) Often, Purgatory is needed for us to be cleansed of any defects or attachments that keep us from loving God with our whole heart. Purgatory is thus defined as the state of those "who die in God's grace and friendship" and are "indeed assured of their eternal salvation," but who still have need of purification to enter into the happiness of Heaven (*CCC*, 1030).

Most people who die suddenly pass away without the benefit of the Sacraments, and most often they will have died with some sin, or temporal punishment due to sin, on their soul. Consequently, they may find themselves in Purgatory and not hell, because they are not guilty of an unrepented mortal sin. The purpose of Purgatory is therefore to purge us of all unrepented venial sin (as well as to remit the punishment due for all imperfectly repented sins, venial or mortal).

To some of us, venial sins may not seem like anything in need of serious rectification, but the need to purge them is important, nonetheless. Purgatory is nothing other than an intensive purification of the soul to make it perfect in love. It is analogous to the refining process in the purification of metal through fire, burning away the impurities of dross. As St. Paul instructs the Corinthians:

> Now if anyone builds on the foundation with gold, silver, precious stones, wood, hay, straw — the work of each builder will become visible, for the Day will disclose it, because it will be revealed with fire, and the fire will test what sort of work each has done. If what has been built on the foundation survives, the builder will receive a reward. If the work is burned up, the builder will suffer loss; the builder will be saved, but only as through fire (1 Cor 3:12-15).

To illustrate this point, would you want to meet your future spouse on the day of your wedding without looking your very best, totally cleaned and prepared to enter into the wedding celebration? Of course you wouldn't! You would not want the slightest stain on your wedding garment. Neither does Christ, our Bridegroom, want any stain on our wedding garment (our soul) when we enter into the wedding feast of Heaven.

As evangelist and author Sr. Emmanuel Maillard notes, "In Purgatory, Christ's presence fills the soul with a joy which is somewhat tinted with pain. ... [I]t happens because the soul isn't fully prepared to bear His light."[92] Sister Emmanuel's statement may surprise some of us; we may not have realized that Purgatory, often viewed only as a place of extreme suffering and punishment, is also an extreme mercy of God. Purgatory is punishment that at the same time heals and sanctifies. Or, to put it the other way, it is a spiritual healing process, the pain of which at the same time remits temporal punishment due for sin.

Why? As St. Catherine of Genoa says regarding the souls in Purgatory, "[I]t seems to them that He has shown them great mercy. For if His goodness had not tempered justice with mercy, making satisfaction with the precious blood of Jesus Christ, one sin would deserve a thousand perpetual Hells."[93] Her statement is in line with the testimony of many saints who have spoken of a great number of souls in Purgatory, a detail that only underscores God's tremendous and merciful endeavor to save as many souls as possible. Thus, it is a mercy when He avoids giving us what we really deserve.

Taking this point further, in St. Catherine's *Treatise on Purgatory* she writes of the soul in need of purification:

> As it also sees in itself the impediment to its union with God, the soul understands that this can be taken away only by means of Purgatory and casts itself therein swiftly and willingly. For it sees that sins for which no atonement was made prevent it from drawing near to God. It casts itself therein because it understands that Purgatory is God's great work of mercy. ... [T]he souls in Purgatory enjoy the greatest happiness and endure the greatest pain; the one does not hinder the other.[94]

Believe it or not, the souls in Purgatory are actually *happy* because all of them will eventually enter Heaven. The mercy of Purgatory, then, is yet another reason we can have hope for our departed loved ones.

*H*ELL. Hell is a difficult reality to talk about, yet I would be remiss if I didn't. So please bear with me for a bit. We'll get through this quickly.

Ironically, hell exists because God is love. I know that sounds "strange as hell," but think for a moment: God is love, and God desires the freely given love of His creatures. As we've previously mentioned, if He simply forced us to love Him by manipulating our wills, then we wouldn't truly be giving Him love, would we? In fact, it wouldn't be real love at all. Love, to be true, must be free. It can't be forced; it has to be offered and received. In that case, the choice *not to love* must be a possibility as well.

The truth is that we were made as persons in the image and likeness of God; therefore, we are patterned after the persons of the Trinity, who live in total love. If we refuse to love God and neighbor, then we are denying our very nature as a person. We are denying the very thing that will fulfill us and answer our deepest desires. In that case, we set ourselves up for hell.

But why is hell everlasting? Why can't the damned leave it at some point?

Firstly, consider that whatever spiritual state we die in becomes a fixed state. When the angels made their choice to serve God or not, they were either blessed or damned (and became demons) in an instant, fixed forever in that state, because unlike us, they could see the full consequences of their decision. If we humans turn away from God's love (via sin) we still have the opportunity in this life to repent and turn back to God (most perfectly in the Sacrament of Confession). But once our soul separates from our body, our final choice for or against God is definitive for us as well, and we will be judged accordingly. We'll have our orientation toward God or away from Him, and we'll remain in that state for all eternity.

Secondly, remember that even though God is love, and His love is everlasting, He will respect our free-will choice. Even though He loves us and will never — indeed, *can* never let us go, we may refuse to reciprocate His love and ultimately choose hell.

So hell is a real option. C.S. Lewis once wrote that "the gates of hell are locked from the inside."[95] That explains why a merciful God allows some souls to go to hell, because in their own twisted way, they want to be there. Their hatred of God would make them miserable serving Him in Heaven, so they separate themselves from Him. That is the heart of what hell is: separation from God for all eternity. Evil is simply a privation of the good, and the choice to be separated from God, who is the ultimate good, results in the ultimate evil, which is hell.

But the fact that we can choose God even in our last moments should give us hope, even for the most miserable soul. I don't know your lost loved one, but I knew my grandmother. The odds are pretty good that my grandmother and your lost loved one were similar in that both may have wanted to end their suffering — but it's likely that neither of them wanted to reject God for all eternity. Even if a person were a wretch in this world and took their own life, they would have the same chance I believe that my grandma had, to encounter and accept Jesus, who is Mercy itself. That is why I have so much hope for her salvation and for those close to you.

It is the devil who desires our damnation, who accuses us of our sins, and who wants to see justice without mercy. Yet God sent His Son to save, not to damn; to open the gates of Heaven, not to throw people into hell. God is love, and He loves us all and desires that we all be saved, although some will reject His love and not be saved. The point is that we must try to aid our brothers and sisters through our intercessory prayer; we never know if they will accept or reject that final grace at the moment of their death. As we've learned, we can have the real hope of helping others, through our prayers and sacrifices, to avoid hell and enter the eternal embrace of God's merciful love, which is Heaven.

I want to close this discussion by emphasizing that the Church's teaching on life after death is a source of great consolation to me. Why? Because I have good reason to hope that I will see my loved ones again. We will all meet again at the resurrection of the dead, at the general judgment, and hopefully I'll meet all of them in Heaven before that.

As Fr. William Byron, SJ, once said regarding God's judgment of those who have succumbed to suicide:

> Divine decisions ... are filtered through divine mercy. Tragedy at the end of this life is no sure sign of an eternal tragedy in the next.[96]

Divine Mercy — this is what our faith is about. This is what God in His wisdom and in His love has intended for us to receive. Thus, we have hope.

The Bridge of Trust:
You Can Confidently Hope
in Their Salvation

Our hope is always essentially also hope for others;
only thus is it truly hope for me too.[97]

— Pope Benedict XVI

This section is entitled "The Bridge of Trust." Typically, a bridge connects two bodies of land, facilitating movement from one location to another. Here, the "bridge of trust" connects the hope for your deceased loved one (Part One) to hope for you (Part Two). Trust in God is the bridge that links these two hopes together. We can conclude from the quote above from Pope Benedict XVI that your hope for your loved one's salvation is also a true hope for you, too.

If you are reading this book, I think it is safe to say you have come looking for such hope. You have come hoping that your deceased loved one — your husband, wife, son, daughter, niece, nephew, grandson, granddaughter, friend, or friend of a friend — will have eternal life with God. I, too, share your hope. I trust in God's goodness, His infinite loving mercy, even more than I trust that my very own parents love me — and I *know* that my parents love me without a hint of doubt. Based upon this trust in God's infinite goodness and mercy and your prayerful hope for your loved one, I am going to make a bold claim:

I confidently hope that your deceased loved one *does* have eternal life with God.

"Did I hear you correctly, Fr. Chris?"
Yes, you did. Regarding those deceased loved ones who were like my grandmother, a soul with some very good qualities, but crushed by life's misfortunes and chronic suffering, **I confidently hope that they have eternal life with God.** And even regarding those whose lives were much darker, who may have also died by their own hand, whose

87

souls were (as far as we can tell) much further from God, and who manifested in their lives only the smallest sparks of virtue, you can still have hope that they can be saved. Why? *Precisely because you can pray for them and offer sacrifices for them now, and help them obtain the final grace that can, if they accept it, lead them to salvation.*

"But how can you as a Catholic priest make such a bold, outlandish, even theologically reckless claim?" you might ask. "The Church teaches that there is the possibility of hell, of eternal separation from God!"

Yes, as we explained earlier, eternal separation from God for all of us is a very real possibility. And we cannot say definitively that anyone does or does not have eternal life with God, except for those few souls identified and canonized by the Church as saints. I stand by my bold claim because I believe in the Revelation of Jesus Christ Himself. I trust in the boundless mercy of God for your beloved, and I trust that you do, too. With St. Faustina, I appeal to the loving heart of the Father: "O my God, my only hope, I have placed all my trust in You, and I know I shall not be disappointed" (*Diary*, 317).

In the conclusion of the Sermon on the Mount, regarded by many theologians as Jesus' greatest public teaching, Christ Himself is the guarantor of His Father's infinite goodness and mercy for His children in need.

He proclaims:

Ask, and it will be given you; seek, and you will find; knock, and it will be opened to you. For every one who asks receives, and he who seeks finds, and to him who knocks it will be opened.

Or what man of you, if his son asks him for bread, will give him a stone? Or if he asks for a fish, will give him a serpent? If you then, who are evil, know how to give good gifts to your children, how much more will your Father who is in heaven give good things to those who ask him! (Mt 7:7-11).

Would you give your son or daughter a stone or a serpent if they were in need? Of course not! You would *ask* for eternal life for those you care about. In reading this book, you *seek* the reward of eternal life for them. Through your prayers and offered suffering, you are able to *knock* at the door of Divine Mercy, that it might open so that those you have lost might have life and have it abundantly for all eternity with God the Father in His Son, Jesus Christ.

Simply put, you long for and desire the salvation of those you love. You, who are imperfect and broken in your own right, want eternal life for them and would give it in an *instant* if it were within your power. Remember: "If you then, who are evil, know how to give good gifts to your children, how much more will your Father who is in heaven give good things to [you] who ask him!"

Well, it *is* within the realm of your power through the vessel of *trust* in Jesus' infinite goodness. How much greater is the goodness of the infinite God than your good desires for those you love? *Infinitely greater!*

In His revelations to St. Faustina, Jesus tells her, **"My Heart overflows with great mercy for souls, and especially for poor sinners. If only they could understand that I am the best of Fathers to them and that it is for them that the Blood and Water flowed from My Heart as from a fount overflowing with mercy ... I desire to bestow My graces upon souls, but they do not want to accept them"** (*Diary*, 367).

But you and I *do* want to accept these boundless graces of Jesus, and we trust that He is "the best of Fathers" in giving these graces to us, His children, who ask, seek, and knock. And Jesus expresses His pleasure in our confident trust in Him, saying to St. Faustina, **"Oh, how I love those souls who have complete confidence in Me — I will do everything for them"** (*Diary*, 294).

We have a Heavenly Father who sees His Son in each of us and gives every good gift that our hearts seek and ask for. You and I trust that this infinitely good Father will bestow eternal life on those we love, even if they took their own life. Our confidence is in Jesus, the Divine Mercy, who told Faustina, **"Every soul believing and trusting in My mercy will obtain it"** (*Diary*, 420).

So let us draw from this boundless fount of Divine Mercy for the eternal salvation of our family and friends, and proclaim with St. Faustina and all the heavens, **"O Blood and Water which gushed forth from the Heart of Jesus as a fount of mercy for us, I trust in You!"** (*Diary*, 84). This prayer in particular is incredibly powerful for the conversion of sinners. Saint Faustina recites it on at least two occasions in the *Diary* (for instance, 187, 309).

Jesus Himself tells Faustina, **"Call upon My mercy on behalf of sinners; I desire their salvation. When you say this prayer, with a contrite heart and with faith on behalf of some sinner, I will give him the grace of conversion"** (186).[98]

Here, we see that Jesus *strongly* desires the salvation of sinners and loves them to such a degree that the flames of His mercy actually burn Him and clamor to be spent to rescue souls most in need. Read this passage again. See Jesus' own words: **"I desire their salvation ... I will give him the grace of conversion."**[99]

As you recall in Part One, we discussed how our prayers transcend time because God Himself transcends time. (You will read about this more extensively in the "Theological Underpinnings" section following Part Two.) Certainly, our Merciful Lord, who is Love itself, desires the redemption of our loved one even *more* than we do. And He loves us and desires to fulfill our hearts' desires when directed to our ultimate good, which is eternal life with Him. As John tells us in his First Letter, "This is what He has *promised* us — eternal life!" (1 Jn 2:25; emphasis my own).

When we pray for those who took their own lives, we come to trust in Jesus with faith in His goodness and mercy, that He will hear our prayers no matter when we make them, apply the grace of those prayers in their final moments, and offer them what He Himself has promised — *eternal life!* For this reason, I make the bold claim of hope that they will have their share in eternal life with God, because I trust the promise that Jesus Himself has declared. So together with you, I pray the prayer invoking God's mercy: "O Blood and Water which gushed forth from the Heart of Jesus as a fount of mercy for us, I trust in You!"

Having hope for our loved one's eternal life with God, we can begin to have hope for ourselves. We can draw from the deep wells of Divine Mercy to find further healing and peace for our own souls. We may still be grieving. We may still feel the acute, indescribable pain of having lost a beloved family member or friend. If that is the case, we need to gently allow what I call God's "prescription of hope" to echo in our hearts: "Jesus, I trust in You."

Be encouraged. The second half of this journey is intended to inspire *Hope for You*. In Part Two, we will first look at the general types, effects, and stages of grief after a suicide or tragic loss. Then, we will offer three basic spiritual principles, a moving personal story, and additional spiritual aids related to the message of Divine Mercy to encourage you with hope in the aftermath of a life-changing tragedy. Lastly, we'll conclude on a note of confident hope that God's infinite love can bring a greater good out of your suffering, pain, and loss, enabling you to share in the communion of God and the saints with your loved one, both now and most fully in eternity. By continuing this journey with us, we pray that you might have your own "epiphany of hope," as you are restored and strengthened by the One who is Love and Mercy itself.

~ PART TWO ~

There Really Is Hope for You

*For I have come down from heaven, not to do my own
will, but the will of him who sent me; and this is the will of
him who sent me, that I should lose nothing of all that he
has given me, but raise it up at the last day. For this is the
will of my Father, that everyone who sees the Son
and believes in him should have eternal life;
and I will raise him up at the last day.*

— Jn 6:38-40

INTRODUCTION
Two Brothers Reunited

My name is Jason Lewis. When Fr. Chris asked me to join him in the
mission of the Association of Marian Helpers, I was rather elated. It
meant that I would be reconnecting with the charism, mission, and
heart of the Gospel — Divine Mercy — for which I am more passionate
than anything else on earth. As a former seminarian with the Marian
Fathers of the Immaculate Conception and now a religious brother
with Fr. Chris, it was a long road coming home. But there could not
have been a better fit for me.

We reconnected in the Fall of 2018 in Stockbridge, Massachusetts, home of the National Shrine of The Divine Mercy. Agreeing to
work on several future projects, I was enthusiastic to get started. However, there was one project that weighed heavily on Fr. Chris' heart.
It was the book you are now reading. He shared with me his personal
experience of the loss of his grandmother, and it touched *my* heart.
Extremely busy as the director of the Association of Marian Helpers,

the epicenter of the Marian Fathers' ministry outreaches, he expressed disappointment at being unable to devote all the time he needed to complete the book; so he proposed that we begin working together on this particular project.

He said, "Jason, people need this book. This book has to touch those who are in pain and grieving deeply from the loss of someone special, especially the incalculable pain that results from a suicide. It needs to touch their hearts and give them the hope of salvation for their loved one and hope for themselves in their present grief. This is what Divine Mercy is all about."

Immediately, I knew he was right. It was a little "epiphany." Having had experiences of grief myself, even recently, I wanted to give more of myself to encourage hope for others who might be grieving a recent or a long-past loss. Although this book is directed toward grief related to suicide, its tenets are applicable to other forms of grief and loss, drawing from foundational principles of the Gospel and Divine Mercy spirituality. These sources attest to an all-powerful and loving God, a tremendous reality and gift that our faith has given us though the redemptive action of Jesus Christ. Not only are we offered the greatest of hopes for our loved ones — the hope of eternal life with Him — but we can have *confident hope for our own healing in the present* in and through Divine Mercy. That means there is *hope for you.*

*O*UR PATH OF HEALING IN GRIEF. Based upon our confident hope for the salvation of our loved ones, arising from the "bridge of trust," we also have the confident hope of being reunited with them some day in Heaven. Our Lord assumed human nature and became one of us for that very purpose; He suffered gruesome agony, Passion unto death, so that we might have life eternal and the hope to share it with those we love.

Christ shows us that death is not the final word. This hope should impart a considerable degree of consolation to us in the present. It is the "great hope" that offers meaning to our existence and gives us the courage to persevere through this valley of tears.

Nevertheless, the painful effects of losing someone we love are bound to persist, often with a sting that can be debilitating. The suicide of someone close is one of the greatest traumas we can ever experience. It's certain that life after a suicide will never be the same. Father Chris recounted to me his meeting with Dr. Mollie Marti, founder and CEO of the National Resilience Institute, and a nationally recognized expert on community resiliency after a suicide. She said to him, "Father, suicide has all the force and effect of a bomb going off in a community. It leaves behind many deep wounds, often unexpected ones, and many times hidden ones. You and those around you are survivors of one of the hardest tragedies to handle in life."

The good doctor's observations are spot on. We should take them to heart and remind ourselves that painful, sudden blows to our hearts — particularly those inflicted by a suicide — can have crippling effects on us, leaving us emotionally paralyzed. The impact of a suicide is far-reaching, touching countless lives. This is a hard reality. But there is another reality — the reality that healing *is* possible.

It should be established up front that healing in grief is a process. You may have to confront the effects of the tragedy repeatedly, much like those suffering from PTSD have to relive their traumas. In the following chapters, it is my wish that we can walk the road of recovery in grief together, and that along the way, you will experience an "epiphany of hope," as I did in my healing process.

As the first step in this journey, we will consider an overview of grief, looking at its types, effects, and stages. Then we will introduce you to our very dear friend, Sammie Wood, and her incredibly moving journey through grief from the loss of her daughter by suicide. Next, we will consider three spiritual principles that can be applied toward healing in grief, and then offer some additional spiritual aids to recovery. Finally, we will discuss the ultimate hope of sharing eternal life with our loved ones. On these "shores of hope," you just might find renewed consolation as you contemplate the wonders of an all-loving and merciful God who brings healing from grief, joy from pain, and life from death.

For now, let us take a closer look at the nature of grief and its manifestations. If you are already familiar with the categories, effects, and stages of grief, or if the material becomes too weighty, you might proceed to the section "Grieving with Others" at the end of this chapter.

CHAPTER ONE

An Overview of Suicide Grief and Its Effects

Our discussion of hope for you, as a survivor of a suicide, will be from a spiritual perspective. Throughout salvation history, this approach has been a proven way of responding to grief. Father Chris and I have specialized in the tenets of the Catholic faith, spirituality, and pastoral direction, preparing us to approach grief in the aftermath of a suicide from this vantage point.

However, we would be remiss not to mention some common information that is available and specific to grief bereavement put out by professionals in the field. Due to the complexities of suicide bereavement, we strongly encourage you to employ professional help in striving to pick up the pieces and regain some semblance of a "normal" life. We do not want to offer any false promises or ill-conceived hope.

Any loss of a close relationship is bound to cause serious grief. Admittedly, the trauma from a suicide may be the most gut-wrenching, perplexing, and acute pain that you will ever endure. It might feel as if your world is spinning out of control, as if you will never experience any degree of peace or "normalcy" again. In the words of a dear friend, Sammie Wood, whose story we will explore in greater detail later in the book, you never "get over" the loss of a loved one to a suicide, but you *"can and will* get through it."

In order to begin this process of hope and healing, we need to look at the effects that suicide can have on our lives. An online article in the journal *Dialogues in Clinical Neuroscience* summarizes the multidimensional effects of suffering that are often the plight of a suicide survivor:

> The feelings of loss, sadness, and loneliness experienced after any death of a loved one are often magnified in suicide survivors by feelings of guilt, confusion, rejection, shame, anger, and the effects of stigma and trauma. Furthermore,

96

survivors of suicide loss are at higher risk of developing major depression, post-traumatic stress disorder, and suicidal behaviors, as well as a prolonged form of grief called complicated grief.[100]

These symptoms and consequences experienced by suicide survivors are severe and have no "quick fix" or "over-the-counter" remedy. Typically, they will require the survivor to trudge through moments of great darkness, pain, and confusion.

THREE CATEGORIES OF GRIEF. Mental health professionals often identify three categories of grief: acute, integrated, and complicated. They are widely employed to describe the kinds of grief one may be undergoing.

Acute grief is the grief experienced in the early days or weeks after the loss of a loved one. "Shock, anguish, loss, anger, guilt, regret, anxiety, fear, intrusive images, depersonalization, feeling overwhelmed, loneliness, unhappiness, and depression are just some of the feeling states often described."[101] The word "acute" connotes the sharpest point, where the pain of one's loss is most fresh and even raw.

Integrated grief is the ongoing grief typically experienced in the months following the loss. Here, the survivor begins to reintegrate typical activities, such as normal work patterns, ordinary duties, and social relationships, into their daily lives. They begin to experience the joys of life again, even if only partially. If someone is moving through the processes that occur in the integrated grief phase, changes are very likely to occur within the person. Oftentimes, they discover meaning in their lives and find healing and wholeness at a new level. Life begins to become more manageable. Survivors in the integrated grief stage often realize "new capacities, wisdom, unrecognized strengths, new and meaningful relationships, and broader perspectives emerge in the aftermath of loss."[102]

Recently, the psychiatric community has developed the concept of posttraumatic growth (PTG), which shows that a positive psychological change can actually occur as the result of one's struggle with a traumatic event. Knowing that growth after a difficult loss is possible provides hope for the individual, said Dr. Melinda Moore, but also "gives them tools for rebuilding their lives by giving them a real understanding of how they have been changed as a result of this trauma."

Fostering posttraumatic growth is an important approach that both professionals and organizations may opt to employ. It provides a way for some families who have been through devastating events, said Dr. Moore, to grow "in a way that their lives are forever changed, but more resilient and robust than they might have otherwise been."[103]

Certainly, if you are still reeling from the effects of acute grief, the potential for self-discovery and healing in the integrated stage offers hope in your present trials. As we saw in Part One, this self-discovery can take the form of little, and sometimes big, "epiphany moments" that God grants us in our journey through grief. The state of integration and some of its effects, however, may take months and even years to manifest, especially given the poignancy of a suicide. The smaller percentage of survivors who may not be able to arrive at such an integration develop a state of complicated grief.

Complicated grief is an extension of acute grief, whereby the survivor of a loss is unable to reintegrate their lives in a meaningful way without their beloved departed. Daily activities may remain arduous, and the sting of the loss persists over time and is recurrent. Deep depression and symptoms of PTSD are conditions often experienced in complicated grief.[104]

Moreover, those with complicated grief from suicide are much more prone to suicidal ideation themselves.[105] It is estimated that 25-43 percent of suicide survivors who lose someone particularly close to them — a son or daughter, mother or father, husband or wife, brother or sister, or another person intimately connected to them — will undergo complicated grief. That's approximately double the percentage of those who will undergo complicated grief resulting from other kinds of loss.[106] Some research suggests that it can take three to five years for those suffering from the impact of a suicide to arrive at integrated grief.[107]

If you are experiencing acute or complicated grief for an extended period of time, we urge you to immediately seek out health care professionals who are trained to assist you in reconciling the painful effects of your loss. There is absolutely no shame in asking for help. Think of Jesus, the God-Man, who accepted the caring support of His followers — Simon of Cyrene, Veronica, the women at the Cross, John the Apostle, and of course, His own mother — while bearing the agonizing weight of the Cross on the walk to Calvary.

*T*HE *EFFECTS OF GRIEF.* Research by experts in suicidology, the scientific study of suicidal behavior, indicates that the effects of bereavement in suicide survivors are qualitatively different than the effects of typical grief in response to a more common sort of loss. "In addition to the inevitable grief, sadness, and disbelief typical of all grief, overwhelming guilt, confusion, rejection, shame, and anger are also often prominent" in suicide grief.[108]

According to Dr. Melinda Moore, grieving from suicide has been associated with psychiatric disorders such as PTSD and prolonged grief disorder,[109] and with major depression and anxiety disorders,[110] all of which can place people at increased risk of taking their own lives.[111] Research indicates that the risk of suicide for someone who has lost their spouse is higher than that from bereavement from other causes.[112] Moreover, losing a child to suicide increases the suicide risk for a parent more than for a parent mourning the death of a child who died by other means.[113] If the suicide is within the immediate family, a twofold increase in death by suicide has been observed among family members.[114]

Survivors often assume a far greater personal responsibility for their loss than reality supports. As we mentioned in Part One, it is common for suicide survivors to seek answers to questions like "Why?"; "What could I have done to prevent it?"; or "What signs did I miss?" for months or even years. With their need to make sense of the occurrence, oftentimes a survivor leaves no stone unturned while replaying in their minds the events leading up to the act. Shame from the stigma of suicide is common, and survivors can be plagued with guilt for having somehow "failed" to prevent the tragedy. This effect is very common, for instance, in the lives of parents who have lost a child to suicide.

It is important to recognize and to reinforce the fact that no two people experience grief in the same way. You might be experiencing many different effects of the grieving process in the midst of acute, integrated, or complicated grief.

Our personhood consists of spirit, soul, and body. Therefore, the effects of losing someone dear to us are going to be spiritual, mental-emotional, and physical. These trifold effects are often manifest in various forms after the loss of someone we loved. Identifying these effects can help us understand what we are going through. For

instance, we may experience the following "symptoms," or effects, of
grieving suicide in the three spheres of our personhood:[115]

Physical (Body)

• Numbness	• Nausea
• Short attention span	• Headaches
• Inability to concentrate	• Physical pain
• Inability to sleep	• Nervousness
• Fitful sleep patterns	• Anxiety
• Apathy	• Inability to eat
• Exhaustion	• Overeating
• Emptiness	• Crying often
• Heaviness in the chest	• Inability to cry

Mental-Emotional (Soul)

• Shock	• Anger
• Guilt	• Yearning
• Deep sadness	

Spiritual (Spirit)

• Loss of faith	• Increased faith
• Strong doubts	• Increased awareness of
• Inability to pray	and attachment to God
• Anger toward God	

Certainly, this is an extensive list of the potential effects of grief.
But it can be helpful to know the wide and varied range of how grief
can manifest itself during our suffering. Indeed, these effects can be
debilitating. They can impose a sense of insecurity and instability in
our lives. Sometimes what we used to know as "reality" doesn't seem
as certain as it once did. We might lose our bearings, emotionally,
spiritually, and even physically. With such dramatic changes, we might
feel as if we are living in a completely foreign land.

Now that we have covered the three types of grief often identified
by medical professionals and the possible effects of grief (physical,
mental, and spiritual), let's consider the widely recognized five stages of
grief. Swiss-American psychiatrist Elisabeth Kübler-Ross first identified
these stages decades ago. Ever since, many people have found them to
be helpful in understanding what they're experiencing after a loss.[116]

*T*HE FIVE STAGES OF GRIEF. In order to move forward in healing from the loss of a close loved one, we inevitably will have to walk through the pain of the loss, a process that typically takes place in certain stages. Everyone will grieve at some point during their lifetime, and sometimes grieve repeatedly. Every loss of love is unique because every personal relationship is unique; no two relationships are identical. Therefore, the grief that we undergo is unique to us. However, it is widely understood that the grieving process can include universally common features.

The five stages of grief can help us to comprehend some of the effects that occur in the wake of a personal loss that hits close to home. These stages are:

1. Denial
2. Anger
3. Bargaining
4. Depression
5. Acceptance[117]

It must first be noted that these stages provide only a framework for understanding the phenomena that grieving presents. They are not an exhaustive list of a survivor's possible dispositions. In their most recent work, *On Grief and Grieving: Finding the Meaning of Grief Through the Five Stages of Loss*, Kübler-Ross and coauthor David Kessler insist that those who grieve may not experience all of these stages or even in the same order. One may go back and forth between stages and even return to certain stages again and again.

There's also no preset timeline for how long it takes to get through the stages of grief. As Kübler-Ross says, "There is not a typical response to loss as there is no typical loss. Our grief is as individual as our lives."[118] Let's now take a more in-depth look at what each of the five stages may look like.

(1) *Denial.* Denial in grief is often a necessary first step. The shock of a tragedy can paralyze us. Denial is a way of coping with that first, enormous shock, the first encounter with this new, painful reality, which can leave us in a state of disbelief. Denial is and can be "a grace" in the initial healing process, since it allows us to continue to function while emotionally, spiritually, and sometimes physically maimed from our

loss. It is a period in which we might feel numb or dazed. In time, we begin to feel the pain of the loss,[119] but denial allows for a more gradual, "manageable" pace leading into the feelings of pain.

(2) Anger. Anger is often the first *emotion* that emerges in the grieving process. It is a normal and often necessary part of that process. It is often perceived that anger is a negative emotion that should always be suppressed. Kübler-Ross and Kessler believe differently. They hold that "anger is strength and it can be an anchor, giving temporary structure to the nothingness of loss."[120]

It's right and even healthy to feel anger, as long as our anger doesn't reach dangerous levels or last for an inordinate amount of time. Anger can often be directed at one's own self, the deceased, coworkers, family, friends, or even God. (This will be treated in greater depth in Chapter Three.) Feeling anger in the present moment enables its eventual lessening and passing, but refusing to feel and face anger will prolong it.[121] Anger is a sign that we are hurt. We lost someone whom we cared about deeply, who can never be replaced. It is natural to feel angry.

Allow yourself to feel your anger. Get it out in safe and healthy ways by sharing it with trusted friends, family, spiritual advisers, and/or mental health professionals. Some find that exercise can help to manage anger and work through the emotional pain of loss.[122]

(3) Bargaining. This stage can be especially hard for those of us who have to grieve an unexpected, sudden loss, such as a suicide. We experience the "what ifs," the "if onlys," and the "coulda, woulda, shouldas" as we long to have our loved ones back again. It is also the stage where guilt emerges more intensely.

Again, it is important to remember that the stages aren't always linear. They don't happen in a tidy progression, come once, and disappear. They can and do recur over weeks, months, and even years, but also over the hours and minutes of our day.

Bargaining can be an important part of the grieving process. It's our attempt at making sense of the apparent senselessness of a loss, our attempt to wrap our minds around our loved one's death and to find meaning in our lives again.[123]

One helpful tool for walking through this stage is journaling one's feelings, a tool we will also look at in more detail later. For those who choose to keep their writings, these reflections can be invaluable for future review, allowing them to see where God's grace has been working in their lives.

(4) Depression. Depression can feel like being stuck in a swamp on a gray, rainy day. It can seem like it goes on forever with no end in sight. Everything seems empty and meaningless. This stage often occurs when the full reality of our loss sets in.

Be assured, depression after the death of someone close to you is quite common. If ever a person has a reason to be despondent, it's when they have lost someone whom they loved deeply, especially when the loss is sudden and without resolution. Depression is usually a necessary stage of grief and can serve a constructive purpose as a damper on unruly or extreme emotions. When in the depression stage, it may be difficult to get out of bed, make it to work, concentrate, eat, or have any will to engage with life. Participation in daily activities can seem like climbing Mt. Everest.

Some people have found it helpful to treat depression as an uninvited and unwelcome, but unavoidable guest. Sometimes it seems this guest is never going to leave. But it might be helpful, to a degree, to simply sit with the depression, and simply feel it. Again, it is a natural part of grieving.[124]

When we're depressed, our usual practices of prayer may become next to impossible. Our daily vocal prayers or our meditations may seem far too demanding. In this case, it's best to go easy on ourselves. God understands what's happening, and He therefore draws very close to us in our darkness.

Sometimes, all we can do in our depression and pain is be silent amidst the mystery of suffering, knowing that the Father sees in us His suffering Son, who experienced loneliness and abandonment many times, and His Heart is deeply moved for us. As Fr. Chris mentioned in Part One, St. Teresa of Avila purportedly wrote, "One must not think that a person who is suffering is not praying. He is offering up his suffering to God, and many a time he is praying much more truly than one who goes away by himself and meditates his head off." Simply allow Jesus to be with you and rest in the silent embrace of His love. Let your silent suffering be your prayer.

Being depressed off and on for a lengthy period — months or even years — isn't unusual for those dealing with serious grief.[125] Despite the intensity of your present feelings, remember that this intensity will indeed ease with time. You may have heard the adage "time takes time." As annoying as it might presently sound, it's true; time is a necessary component of the healing process.

(5) Acceptance. Many misunderstand acceptance as arriving at a place where we're "okay" with the loss of our beloved, but that's not necessarily the case. Acceptance *does* mean that we are able to live life again, a new kind of life without the physical presence of our loved one, through a process that evolves over time. But what makes acceptance possible, in part, is knowing that we have the hope of spiritual communion with them, as we will see in Chapter Five.

When we're in the acceptance stage, we often begin to have more good days than bad. New relationships, structures, and adjusted routines often become part of our new reality. Like all the other stages, acceptance may come and go.[126] It may also seem impossible at the present time. In fact, even hearing about acceptance may be repulsive and incite more anger in us if the pain is still fresh. The one thing we may be able to accept in the present is that "we are where we are" in the grieving process, and that we will have ups and downs, often feeling disoriented or unlike our "normal" selves. Again, this is fine. Eventually, a deeper acceptance and peace will meet us if we simply allow grief to take its natural course.

GRIEVING WITH OTHERS. Unfortunately, many survivors of suicide may find themselves unable to experience any degree of post-traumatic growth. We already mentioned that your particular grief is unique, due to the unrepeatable relationship you shared with the deceased person. If your loss is recent and acute, you might feel so overwhelmed, confused, lost, and disoriented that you cannot imagine any end to your suffering. Your world may feel like it's spinning out of control, and any "epiphany of hope," as shared in Fr. Chris' personal story, may seem entirely out of reach.

First of all, let me assure you that absolutely *no one* knows the extent of your pain and sorrow other than you and God. Even with the most sympathetic support network around you, there are going to be times when no one can completely understand what you're going through. But as you read this book, know that Fr. Chris and I come to you as friends who have walked through deep, heartbreaking pain ourselves. Of course, there's no "magic pill" that will take away your suffering. If there were, we would give it to you — except that we *know* of the gifts that await you as you persevere through these trying times. That being said, please understand that we are here for you in prayerful spirit. In fact, we have been praying for those who will read this book.

Sometimes, the very best gift you can receive in your pain is the simple presence of another person who cares, someone who lets you know that it's okay to feel the way you do. It's okay to be confused, disoriented, and even out of control in a certain way. It's okay to be angry. It's okay to feel lost. It's okay to simply collapse in the arms of Jesus and allow Him to hold you. If you are in the early portion of acute grief and the pain seems entirely overwhelming, unmanageable, and never-ending, it is a blessing to have someone around who will remind you that you are *not* going to feel like this forever, and that this all-consuming pain will lessen.

In my own journey through grief, I found it essential to have certain people near me who understood, to some degree, what I was having to endure. I called them my "circle of trust" — Mary and Billie, Mom and Dad, Frs. Tom and Kurt ... and Charlie Bear. Without that immediate circle of trust, I am not sure how I would have made it through the roughest times.

Each person in my circle was present in a unique way. None of them could have shouldered all of the weight I was bearing from moment to moment. They had lives of their own. But each of them walked through recovery in grief with me and were there in a way that only Providence could have arranged.

Moreover, a special "heavenly circle" assisted me. I didn't choose them; they chose me. My heavenly circle (I felt in my heart) included Faustina, Theresa of Avila, Augustine, and Mark, and later John Paul II, Monica, and John, the Beloved Disciple. I'm sure there were more. I now see that both circles were gathered and led by one who understands the pain of suffering like no human person who ever lived on earth — Mary, our mother. And throughout it all, of course, there was Jesus — loving, tender, merciful, and strong.

I pray that you allow your own "circle of trust" to form around you. God will provide just the right people, both on earth and in Heaven, if you allow Him to surround you with love and care. It's all right to have moments of solitude; in fact, those times will be necessary. But we should be careful not to allow healing solitude to grow into harmful isolation, where we place ourselves beyond the reach of love. This can happen even when we are surrounded by people daily but still choose to wall off our hearts.

Remember, as human persons we are not made to bear heavy burdens alone. God created us to be social, communal beings. We are meant to live in relation with Him and others — both on earth and in Heaven. Talk with those in your circle. Also, talk with your pastor, who can be a great source of consolation, grace, and spiritual direction. If you find your grief unbearable, meet with a grief counselor who can offer an understanding ear and a shoulder to lean on. They have a special, blessed calling and are trained in the stages and effects of grief. Also, consider attending a grief recovery group at a local parish or as part of a community outreach program. We do well to share our grief with others who have endured a similar experience. (Please see Appendix D for some support resources.)

Most grief professionals agree that sharing the story of your loss can be instrumental in helping you over time. Bottling it up internally, refusing to talk about your trauma, or never acknowledging how your departed loved one died will not allow you to pass through the process of grief. That's a recipe for deeper difficulties down the road. It's also important to remember that Jesus is present with you and that our Sorrowful Mother walks beside you, so you can know that you are never truly alone. Remember, God loves you, and He is with you, and when you avail yourself of Him, you will begin to heal and have hope.

CHAPTER TWO

Three Spiritual Principles in Suicide Bereavement — An Introduction

Now that we have discussed the nature of grief and some of the unique complexities of a suicide, drawing from resources offered by grief professionals, let's shift our focus to the critical spiritual approaches we can take in the healing process. Here are three spiritual principles that can assist you in your healing from bereavement and offer you real hope.

1. We admit that we are powerless over the loss of our loved one.
2. We come to trust that Jesus, the Divine Mercy, can restore our lives to manageability.
3. We make a decision to entrust our will, our lives, and our loved one to the loving care and protection of God.

One thing is for certain: If you are grieving from a suicide, many things will not make sense about the circumstances in which you find yourself. It will be impossible to "figure out" the chain of events that has overwhelmed you. However, these three spiritual principles for coping with suicide bereavement can work together to help place you on more solid footing. Of course, the time it takes to return to "manageability" — to get things "back on track" — will vary for each person. It may be difficult to see right now, but the Father loves you and will not leave you orphaned in your anguish. He *will* help you.

In the following chapter, we will elaborate on how these three spiritual principles can be an aid in your personal healing, offering further hope in the wake of a tragic and traumatic loss. But before we do that, let us consider the story of a friend and her family who survived one of the most unimaginable tragedies — the death of their 17-year-old daughter by suicide — and how the three spiritual principles factored into their healing in grief.

A MOTHER'S HEART IN SORROW AND LOSS. We would now like to introduce you to a very dear friend of ours whom we mentioned earlier. Her name is Sammie Wood. When Fr. Chris shared her amazing story with me, to say I was deeply moved is an understatement.

While working on Part Two of this book, I knew that I needed to contact Sammie directly to have a conversation. Before ever talking with her, I sensed interiorly that we would have a spiritual connection. My intuition was right. Although I have yet to meet her in person, I feel like Sammie and I have been friends for years. She is now an expanded part of "my circle." Her experience with the devastating aftermath of a suicide is heartfelt and encouraging for those who have loved and lost. In many ways, Sammie is like a coauthor of this book with us as well. The contribution of her experience, strength, and hope has been invaluable.

Sammie initially shared her soul-stirring story of the loss of her teenaged daughter in the summer 2017 issue of *Marian Helper* magazine in an article written by Melanie Williams, a staff writer at the Marian Helpers Center. We've reprinted it below:

"The sun could have *not* risen that day and it would have been less surprising than what actually happened." Sammie Wood, a mother of three, homemaker, and cattle rancher from Clayton, New Mexico, spoke through tears as she recalled the events of Aug. 10, 2014.

The night before, a Saturday, Sammie, her husband, and her daughter Clare, 17, went to Mass. Afterwards Clare, her youngest, went to a dance before the start of her senior year of high school.

Tall, slender, beautiful, and fun-loving, Clare valued laughter, friendship, and faith. She often would dance and sing around the kitchen with her mom and two siblings. She played volleyball, and was a cheerleader and National Honor Society member. She would tell people she would pray for them. She loved the Lord and wrote little notes to herself that said things like, "Make God loved."

She was no saint. She did many, many good things and also made mistakes. For her Confirmation saint, after much research, she chose St. Margaret of Cortona, famously willful.

That Sunday morning, Sammie went to Clare's bedroom to check in and to snuggle. She asked her how the dance went. Clare wasn't too responsive. She didn't want to talk. She said she was tired. Sammie held her for a moment, then, as she did every morning, she took her rosary beads with a relic of St. Faustina and went for a walk to pray the Rosary and Chaplet of Divine Mercy for her daily intention of praying for someone who would die that day.

When Sammie returned home, Clare was up and asked her, "Mamma, where were you?"

"Out for my morning Rosary and Chaplet, praying for someone who will die today," Sammie said.

The sunny New Mexico morning turned uncharacteristically overcast. Chip, Sammie's husband, grilled steaks outside for lunch, but the foul weather drove the family inside. Sammie and Chip eventually settled in to watch a golf match as Sammie worked on a needlepoint Christmas stocking. Clare settled in another room to watch a different program. At one point, Sammie checked in on her. She knelt beside her and asked her if she wanted to join them. Clare still seemed despondent, and she declined, saying she didn't really like watching golf.

Before leaving her be, Sammie leaned in and told Clare she knew that returning to school for the fall semester wouldn't be easy, with all of the preparation Clare needed to do for college. But Sammie told Clare that she loved her, and Sammie blessed her. She made the Sign of the Cross on her daughter's forehead. That was the last time Sammie saw her baby girl alive.

Clouds continued to roll in across the high plains when Chip and Sammie heard what sounded like a sharp "pop" coming from outside. They figured it was weather-related. But minutes later, Sammie's father rushed into the house screaming, "Clare shot herself! Clare's dead!"

Sammie's parents live on the family ranch, in a house close to the barn. They had heard the gunshot. Clare had driven her car up to the barn, stepped out onto the cement apron, and taken her own life. She was wearing her scapular, which was not typical. She had left a note in her car that read, "I love you guys so much. Please forgive me. I'm so sorry."

As Sammie and Chip came upon their daughter's lifeless body, the skies began to pour. They carried her body inside the barn for shelter and called 911. The Wood family lives 33 miles away from the nearest town. The emergency responders took three hours to get there.

All the while, as family gathered at the ranch to mourn, Sammie embraced her daughter's body. She wailed, wept, and prayed.

The Woods would eventually discover that Clare had been having trouble with girls at school and was a victim of cyberbullying.

She had shared with her sister that a fellow volleyball teammate's ex-boyfriend was romantically interested in her, and though Clare wasn't interested in him, some girls in her class were giving her a hard time about it all.

The Woods also would learn that at the dance the night before, the boy had asked Clare to dance. They were seen kissing on the dance floor. Clare was upset with herself that she had allowed that to happen and wanted to call and apologize to her teammate, but the girl and some others had already started talking about it. In a small town, in a class of 50 people, gossip and rumors spread like wildfire.

"I never saw anything in Clare that I thought was unusual," Sammie said. "She was a typical teenager. But the day Clare died, she was going through the 'perfect storm' in her mind to cause her to take her own life."

Clare also suffered from extreme eczema, asthma, and allergies, for which she was on medication. Sammie later found out that the medication can have a serious side effect — suicidal thoughts.

Sammie immediately turned to the Blessed Mother, who knows as well as anyone what it's like to lose a child.

"The night Clare died, of course I didn't sleep much — tossing, turning, weeping, pacing," Sammie recalled. "We have a big window in our living room with rocking chairs in front of it. In the early morning hours, I got up and went to sit in one of those chairs. The skies had cleared, and it was the night of the big 'honey moon.' The moon was huge in that big window. As many people say, I believe the moon stands for Our Blessed Mother — reflecting the light of her Son. I believe she was silently keeping vigil with me — praying and standing with me."

At the funeral, many students approached Sammie to tell her that Clare had helped them through difficult times, including deep depression. Some shared that Clare had protected them from bullying.

Sammie racked her brain for days and months trying to make sense of it all. Had she missed something? Did she somehow give Clare "permission" to kill herself by telling her that her daily prayer intention was for someone who would die that day?

Why didn't God save her daughter? Why didn't He show her what Clare was going through? Why did she go out to pray instead of staying at home when she saw that her daughter was downcast? But she came to realize that she would never understand all of the "whys," and even if she did, it would still never make sense to her or be enough of a reason for her daughter to have done what she did.

Seeking help and support in her grief, Sammie looked in her parish and in her Catholic faith, but could not find any specific program or ministry that could help her.

"I knew the devil wanted to use this to annihilate my family," Sammie said, "but I refused to let that happen."

Two months after Clare's death, Sammie took one of the notebooks that she had bought Clare for school and began to record suitable passages from Scripture, the *Catechism of the Catholic Church*, and quotes from saints who had made it through hard times. This notebook has become the makings of her new life's mission — to create a Catholic grief ministry program that can spread from parish to parish so that no one would have to grieve alone.

In the meantime, Sammie, her friends, and her family have offered hundreds of Masses for the repose of Clare's soul. Sammie wants others to know the importance of praying for the souls in Purgatory.

"People need to remember to pray for their loved ones who have passed," she said. "Don't just assume they went to Heaven."

One night about six months after Clare died, Sammie begged her "Clara" to come to her in a dream and let her know that she was OK. She needed a sign.

That night, Sammie couldn't sleep. She walked around the house most of the night. Not until the early morning hours did she finally fall asleep — and she got her sign. She dreamed she was in a big hotel. Two girls were playing inside a gift shop and trying very hard to make her laugh. She laughed and smiled at them. She couldn't see their faces because they had donned masks and feathers from the gift store to cover their faces. At one point, though, the girls exchanged masks, and Sammie saw that one of the girls was Clare. She ran up to her and called her name and kissed her on the cheek. Clare had a huge smile. She took Sammie by the arm and led her down a hallway.

In the dream, Clare said, "I have to get back now, Mom. I have to get back!"

Sammie replied, "Clare, why do you have to get back?"

"I've tasted everything here, Mom," she responded, "and everything tastes so much sweeter there. I've done everything here, Mom, and everything's so much greater there."

Sammie said, "What's so great there, Clare?"

She said, "I gaze on the beauty of God."

At that moment, Sammie's alarm went off, and she awoke. This dream brought great consolation to Sammie, and she even wondered if the other girl was the baby she had miscarried before having Clare.

Since then, Sammie's journey has been one of healing and forgiveness.

"I don't seek out the girls who bullied my daughter," she said, "but I do forgive them, and I pray and sacrifice for them so that their lives go well and they be good and holy young women."

Forgiveness, she said, is a process that sometimes requires a bending of her will.

"Eventually the bending of your will softens your heart," she said, "and forgiving becomes much easier."

Even more difficult, though, has been forgiving herself. Even today she still struggles with guilt. "She was my baby," said Sammie. "There are days when I scream out into the air, 'Clare, please forgive me!' I pray to the Blessed Mother to lend me her hope, her trust, and her faith."

She said, "The future is hard, but I stay close to Jesus and the Blessed Mother, and I feel closer to Clare now more than ever before. I'm a simple woman, I don't have much to offer, but I don't want anyone to have to grieve alone or turn to other things like mediums or 'seers' or anything else. In our Catholic faith, we have redemptive suffering, the saints, the Blessed Mother, the Eucharist. These are what can bring us through anything in life, even the most difficult times."

Her other children, Sally and Gus, have been tremendously helpful in reminding her that she is, and always has been, a good mother. Sammie continues to pray the Chaplet of Divine Mercy every day for Clare.

"I know that God is outside of time and space," she said. "I know He can apply graces from my prayers to the moment of her death. I leave it in His hands, knowing that mercy is His greatest attribute. I know He loves Clare infinitely more than I am capable of. I trust that my God has Clare in His loving care. As St. Faustina taught us, our words have to be 'Jesus, I trust in You'!"

What an incredible story. Sammie has been able to find hope and peace in the depths of a shattering loss. Although no loss of a loved one is the same, her response to these tragic events can inspire us and teach us in so many ways. As mentioned, she has told us that you don't ever "get over" the loss of a loved one to suicide, but you can "get through" the grief and trauma.

Let's look at this story in greater detail, specifically as it relates to the three spiritual principles of powerlessness over loss, trust in Jesus, and entrustment to God.

*P*OWERLESSNESS *OVER* *LOSS.* First, let's consider some areas in the Woods' tragedy that rendered them powerless over the loss of their beloved Clare. We see from their story that Clare was a very popular girl, well-liked by her friends and deeply loved by her family. She was a person of faith who encouraged others to "make God loved." Clare was also quick to help younger and less-fortunate teens in their struggles, especially with peers. Her act of suicide came as a complete shock to her family and her community. Nobody saw it coming.

As one could imagine, the scene of Clare's death was graphic. Moving Clare out of the rain and into the barn, Sammie held her daughter's lifeless body in her arms for some three hours while waiting for emergency personnel to arrive. Prior to their arrival, Sammie recounts that a "very dear" deacon of their parish church arrived on the scene as she held Clare, sobbing. Peering up at him through tear-filled eyes of angst, shock, and bewilderment, she said to him, "There is nothing for this. There is *nothing.*"

No words, no spiritual insight, not even the immediate presence of God's minister could bring any consolation or explanation for the events that had just unfolded. The reality of the raw emotion and trauma that Sammie and her family experienced has to be left for what it is; it cannot be downplayed or ignored, only endured. That is powerlessness.

The scene is reminiscent of the one immediately following our Lord's death upon the Cross, when Jesus is placed in the arms of His mother. Given the description, who can't help but think of Michelangelo's depiction of the Blessed Virgin holding her Son in her arms immediately after His death? No doubt, Sammie and her family will replay these events in their minds for years to come. How could they not?

The subsequent weeks and months were nearly impossible for the Wood family to bear. Sammie describes the immediate effects of the acute grief she felt after the loss of Clare:

When we first lost our daughter suddenly and tragically, the world became foreign to us. The unthinkable could actually happen. It was as if we had been plunged into the middle of the ocean, in the dark of the night, in the midst of a perfect storm. The waves of grief, shock, and despair were crashing down upon us from all sides. At times we were in the trough of the wave, barely able to draw our next breath. Other times we were at the crest of the wave; we could actually see a shoreline in the far-off distance. Our only hope was to cling to the cross as to a life preserver. We knew it was the only way — we knew only Jesus could bring us through this storm. Only He could "set us high upon a rock" and save us.

Here, Sammie offers a powerful description of the desperation one can experience when grieving. She had nowhere else to go. Feeling completely lost and helpless, her family turned to the one unfailing source of hope that they knew — the Cross of Christ.

Clare's decision to take her own life left so many perplexing questions for Sammie, Chip, and the family. Sammie "racked her brain for days and months" trying to make sense of the situation, wondering if her maternal heart had missed some obvious indication of a struggle beyond her recognition. Sammie disclosed that she left no stone unturned in her consideration of the events leading up to Clare's death, mulling them over and over in her mind. As a father who feels it his duty to protect and defend his family, Chip also struggled incessantly to make sense of the situation. Sammie shared with me that, as parents, they felt as if they had failed in the most fundamental task entrusted to them — to care for and protect their child. Again, this is powerlessness.

We also see that Sammie questioned God, even though she is a woman of prayer and faith. Just prior to Clare's act, she walked the ranch praying the Rosary and Chaplet of Divine Mercy for someone who would die that day. Sammie bargained and pleaded with God, asking why He didn't save her daughter from such an incomprehensible tragedy. In time, she arrived at the realization that she was powerless over the death of Clare and that all her questioning and attempts to piece the puzzle together could never be fully resolved. Even if she did have the answers, it still wouldn't make any sense to her.

Questioning or bargaining for answers is a normal part of grief resolution, but it is also intensified and amplified in the case of a suicide. Some mysteries in life are far beyond us, those for which no power of intellect or good will can produce satisfactory explanations. Sammie arrived at the conclusion, "Our only hope was to cling to the cross as to a life preserver. We knew it was the *only* way — we knew only Jesus could bring us through this storm. Only He could 'set us high upon a rock' and save us." Knowing that she was powerless to make any sense of the situation or to bring Clare back again, she turned with trust to God and placed Clare in His hands, along with all her perplexity and unresolved questions.

TRUST IN JESUS. Looking at the Wood family tragedy, we see how Sammie turned to Jesus and Mary with trust to find consolation, strength, and hope in the aftermath of an entirely baffling, senseless loss. Several years prior to Clare's suicide, Sammie and Chip lost a child in a miscarriage. In her pain and anger, Sammie slammed shut the door of her heart to God, a common response from those of us who have been deeply wounded by such an event. She later expressed how she knew that she couldn't have the same response of anger toward God this time around. In the case of her daughter's death, Sammie knew that in her own strength, she couldn't withstand the pain and suffering that lay ahead. She had to have the strength that comes only from God.

Extremely restless and inconsolable on the night of Clare's death, Sammie recognized the presence of the Blessed Mother, symbolized in the large honey moon visible through her picture window. Even in the immediate wake of such a devastating loss, she saw a glimmer of hope in her situation, sensing the care and concern of a mother who could identify with the depths of indescribable pain in another mother's heart. As the Mother of God, Mary saw her suffering Son nearly annihilated before her very eyes. Sammie knows that this mother comprehends maternal agony like no other, and so she looked to Mary as the brightest reflection of God's light in the midst of her darkness.

Sammie told me that she believes that God draws closest to us when we suffer, because the Father sees Jesus in us then. He sees His Son's Passion and draws close to Him, to *Emmanuel* (the Hebrew name for Jesus, meaning, "God with us"). In her weakness and struggles, Sammie draws upon the strength of God in prayer, knowing that He is the most steadfast source of comfort and understanding.

Sammie also recognized the forces of evil that sought to destroy her and her family over the loss of Clare. Like a fierce mother bear ready to battle with an intruder in her family den, she refused to surrender to the taunts and threats of the evil one. She continues to trust in God and to place herself under His protection.

*E*NTRUSTMENT TO GOD'S CARE AND PROTECTION. As a woman of faith who has experienced the love of God at a deep level, Sammie is confident that Clare is in God's care. She trusts in His infinite mercy, proclaiming it to be His greatest attribute. She knows that the Father loves Clare "infinitely more" than she is capable of, even as a mother who has loved her daughter very dearly. She has had hundreds of Masses said for Clare, and continues to offer her to the Father in every Eucharistic celebration. As we saw with Fr. Chris' story in Part One, Sammie knows that God is outside of chronological time as we know it and that her prayers can make a difference for Clare at the moment of her death.

She also prays the Chaplet of Divine Mercy for her daughter every day. She encourages others who have gone through similar tragedies not to presume eternal life for those who have died by suicide. Sammie acknowledges the grave nature of the act of suicide, so she remains persistent in praying for Clare. She recognizes the pain that Clare's action inflicted upon their family and community, but she also refuses to give in to despair or to be angry at her daughter. Sammie knows that Clare loved God, and of course, that God loves her "Clara" more than she could ever imagine.

*C*OMMUNION WITH CLARE IN GOD. Although Sammie turns to God and is consoled by Him in her suffering, the memory of this loss always remains with her. She uses an analogy to describe the phenomena, saying, "It's like there's a pot of boiling water always on the stove. When I discuss Clare with others, it's like lifting the lid off the pot to release the pressure and steam. Clare is always with me, simmering just beneath the lid." Even though she has moved into integrated grief and the acceptance stage of healing, Clare and the events of her death are always a part of Sammie, every moment of every day.

Another observation we can take from the Wood family story is that Sammie continues to love Clare "in God," trusting her to the merciful Heart of the Father, who desires that not one of His little ones be lost. She continues to commune with Clare, knowing that physical death is not the end of her daughter, but just the beginning of a new way of be-ing, a new and fuller way of living. So it is with our departed loved ones. They do not cease to exist; they simply exist in another mode of being. And as the Church teaches, we Christian believers are part of the Communion of Saints, the Body of Christ. We are capable of continued communion with our faithful departed through God's Spirit, even after their death.

Just six months after her death, Sammie begged her "Clara" to come to her in a dream and give her a sign. That night, she dreamt of Clare as a little girl who had visited her from Heaven. Sammie saw Clare smile at her with eyes full of joy and peace. Then Clare had to get back to where things were "sweeter" for her, where she gazes perpetually on the beauty of God. This dream was a great grace given to Sammie, divine solace in the midst of turbulent grief.

Now, five years after her daughter's suicide, Sammie shares that she "feels closer to Clare now than ever before," adding, "I tell her many times a day in my heart that I love her and that I miss her. I pray for her always, especially the Chaplet." She says that, as a mother who is already accustomed to multitasking, she always carries Clare with her throughout the day. As Sammie's experience demonstrates, continued communion with your loved one through the Mystical Body of Christ can offer tremendous consolation and aid you in the healing process.

As a result of her healing in grief, Sammie recognizes the little signs of her daughter's presence around her, simple things that trigger a memory. Sammie shares that she might find something like a penny or feather in an unusual place that reminds her of some precious moment she shared with Clare. It's a reminder that her daughter is near and safe, even though she still grieves her. It is important to recognize and acknowledge these signs of consolation from above regarding our lost loved ones. They might seem insignificant to some, but they can mean the world to you, moments to be cherished as precious gifts from a loving God.

A Survivor's Concern for Others. To assist in alleviating some of her own interior pain from the loss of Clare, Sammie also directs her attention to those she might help in a special way because of her circumstances. She prays for her family and many others who have suffered a similar loss. She even formed the beginnings of a grief program to help others in their need. Some of its content is included in this book. Although she knows she will always bear a certain wound from the physical absence of her daughter, she demonstrates through her journey that "with God all things are possible" (Mt 19:26). Her life and her tragic experience have become not only manageable, but transformational, mysteriously capable of generating blessings and good from her incredibly painful loss.

Most poignantly, Sammie shows us that, along with Clare and all of our loved ones, we are ultimately called as God's children into communion with Him, to "gaze on the beauty of God" as our true destiny, sharing in eternal life with and in God Himself — our ultimate hope. Throughout the remainder of the book, we will reference additional insights that Sammie's testimony offers. For now, let's take a deeper look at how the three spiritual principles can assist us in our journey through grief.

CHAPTER THREE

Three Spiritual Principles Further Explained

In the previous chapter, we introduced three spiritual principles that can be incorporated into your process of healing from grief. However, these principles can be used wherever we might be in our Christian journey. In fact, they are really just a summary of our initial response to Christ when we first heard the Good News of salvation.

After the apostles encountered the Risen Christ and were empowered by the Holy Spirit, they went out to bring this message of hope to those living in darkness. Considering the Acts of the Apostles, an historical-spiritual account of the apostles' mission, we see that three actions are asked of those who hear the Gospel: Repent, believe in the name of Jesus, and be baptized. These three actions correspond to the three spiritual principles for healing in one's grief and can be a helpful aid to all who desire to continue to grow in their love for God.

The first principle calls us to admit that we are powerless over the loss of our loved one and the subsequent effects of grief upon us. In essence, it corresponds to repentance, which also is an admission of powerlessness over the grip and effects of sin in our lives. The second principle is simply turning to trust in Jesus, the Divine Mercy, to restore manageability in our lives, which corresponds to belief in His name and His Person, and to the hope that this belief instills in us. The third principle is a conscious act of entrustment of ourselves and our beloved departed to the care and protection of God, an act that corresponds to our Baptism. It's much like a renewal of our baptismal promises; it is a re-entrustment of ourselves to the loving care of the Father. Let's now look more closely at each of these three spiritual principles.

FIRST PRINCIPLE

WE ADMIT THAT WE ARE POWERLESS OVER THE LOSS OF OUR LOVED ONE.

When we lose someone very dear to us, the loss is akin to losing a limb. If we suddenly lost an arm, for example, the effects would be devastating. Until that arm is no longer there, we probably don't realize how much we depend on it. We use our arms to hold our children, to work, and to do simple tasks like opening doors, picking up laundry, changing channels with the remote, and taking out the trash. We are so accustomed to living and operating with two arms that if we lost one, our everyday activities would suddenly seem unmanageable. We might even continue to act as if our arm was still with us, a phenomenon called "phantom limb syndrome."

Likewise, we never realize how much another person is a part of our lives, a part of our very being, until they are gone. It is to be expected that just as with the loss of a limb, our lives may seem unmanageable without them. They have been a part of us, perhaps even part of our daily lives. We have talked, laughed, and cried with them. We have enjoyed simply spending time with them. Perhaps we have cared for them throughout their lives, as is the case with a son or daughter. Perhaps they cared for us, as our parents did. Maybe we walked hand-in-hand with them through years of marriage, meeting life's joys and challenges together.

When a loved one is suddenly taken from us, life may seem completely out of our control and even foreign to us. We have created a bond of love with them that can never be replaced, at least not exactly in the same way. We will never share those special moments with them again. We're bound to feel a void when they're gone — sometimes a terrible, gut-wrenching void — from which we feel we might never recover.

Like those having the sensation of a phantom limb, we may proceed with the ingrained anticipation that our loved one is still with us — that they'll walk through the door at any moment. We may proceed with the expectation that they will come down the steps for breakfast, or that they'll join us for Mass, or for a walk, or a favorite TV show. As we indicated earlier, this stage of denial is a natural part of the grieving process.

Denial allows us time to adjust and reorient ourselves to life without our loved one. We may feel awkward, frustrated, and afflicted at first. We may think of the person hundreds of times during the day, just as we would continually think about a missing limb.

At some point, however, we must accept that we are completely powerless over such a loss. We are also powerless over some of the consequences that have been brought upon us. This is often very difficult for us to grasp. Perhaps we do not want to accept our loss. We are hurting and we do not like the symptoms of our grief. Our loved one is gone, and the harsh reality is that nothing we do can bring them back. When this fact truly sets root into the core of our being, we will likely experience a sense of complete disorientation and bewilderment.

As previously mentioned, disorientation and loneliness are common companions of acute grief. One point to remember is that, whatever your grief symptoms may be, they are not your fault. They are the effects of a major change in your life. No matter what you are enduring, remember to be gentle with yourself. The important thing is to acknowledge your grief in the present moment. Grief and mourning are a part of life. Remember, even Jesus mourned.

GOOD MOURNING. One of Fr. Chris' favorite Scripture trivia questions often puts people to the test: He asks them to identify the shortest verse in Scripture. Guess it yet? It's from the Gospel of John: "Jesus wept" (11:35). These two words couldn't be more profound.

The context of the surrounding verses is that Jesus had heard of the illness of His friend Lazarus of Bethany, the brother of Martha and Mary. When Jesus and His disciples arrived at Lazarus' home, they found that Lazarus had been in his tomb for four days. Jesus had come because He "loved Martha and her sister and Lazarus" (11:5). As was consistent with Jewish practice, "many of the Jews had come to Martha and Mary to console them concerning their brother" (11:18). Lazarus' friends and relatives were in mourning for him, weeping at the tomb of their beloved deceased.

Jesus demonstrated how intimately He identified with their sorrow. He was "deeply moved in spirit and troubled" over the death of Lazarus (11:33). He felt the pain of loss with Martha and Mary for their brother. And so He wept. As this story shows us, Jesus identifies with our human emotions and sentiments because He is "like us in all things but sin"; therefore, "we have not a high priest who is unable to sympathize with our weaknesses" (Heb 4:15). We can be sure that He feels the pain of the loss of our loved one as well.

Yes, our Lord mourned. And so some of the saintliest of Christians have wept and mourned as well. The fact that we mourn doesn't mean we've lost our faith, doubt our faith, or have somehow failed to trust. Moreover, mourning is not a selfish act. To mourn is natural. To mourn is honest. To mourn means that we have loved and lost someone of irreplaceable value — or at the very least, that we no longer have their presence in the manner to which we were previously accustomed.

In fact, it's important to mourn. It's important to give yourself time. Across cultures, people have different rituals for mourning their deceased. For example, the Irish wake or the Jewish tradition of keeping *kaddish*. Some cultures have a tradition of widows wearing black for a period after the death of their spouse. Consider the mourning of our Blessed Mother, most touchingly portrayed in artist renderings of Our Lady of Sorrows. Despite the grace of foreknowledge of her Son's imminent Resurrection, she mourned His suffering and death at Mount Calvary. Who among us is not moved by Michelangelo's depiction of Mother Mary in the magnificence of the "Pietà"?

A period of mourning and ritual expressions of grief can be an enormous help. The process of a wake, a funeral Mass, and the burial or interment of a family member or friend's remains allows you to grieve with your parish community and close relatives. It answers the perennial problem for those close to the survivors of what to do for them by giving the whole community a ritual to follow.

When grieving, we might ask ourselves the question, "How long will it take to be 'all right' again?" The answer to that question varies from person to person. Generally, the first year after a loss is very difficult. You're dealing with the funeral arrangements and the immediate challenges resulting from a major change in your life. For the very first time, you pass over anniversaries and birthdays, over holidays that come loaded with memories and associations. You're trying to make it through life with a huge hole punched in the middle of it. The first year after the loss of a loved one to suicide is often earth-shattering.

One key recommendation made by secular and spiritual authorities alike is that, if possible, you should not make major decisions during a period of desolation such as mourning. In times of deep sorrow, you may be prone to be unduly influenced by emotions that will eventually pass, rather than by reason and spirit. Let the sharpest pangs of grief subside before making any serious decisions. If necessary, make them in consultation with a trusted confidant.

*C*ONSUMER BEWARE. It is important to mention that one caveat to be careful of during the grieving process is the potential risk of self-medication, that is, using substances that are not regulated and monitored by qualified medical professionals. It is not uncommon for those who suffer a traumatic life event such as a suicide to turn to alcohol, habit-forming prescription medications, or illicit drugs to alleviate the pain. (We are not referring to legitimately prescribed antidepressants or medications, a topic far beyond our expertise. Please consult with your medical professional[s] regarding prescribed medications.)

Unregulated substances will often lift the immediate intensity of the suffering that comes with grief. However, as mentioned in Part One, self-medication can be a dangerous, slippery road that can result in psychological and physiological dependencies, anxiety, greater depression, and lack of control. At some point, we need to walk through the pain of our loss if we hope to regain real peace and a sense of manageability in our lives. Complete avoidance of the pain we are experiencing, especially pursued through alcohol and illicit mind-altering chemicals, only digs our hole deeper and deeper — and in the case of substance abuse, can cause us serious harm or even death.

If you think for a moment that you may be experiencing signs or effects of addiction to alcohol or other substances, please seek help immediately. *There is no shame in getting help.* Talk with someone you trust. Talk with your pastor. Talk with a medical professional. Reach out to those who are recovering from similar afflictions, such as members of Alcoholics Anonymous or similar 12-step programs. They will be only too happy to help, and there will be no judgment attached.

*A*NGER AT GOD. Another factor to consider in regard to accepting powerlessness over our loss is how we feel toward God. During a time of acute grief, it may often seem that our lives are out of control, and that an inescapable avalanche is hanging over us, ready to bury us at any moment. During these burdensome times, we may feel completely powerless, incapable of even lifting a prayer to God. We may even feel that He has completely abandoned us — that He cannot be trusted. After all, isn't He the Author of all life? Didn't He permit the loss of our loved one? Didn't He allow them to take their own life? Doesn't

He have a part in all of this? Where was His mercy in *their* misery and despair? Where is He in ours? Our response to these questions may be anger at God.

Anger at God is a common, understandable reaction to the grieving process. It doesn't mean we're failing to be faithful or to believe in God. In one sense, it's fine to be angry at Him. It can be a good and necessary part of our healing as we walk through our grief. It also means you believe in Him, know Him, and even trust in Him. You wouldn't be talking (or complaining) to Him otherwise.

Once again, we can look to an example from Scripture. Job, too, was angry with God, angry with what was happening to him and his family. Job complained about his treatment at the hands of God, and *Job was right to complain*. He was an innocent man, undergoing terrible suffering that he did not merit by his own actions.

So Job called upon God to give an answer for the woes that had befallen him. God heard Job's grieving plea and came down before His angry, confused servant. Job complained to God, professing his innocence and the unfairness of the injustices that had fallen upon him and his family.

If we look more closely, however, we see that Job did not waver in his trust of God. He humbly called out to the Lord in the midst of his emotional, psychological, and spiritual pain. Confronted with the living presence of God, Job finally found peace through his sincere prayer — through honest communication with God, who gave Job a different perspective than he had previously. The same can happen to us when we call upon the Lord.

Like Job, you can give yourself permission to be upset with God. Speak to Him about your confusion. Eucharistic Adoration is often a great place to have such conversations. Here, the Lord has made Himself our "captive audience," humbly awaiting us under the veiled appearance of bread. Certainly, without fear or trepidation, we can approach such a God who has made Himself so seemingly small.

We can also find consolation and a way to express our anger in the psalms, especially those known as the *psalms of complaint or the psalms of lament*.[127] In these psalms, we can draw upon the strength of Scripture and find words to tell God of our anger, pain, and confusion. The Book of Psalms has been the model of prayer for Jews and Christians for thousands of years. And surprisingly, the psalms of complaint or lament make up a large portion of the Book of Psalms!

Just remember that God wants you to come to Him, even in your sins and weakness, even when you're mad, or sad, or speechless with grief. He wants you to come to Him with confidence and love. He loves you and is listening intently to you, even during those times when He seems far off — in fact, *especially* then. He does not condemn you for your anger. He does not condemn you for the honesty of your prayer. Recall the Lord's agony on the Cross. Identifying with us in the extremes of His own suffering, He cried out, "My God, my God, why hast thou forsaken me?" (Mt 27:46).

If we are angry with God, sometimes it's because there's something we don't quite understand yet. We might ask, "Why is this happening? What kind of God would allow this? I really need to know what is going on here!" We may even question God's motives — does He really love us unconditionally? Or does He just want us to suffer? In this way we acknowledge our powerlessness and lack of understanding over our traumatic circumstances.

*I*S GOD REALLY GOOD? This question can be a real problem for those of us who have endured grave tragedies, especially when we thought God should have prevented them. How can we come back to our previous faith in a good God? We may still believe He exists; we may be confident in His power, but we may reflect on a loss we have experienced and be strongly tempted to wonder, "Was this the best you could do? Did you *mean* for someone who meant so much to me to die like this? Did you *want* me to go through all this suffering and sorrow?"

C.S. Lewis gave this sort of questioning powerful expression in his book *A Grief Observed*. It's about as forceful a literary exposition of the pain of grief as you will ever find. In it, Lewis rails at God unreservedly. He wonders if God is really the "Cosmic Sadist," asking if He delights in pain and suffering and is causing it intentionally. One of the greatest Christian writers of all time, Lewis challenged the goodness of God in his grief — before taking it all back.

Why did he become convinced that God is good and not the Cosmic Sadist?

The answer is that Lewis had two "epiphanies" that pointed to the goodness of God. First, he recognized that he was being tempted to substitute feelings for thought. In other words, he saw that his grief was overwhelming his capacity to reason. In the short term, this reaction may be inevitable. There are times when a person in grievous pain is not able to think clearly. That's understandable — we are more than just rational animals. We are sons and daughters of God, made for love, and so when we lose someone we love, it is supposed to hurt. In the Sermon on the Mount, Jesus proclaimed, "*Blessed* are those who mourn, for they shall be comforted" (Mt 5:4; emphasis added).

Second, Lewis realized that a sadist would not be capable of creating beautiful things like flowers, or giving us simple pleasures like sunsets to watch, or providing for our needs. These goods are completely outside the grasp of someone who only enjoys the pain of others; the Creator cannot imagine the good and the beautiful without already being good and beautiful. Lewis saw that the world is a harmonious wonder and a beautiful mystery despite the pain and suffering present here.

Saint Augustine came to the same conclusion as did Lewis, and issued this challenge:

> Question the beauty of the earth, question the beauty of the sea, question the beauty of the air distending and diffusing itself, question the beauty of the sky ... question all these realities. All respond: "See, we are beautiful." Their beauty is a profession. These beauties are subject to change. Who made them if not the Beautiful One who is not subject to change? (*CCC*, 32)[128]

These two great thinkers assure us that God is good because He made all that is good. The fact that God is good, however, may not be a comfort in the midst of your current challenges. How do you square that goodness with the tragedy you've experienced and the broken and fallen world we live in?

You have to acknowledge that the world is broken — but not broken beyond repair. It's when we turn to the mercy of God that things begin to make sense again.

Our acknowledgment of our own brokenness — of our powerlessness over our loss — actually makes a lot of sense. At first, to admit our powerlessness might be perceived as a sign of weakness, an inability to cope with life on its own terms. Nothing could be further from the truth. It takes tremendous courage and determination to persevere through deep anguish and sorrow. It takes just as much courage to admit that we are powerless over loss and its effects upon us.

We are often taught and conditioned that we simply need to be strong and "pull ourselves up by our bootstraps." That approach may often work with many adversities that we encounter in life, but applied to grief and loss, it can have dismal consequences. As Kübler-Ross and Kessler observe, "When we shelve our pain, it doesn't go away. Rather, it festers in a myriad of ways."[129] It sits underneath the surface, always present but unaddressed. In this way, healing becomes difficult, if not impossible.

The only way through our darkness is to walk with courage in the grace of God, as we will discuss later. This is a mark of true strength, as we set out on perhaps the hardest journey we will ever have to make. But on the other side of our pain, as we walk through the fire of our suffering, healing awaits, healing that will transform us. Consistent with the message of the Gospel, Kübler-Ross and Kessler assure us that "peace lies at the center of the pain, and although it will hurt, you *will* move through it a lot faster than if you distracted yourself with external outings."[130]

Avoiding, resisting, and repressing our grief only postpones the pain — sometimes for weeks, months, or even years. But it doesn't heal it. Let's once again consider the experience of Sammie. As mentioned in the previous chapter, Sammie and her husband lost a child to miscarriage years prior to the death of their daughter Clare. Sammie became indignant at God, turning away from Him in her pain. She remembers her grief at the time: "The loss made me angry at God — so angry in fact, that I actually told Him, 'I miss my baby ... now You can miss me!' And I walked away. I walked away into anger, bitterness, and resentment. It was dark, cold, and lonely."

Eventually, Sammie realized that anger was not the answer. She explains her transformed perspective, recalling, "Jesus kept calling me back to Himself and, thanks be to His grace, I returned. When we lost another child later in life — Clare — I knew I couldn't grieve in the same way I had before. I wouldn't make it. I knew I needed God to help me."

As Sammie's story illustrates, once we admit our powerlessness over the loss of a loved one and its impact upon our lives, we need to find strength beyond ourselves that will enable us to function normally again. This brings us to the second spiritual principle for healing in grief — trust in Jesus.

SECOND PRINCIPLE

WE COME TO TRUST THAT CHRIST, THE DIVINE MERCY, CAN RESTORE OUR LIVES TO MANAGEABILITY.

We have not a high priest who is unable to sympathize with our weaknesses, but one who in every respect has been tempted as we are, yet without sinning. Let us then with confidence draw near to the throne of grace, that we may receive mercy and find grace to help in time of need.

— Heb 4:15-16

Sometimes, trust in another — even in God — can be difficult. We might feel vulnerable and afraid in our current state of powerlessness. However, this step of trust might not be as big as it seems. Jesus is the Good Shepherd who comes to us in our weakness and need. He does not impose heavy burdens and impossible terms upon us before we can receive His friendship and grace. His yoke is easy and His burden is light (see Mt 11:30). For this reason, He gives us simple aids that can help open the door to trust in Him. Let's consider three channels that can help us to step from powerlessness to trust: nature, silence, and the Image of Divine Mercy. They don't require much from us. They are God's simple gifts that can lead us to trust more easily in Him.

*O*N NATURE. In our grief, we may have difficulty opening up to God, a possible effect that we discussed in Chapter One. After such a serious, life-changing event, it is often easy to retreat into ourselves. Earlier, we briefly presented the risks of isolation — but what might we do to get out of ourselves if we are stuck in this prison?

One simple means of connecting with God is through nature. Much has been written on this topic, but here we only want to mention the positive effects of nature on our mental outlook. Creation can be a powerful way to get out of our "shells" and into healing, a "natural way" of healing through "nature's way." All we have to do is gaze up at the stars on a clear night, contemplate the vastness of the ocean as the waves crash on the shore, bask in a beautiful sunset, or take in a majestic view from a mountaintop. The wonders of nature help us to realize the beauty and immensity of God's creation. Immersing ourselves in nature can be an invaluable way to help us begin to trust in God's love for us, as we behold all He has provided.

A growing number of studies reveal a correlation between our exposure to nature and personal well-being. Research shows that more green spaces in neighborhoods "lower the average body mass index of the children who live there." They alter our mood and lift our spirits.

> Patients recovering from surgery have been found to need one day less in the hospital if trees can be seen from their windows instead of just bricks. A recent study has shown that people become more generous after they see pictures of nature. Time spent in nature has been shown to improve self-esteem and conflict resolution. One hour spent in nature can improve memory and attention span by 20%. Nature can help calm us. It can help us focus. It can even act as an anti-depressant.[131]

Nature awakens our spirit as well as our senses. God can communicate to us through such things as the sounds of water, birds, or a gentle breeze, which are a reflection of His own beauty. The harmony and balance of creation can reveal a God who is ever-present. Nature has a way of lifting us toward realities that transcend our circumstances. It can open us up to God when our miseries are weighing us down and tempting us to close in on ourselves. Just a short stroll outside can lead us to appreciate the reality of the Intelligent Designer who created our universe, as we saw with C.S. Lewis and St. Augustine.

As director of the Association of Marian Helpers in Stockbridge, Massachusetts, Fr. Chris understands this idea well. He logs many hours working for the Lord. I am a first-hand witness to his late-night shifts writing letters and emails to our Marian Helpers. He is also an avid outdoorsman. When the office begins to weigh too heavily on him, nothing eases his burdens as much as an outing in some crystal-clear water, fishing for smallmouth bass. Kayaking down the local Housatonic River, he shares the environment with beavers, eagles, and deer. Having some outdoor fun with his Marian brothers becomes therapeutic and re-energizes him for his work. As it does for all of us, nature has a way of giving him a greater perspective and appreciation for God, with a simple, all-access pass to beauty.

One other aspect of nature's healing power is worth considering here. Some might laugh at this notion, but those of us who have pets as part of our "circle of trust" will understand all too well how consoling they can be in our grief. All of creation is a gift from God and reflects His goodness and love for us. I once heard a homily where the priest expressed emphatically that our pets are God's gift to us, and that we should thank Him for them. I'd have to agree.

Charlie Bear, my 20-pound Shih Tzu, was a tremendous source of comfort for me at a time when I was grieving heavily. He always seemed to "just know" when I needed some Charlie Bear lovin'! And science seems to support my experience. Studies show that humans release two "feel-good" neurotransmitters — serotonin and dopamine — into the brain when petting a dog.[132] I saw this effect firsthand when I would take Charlie Bear to visit senior centers. Many nursing homes have adopted this natural, therapeutic practice for their residents. The "Charlie Bear effect" was also evident among high school students during his visits with them at stressful exam times. They seemed instantly relieved from their stress and were calmer going into their exams. Some schools have even experimented with the beneficial effects of service animals in the classroom.[133]

Amazingly, recent studies have proven that dogs and humans both release another chemical, oxytocin, in the brain during prolonged interactions, the same chemical released when mothers bond with their babies. Some call it the "love chemical."[134] This evidence shows what you may already know — that our furry friends can be a steady, reliable source of companionship through our grief. (If you have a pet by your side right now, I'll bet you are smiling as you read this. They have that effect on us!)

SOUNDS OF SILENCE. Sometimes in our grief, it's difficult to formulate any kind of prayer. Sammie expressed that there were many days when she could "hardly lift a prayer" under the weight of her suffering. Many of us have probably felt the same way. But God understands. When we are enduring the sorrow associated with the loss of a loved one, especially when it was by their own hand, it is precisely then that our God draws all the closer to us.

When we are weak, our prayer doesn't have to be complicated and full of drawn-out litanies or recited devotions. It may be as simple as "just being" with Jesus, sitting in His Presence and allowing Him to love us. As Jesus told St. Faustina, **"Tell aching mankind to snuggle close to My merciful Heart, and I will fill it with peace"** (*Diary*, 1074). During this kind of prayer, we don't have to say anything. We can simply allow ourselves to *be* in the silent presence of our loving God. In fact, this is often the most pleasing kind of prayer to our Lord, because it helps us come to Him as "little children," powerless and incapable of lifting ourselves up from the mire of suffering.

We know that little children are entirely dependent upon their parents to meet their every need. Infants cannot even verbalize their needs. They cannot feed themselves when hungry or change themselves when soiled. Are we not delighted to provide such basic necessities for them? In the same way, our good and loving Father recognizes the suffering of our grief and provides beyond measure for the needs of our hearts.

If you do absolutely *nothing* else with your grief, come to Jesus and sit at His feet. Come to Jesus, broken as you may be, and trust in His infinite goodness, even if you cannot lift your head to pray. Several times in difficult moments in my life, I recall entering the chapel before Jesus in the tabernacle, only able to sit slumped over and say, "Lord, this is all I got. This is all I can be right now." It is there that we just might find the most tender embrace we can possibly receive.

G*AZE* U*PON THE* I*MAGE OF* D*IVINE* M*ERCY.* Along with silent prayer, the visual image of Jesus, the Divine Mercy, can bring us tremendous grace and consolation without much effort on our part. This Image, in particular, bears abundant grace for those who use it to contemplate and adore the Lord, allowing them to be present in their powerlessness before a tender and loving God. It has a supernatural way of engendering trust in God.

If you look at the Image of Divine Mercy, you will see that Jesus is emerging from thick darkness as a new light of hope in your life. Notice His left foot; Jesus is taking the first gentle step toward you, meeting you wherever you are in pain, suffering, and even despair. His step is not an aggressive one. He comes clothed as a gentle High Priest, with His right hand lifted to impart blessings to you. His eyes are full of compassion, looking at you with love; as He tells St. Faustina: **"My gaze from this image is like My gaze from the cross"** (*Diary*, 326).

As a tender, loving friend, He understands your heartache. He bears the wounds of the most brutal of sufferings, betrayal, and rejection in the nail marks of His hands and feet. He is both priest and victim, able to sympathize with your every weakness because He has made Himself just like you in every way except sin (see Heb 4:14-16).

Jesus' love knows no limits of space or time; it is boundless. As pure merciful love, He is drawn to those of us in the greatest need of a Divine Physician — in greatest need of healing. In the Beatitudes, Jesus teaches us, "Blessed are the poor in spirit, for theirs is the kingdom of heaven" (Mt 5:3), and He tells St. Faustina that His kingdom on earth is His life in the human soul (*Diary*, 1784). Nowhere can He reside more fully than in a heart that is broken with misery. This is because a broken heart has found no other answer — it is powerless and knows it. God is its only remaining hope.

The mercy of God cannot resist such a heart. Jesus desires to hear every murmur of your very own heart in sorrow. He offers you an exchange of hearts as He pulls back the veil of His own Heart, revealing its infinite depths, saying, **"Look into My Heart and see there the love and mercy which I have for humankind ... look, and enter into My Passion"** (*Diary*, 1663). In the Heart of Jesus, you will find every grace to help you in your time of need. And in your heart, you will find His kingdom, where He desires to dwell at your invitation.

As you gaze upon Jesus in the Image of Divine Mercy and look into His Heart, draw upon the graces flowing from the fount of His mercy. Allow this gentle and understanding friend to console and heal your sorrowful heart. Your trust in Jesus will grow because He is a faithful, unwavering companion. You will find confident hope in the words He spoke to St. Faustina:

> I am offering people a vessel with which they are to keep coming for graces to the fountain of mercy. That vessel is this image with the signature, "Jesus, I trust in You!" (*Diary*, 327).

*T*RUST IN JESUS, THE DIVINE MERCY. Aided by such channels of grace as nature, silent prayer, and the Image of Divine Mercy, we might now be ready to take the definitive step of trust in Jesus. In the first spiritual principle of recovery in grief, we admit and accept that we are powerless over the loss of our loved one and its impact upon our lives. We know that we cannot bring our departed loved one back and restore our life to what it once was. We also know that it is nearly impossible to make sense of the senseless act of suicide. Likewise, we are powerless over the adverse effects of our loss, effects that often seem to dominate every waking and sometimes sleeping moments. Yet we are not alone in our misery. Saint Faustina herself said:

> [I] understand souls who are suffering against hope, for I have gone through that fire myself. But God will not give [us anything] beyond our strength. Often have I lived hoping against hope, and have advanced my hope to complete trust in God. Let that which He has ordained from all ages happen to me (*Diary*, 386).

This brings us squarely to the second spiritual principle: We come to trust that Jesus, the Divine Mercy, can restore our lives to manageability.

This principle places all its emphasis on trust. Trust in Jesus, the Divine Mercy, is the bridge that leads us to the shore of hope, sanity, and peace where we find the security of our Lord's embrace. Trust in Jesus is the linchpin (a pin that prevents a wheel from slipping off its axle) of our spiritual life. It truly is the master key that unlocks every grace we need in our lives.

We have mentioned the Image of Divine Mercy many times. When Jesus appeared to St. Faustina in several visions, He asked her to paint this Image according to the "pattern" that she had seen (*Diary*, 49). He also *insisted* that a "signature" be included with the Image — "Jesus, I trust in You." Of all the inscriptions He could have asked her to put under the Image, He asked for one that would include the word "trust." But why?

Trust inherently implies a relationship between two or more parties. It involves persons, beings capable of love, of communion and a bond of hearts. Trust may be the most precious quality for those in a relationship. Trust is the bridge of love between persons, enabling us to give ourselves entirely to another. We see it in all personal relationships in varying degrees, but especially in our closest ones, such as those between a husband and wife, mother and daughter, father and son, and so on.

It's no wonder that in battle, commanders target bridges. After all, bridges facilitate the flow of traffic. Take out the bridge, and the enemy is isolated and unable to move. Is it not the same with human persons in our relationships? Take out the bridge of trust, and married couples cannot reach one another. They grow apart on isolated "islands" of self. They "fall out of love."

Trust is the response that God has desired from humanity since its creation. Consider Adam and Eve in the Garden of Eden. God called upon them to trust Him, to believe in His words and rely upon His loving care and protection. But Adam and Eve demonstrated their *distrust* in God, instead trusting the words of the serpent. Their trust was entirely misdirected, and they became reliant upon themselves. The evil one knew to strategically target the "bridge of trust" in God, the linchpin of communion and of intimate relationship with Him. Strike the linchpin and the wheels fall off — literally.

As the Church teaches us in the *Catechism*, "Man, tempted by the devil, let his trust in his Creator die in his heart and, abusing his freedom, disobeyed God's command. That is what man's first sin consisted of. All subsequent sin would be disobedience toward God and *lack of trust in his goodness*" (397; emphasis added).

In your own unfolding journey, you have been hurt. You very well may feel that the "bridge of trust" connecting you to your lost loved one, as well as to others, has been targeted and taken out. You have loved another person and they are no longer here. Perhaps others around you have hurt you, too. When we have been hurt by another, distrust tends to enter our hearts, and we pull back to protect ourselves. We may want to build walls to shield us from any additional pain.

Trust in God might seem like a difficult step to take if you are in that state of mind, but recall the Image of Divine Mercy. Jesus Himself takes the first step toward us. Jesus is the Good Shepherd who sees your need for a friend, and He takes you upon His shoulders and carries you when it seems you cannot take another step. As Pope Benedict XVI wrote in his encyclical letter *Spe Salvi* (*Saved in Hope*):

> The true shepherd is one who knows even the path that passes through the valley of death; one who walks with me on the path of final solitude, where no one can accompany me, guiding me through: he himself has walked this path, he has descended into the kingdom of death, he has conquered death, and he has returned to accompany us now and to give

us the certainty that, together with him, we can find a way through.[135]

Pope Benedict's words should reassure you that Jesus does indeed go before you. By dying on the Cross, He guaranteed you sure passage through your suffering. He gave His life for you and established an eternal bridge to the Father. He Himself is the bridge. He *is* the Way, the Good Shepherd who leads you to the shores of hope. He can be trusted because He paid for our sins by the Blood of His Cross. For this reason, He insisted that the words "*Jesus, I trust in You*" be placed on the Image of Divine Mercy. He is unfailing in His love for you and cannot lead you astray in your trust in Him. He can only be true to you because He is Truth itself.

So choose to trust in Jesus, who is Mercy itself. He knows the way through your sorrow and the "valley of death" to greener pastures of healing, wholeness, and peace. Unlock the fountain of mercy with the precious key of trust in the Good Shepherd. As Jesus said, **"The graces of My mercy are drawn by means of one vessel only, and that is — trust. The more a soul trusts, the more it will receive"** (*Diary*, 1578).

Trust in Jesus, the Divine Mercy, is the bridge that can bring a solid foundation of hope for you and your loved one. While doubts may reenter your mind, you can always cross the "bridge of trust" again, returning to the loving and merciful Heart of Jesus. "Lord, to whom shall we go? You [alone] have the words of eternal life" (Jn 6:68). You alone bestow the mercy that restores us to manageability and hope. *Jesus, I trust in You!*

THIRD PRINCIPLE

WE MAKE A DECISION TO ENTRUST OUR WILL, OUR LIVES, AND OUR LOVED ONE TO THE LOVING CARE AND PROTECTION OF GOD.

Having regained our hope by trusting in Jesus' mercy, we are ready to entrust our will, our lives, and our lost loved one to the care and protection of Jesus, the Divine Mercy. As stated previously, this principle is nothing other than the renewal of the promises we made at our baptismal vows. Perhaps we were not then fully aware of what our Baptism entailed. Now, fully conscious of our intention to entrust ourselves and everything that is ours to Jesus, we draw upon the graces initially received at our Baptism and always available to us. This is a determined act that will have immediate effects if taken seriously.

But what does this act of entrustment entail for us as those who are grieving?

First, it means that we choose to give all of ourselves to Jesus, including our mind, our will, our heart, our emotions, and our body. We bring to Him our pain and the effects we have suffered from the loss of our loved one. We bring Him our misery, guilt, and shame. We bring Him our sinful inclinations and all our weaknesses. We entrust ourselves into His care and protection just as we are, along with our fears, insecurities, doubts, and shortcomings. We give ourselves entirely to Him without reserve.

Second, we also entrust the one whom we mourn to Jesus' care and protection. We trust in His love and goodness, and we know that He desires the peace, joy, and happiness of our loved one infinitely more than we ever could. Think about that. Think about how much you love the one whom you have lost. Then consider how much greater is Jesus' love and care for them. With bold confidence, entrust them to His mercy — *now and forever!*

Father Seraphim Michalenko, MIC, vice-postulator for St. Faustina's cause for canonization and renowned expert on the message of Divine Mercy, once told me an impressive story about his personal visit to Caesarea Philippi, the location of a massive wall of rock that is the backdrop of Peter's confession of faith. There, Peter said to Jesus, "You are the Christ, the Son of the living God." Jesus responded, "Blessed are you, Simon Bar-Jona! For flesh and blood has not revealed this to you, but my Father who is in heaven. And I tell you, you are Peter, and on this rock I will build my church, and the powers of death shall not prevail against it" (Mt 16:13-20).

Father Seraphim explained how astonishing it is to see this rock wall in person. He described the folds wherein doves find rest and protection from the harsh elements and how you can see the eyes of the doves looking out from the protected crevices of these folds. (In Church tradition, doves are a universal sign of peace, as well as the Holy Spirit and Mary's motherhood.) Then he explained how the folds serve as a natural representation of the pierced side of Christ, the Rock, where His bridegroom the Church securely dwells.

When you entrust yourself and your loved one to Jesus, you are like the doves sheltered in the crevices at Caesarea Philippi. You are hidden in the side of Christ, where the Blood and Water from His merciful Heart was poured out for the world. In your prayer, picture yourself and your loved one enfolded in the side of Christ, where His grace constantly pours over you to bring healing, restoration, and new life. As you were encouraged to do in Part One, pray this powerful prayer of trust: "O Blood and Water, which gushed forth from the Heart of Jesus as a fount of mercy for us, I trust in You." Pray it over and over again. This prayer is a sure source of healing and new life for souls in need of refreshment.

*A*CT OF *ENTRUSTMENT.* If you are now ready to fully give yourself and your loved one into the care and protection of God, you can make your entrustment concrete by offering this prayer (or one that is similar):

> Jesus, I trust in You. You are mercy and goodness itself. In this very moment and forevermore, I offer myself to You entirely to do with me as You will. Remove from me any obstacle that stands in the way of Your grace. I also offer and entrust to You my beloved _____ (name loved one). Take them fully into Your care and protection, now and for all eternity, and may I be fully reunited with them in Heaven. May Your will always be done in my life. Jesus, I trust in You!

You may want to make this prayer with another person at your side. I recall making a similar prayer when I was grieving a very difficult loss myself. I united my prayer to the Mass and included an interior offering of my will, my life, and my lost loved ones. Then I offered a prayer like the one above after the Mass. I chose to make these prayers before Jesus in the Blessed Sacrament with my parents and pastor alongside me, and with the invisible accompaniment of countless hosts of angels and saints in our great "cloud of witnesses" (Heb 12:1).

When you make this offering with a sincere heart, you can think of it as planting a "mustard seed" of hope, with the anticipation of growth. Growth in what? A sense of peace and harmony. You may begin to feel relief from the deep-seated agony that has seized control of your daily life. The hopelessness that pervaded your mind will begin to fade away. You will grow more confident in Jesus' care for the one you lost. A new sense of power and strength may emerge, along with love and gratitude for the nearness of Jesus and His loving mercy. These are all consequences of the integrated grief stage, whereby new strength and understanding often begin to take hold (as we saw in Chapter One, Part Two). The mustard tree of hope will blossom through our continued trust in Christ's loving mercy, sometimes quickly, sometimes gradually.

When times of doubt, heartache, and grief reemerge — as they undoubtedly will — seek to renew trust in Jesus, and recall your decision to offer yourself and your departed loved one to His care and protection. Repeat the words of our "prescription of hope" — Jesus, I trust in You. He has proven Himself in countless ways and will unfailingly come to you in His mercy again and again. He cannot and will not deny your plea, even if you don't clearly see His response or fully understand how He is present. In time, you will again rest securely in the hope of His never-ending love.

*T*HANKSGIVING AND THE *MASS*. We can fortify our decision to entrust ourselves and our loved one to Jesus, the Divine Mercy, through the offering of the Holy Mass — the *Eucharist*. The word itself means "thanksgiving." Every time we attend Mass, we offer thanksgiving for the presence of God in our daily lives. Here, we encounter and renew our bond of love with Him and the whole company of His chosen ones, on earth, in Heaven, and in Purgatory.

In Part One, we described the concluding doxology as the "supercharged" moment of the Mass. To refresh our memories, it is the offering of Jesus Christ, the Son of God, to the Father with a perfectly redeemed humanity in His Person as both High Priest and Victim at Calvary. The Paschal Mystery is not a re-crucifixion, but a re-presentation of the "once-for-all" sacrifice of Cavalry, made present again in the here and now.

In the Mass, particularly in the consecration of bread and wine through our reception of Holy Communion, we are united with Him in His offering to the Father. His sacrifice was made for us, and for all the suffering and agony we have endured from the loss of the one we mourn — past, present, and future. Therefore, the Mass is the perfect time and place to solidify and consecrate our decision to offer ourselves and others to the Father in union with Christ our Lord.

When we are ready to do so, we may choose to express our entrustment with a consecratory prayer similar to that of St. Faustina's:

> Today I place my heart on the paten where Your Heart has been placed, O Jesus, and today I offer myself [and _____ (name lost loved one)] together with You to God, Your Father and mine, as a sacrifice of love and praise. Father of Mercy, look upon the sacrifice of my heart, but through the wound in the Heart of Jesus (*Diary*, 239).

So, too, do we place our hearts, our lives, and our loved one on the paten with Jesus. Especially during the concluding doxology ("Through Him, and with Him, and in Him, O God, almighty Father, in the unity of the Holy Spirit, all glory and honor is yours, forever and ever"), we make our offering in union with Jesus to the Father in the hands of the priest. Definitively, we have now consecrated our decision. We are His entirely, and so is the one whom we entrust into the hands of God.

If we are Catholic and properly disposed, we can now consummate our offering by receiving the healing fruit of Jesus' perfect self-sacrifice at Calvary — His Body, Blood, Soul, and Divinity — from the "Tree of Life" in the Holy Eucharist. Our decision is complete. Entirely united with Jesus in the Holy Eucharist, we can say with Him, "It is finished." Our will, our life, and our loved one are entirely under the care and protection of Jesus, the Divine Mercy. Again, we might do well to unite ourselves with Jesus in a prayer after receiving Communion, as did St. Faustina:

> [Oh my Jesus] do with me as You please. I subject myself to Your will. As of today, your holy will shall be my nourishment, and I will be faithful to your commands with the help of your grace. Do with me as You please. I beg You, O Lord, be with me at every moment of my life (*Diary*, 136).

You can renew your entrustment at every single Mass. You can also have specific Masses celebrated and offered for your cherished departed. Here, the Church on earth intercedes directly for their needs in every single Liturgy. During the Eucharistic Prayer, we intercede on behalf of our departed loved ones as the priest prays:

> Remember our brothers and sisters (N. and N.), who have fallen asleep in the peace of your Christ, and all the dead, whose faith alone you have known. Admit them to rejoice in the light of your face, and in the resurrection give them the fullness of life.[136]

Furthermore, as we saw in Part One, we can also unite our prayers outside of the Mass to the same sacrifice offered on Calvary, the source and fount of all salvation and Divine Mercy. The Rosary and Chaplet of the Divine Mercy are particularly powerful. These devotions are a spiritual extension of the Mass that can be employed wherever we may be throughout our day.

REVIEWING THE THREE SPIRITUAL PRINCIPLES. Our three spiritual principles of healing can be summed up simply: First, we recognize our powerlessness over the loss of our loved one and the effects of grief upon us. Second, we pass over the "bridge of trust" in Jesus, the Divine Mercy, to the shore of hope that Jesus can restore manageability to our lives. Third, given this assurance of hope, we make a decision to entrust our will, our lives, and our loved one to Christ, the Divine Mercy.

The fact that we've made an act of entrustment, however, does not mean that we will stop experiencing the effects of grief and its various stages. It is still quite natural to experience some of these effects and stages over again. Remember, there is no set timetable or predetermined linear progression through this process. As is common, we will still undergo periods of denial, anger, bargaining, and depression. Again, this is a natural response to the loss of someone special in our lives. It has been said that "grief is nothing other than love with no place to go."

One of my favorite Academy-Award winning movies, "Good Will Hunting," powerfully captures the painful impact of loss that only comes from deep love. Although I know that "Good Will Hunting" has some adult language and content, its message is very pertinent, so I'd like to share it with you here. Sean, a psychology teacher played by Robin Williams (who tragically died by suicide himself in real life), is in conversation with Will, a boy-wonder genius, played by Matt Damon. Will has an answer for everything with his photographic memory and unparalleled IQ, but he is deeply wounded from childhood abuse as a foster child. Sean challenges Will's resistance to therapy and "real-life knowledge," which only comes through lived experience. In an unforgettable scene, Sean says to Will (emphasis added):

> If I asked you about love, you'd probably quote me a sonnet. But you've never looked at a woman and been totally vulnerable; known someone that could level you with her eyes. Feeling like God put an angel on earth just for you, who could rescue you from the depths of hell.
>
> And you wouldn't know what it's like to be her angel, to have that love for her, be there forever, through anything, through cancer.
>
> And you wouldn't know about sleeping sitting up in the hospital room for two months, holding her hand, because the doctors could see in your eyes that the terms "visiting hours" don't apply to you. **You don't know about real loss, 'cause it only occurs when you've loved something more than you love yourself. And I doubt you've ever dared to love anybody that much**.

This scene shows us the incredible power of love. When you're grieving, you feel true pain and true loss because you loved. *You dared to love someone more than you loved yourself.* As the saying goes, "'Tis better to have loved and lost, than to have never loved at all." The capacity to give and receive love sacrificially is what makes human beings the crown jewel of God's visible creation. This is precisely what we commemorate in every single celebration of the Eucharist.

Remember, allow yourself to grieve. Allow yourself normal, healthy anger, depression, and bargaining, all of which can be a source of healing for you, most particularly when you practice the three spiritual principles of accepting personal powerlessness, trust in Jesus, and the decision of total entrustment to Him and thereby to allow Him to console you. He will never abandon or betray you. He is yours, and you are His.

CHAPTER FOUR
Additional Spiritual Aids

In the previous chapters, we discussed three spiritual principles to help guide our journey of healing from the loss of our loved one. They lead us to vital practices for our ongoing grief management and recovery. In the context of these three principles, we examined particular sources of grace and mercy that will help us to heal: nature, silent prayer, and the Image of Divine Mercy. We also included the Mass, the Eucharist, the Rosary, and the Chaplet of Divine Mercy, as well as the need to be supported by other people from Heaven and on earth.

In this section, we want to focus on other sources of grace and healing, all of which can also be practiced in the context of our three spiritual principles.

MOTHER OF SORROWS, STAR OF HOPE. Earlier, we shared the story of the Wood family and mentioned that Sammie found refuge and understanding in Mary, the Mother of God. After losing her daughter by such incomprehensible means, Sammie turned to the Blessed Mother for consolation.

Looking up at the large honey moon outside her window on that unforgettable evening after she had lost Clare, Sammie saw in it a symbol of the Blessed Virgin of Nazareth. As the moon reflects the light of the sun, so, too, does Mary reflect the image and likeness of her own Son, Jesus, as no human being ever has. She alone accompanied Jesus from the instant of His human existence in the Incarnation to the very last breath of His earthly life at the Crucifixion. She bore His pain and suffering in her Heart as only a mother could.

When the Angel Gabriel appeared to Mary announcing that she would be the Mother of God and the instrument through which the Savior was born, she began her unique participation in salvation history, seeing it as "her 'destiny' to share, in a singular and unrepeatable way, in the very mission of her divine Son."[137] She gave her Son His human nature, His flesh that would redeem humanity, flesh that would be incomprehensibly mutilated, beaten, whipped, scourged, spat upon, mocked, and then mercilessly crucified.

Participating uniquely in the salvific suffering of her Son, Mary heard it prophesied during the presentation of Jesus in the Temple that a sword would pierce her Heart as well (see Lk 2:35). As Pope St. John Paul II observed:

> It is especially consoling to note — and also accurate in accordance with the Gospel and history — that at the side of Christ, in the first and most exalted place, there is always his Mother through her exemplary testimony that she bears *by her whole life* to this particular Gospel of suffering ... [and] with acute sensitivity, it was on Calvary that Mary's suffering, beside the suffering of Jesus, reached an intensity which can hardly be imagined from a human point of view but which was mysteriously and supernaturally fruitful for the redemption of the world.[138]

For this reason, the Blessed Virgin has been referred to in Church tradition as "Our Lady of Sorrows," a title that refers to the seven sorrows Mary endured in relation to the suffering of her Son (see Appendix F). Understanding from experience the agony and grief of indescribable suffering, this Mother of Sorrows is uniquely able to understand your grief with "acute sensitivity," having been "spiritually crucified"[139] with her Crucified Son upon Calvary. She is the new Eve, standing at the new Tree of Life (the Cross) with her Son, the new Adam.

It is for this reason that, in His final moments of earthly life, Christ assigned to Mary such a unique role:

> [T]he dying Christ conferred upon the ever Virgin Mary a *new kind of motherhood* — spiritual and universal — towards all human beings, so that every individual, during the pilgrimage of faith, might remain, together with her, closely united to Him unto the cross, and so that every form of suffering, given fresh life by the power of this cross, should become no longer the weakness of man but the power of God.[140]

Amidst acute and complicated grief, you may experience periods when no one can console you. Turn to Mary, your spiritual mother, given to you as a gift by Jesus Himself from the Cross. In His final moments, Jesus instructed Mary, "Woman, behold your son!" (Jn 19:26) referring to John, the Beloved Disciple, who at the Last Supper laid his head upon Jesus' chest to hear the whispers of His Heart (see Jn 13:23). John represents all of God's beloved children at the foot of the Cross. Christ then instructed John — and thereby all of God's beloved children — to "Behold, your mother!" (Jn 19:27).

To you who suffer a crippling trauma, to you who endure a soul-wrenching agony, follow Christ's instructions given from the Cross and behold your mother. Behold the woman who is the Mother of Sorrows, the woman who desires to hold you in the depths of her Heart. Like John, take Mary, the Star of Hope, into your home, which, according to a richer understanding of the Scripture text, means, *take your mother into your "inner life-setting,"*[141] and let her console that which is inconsolable.

As St. John Paul II grasped at a very deep level, "The divine Redeemer wishes to penetrate the soul of every sufferer through the heart of His holy Mother, the first and the most exalted of all the redeemed."[142] Like no other creature in human history, she alone is fully acquainted with the incomprehensible pain you feel in your heart. As your mother, she will bring you consolation and hope in the midst of darkness, as she did for her Son and the Beloved Disciple upon Mount Calvary. Allow her to comfort your suffering heart, for a sword of sorrow pierced her own Heart as surely as it has pierced yours.

*S*UFFERING: *U*NITIVE AND *R*EDEMPTIVE. Having undergone deep sorrow from a suicide, you are well acquainted with the anguish incurred by the shock of a friend or loved one's sudden death. As mentioned, its crippling effects can impact the body, mind, and spirit.

Let's face it: Even in its lesser forms, suffering is not an appealing option for most of us. We tend to flee from suffering, seeking to eliminate and alleviate its effects, whether physical, psychological, or spiritual. We naturally tend to avoid pain and seek pleasure. This is a natural, God-given response, designed to protect us and prolong our lives. However, suffering, pain, and death are unavoidable effects of our fallen human condition.

In his apostolic letter *Salvifici Doloris*, Pope John Paul II explains:

Suffering is, in itself, an experience of evil. But Christ has made suffering the firmest basis for the definitive good, namely the good of eternal salvation. By His suffering on the cross, Christ reached to the very roots of evil, of sin and death. He conquered the author of evil, Satan, and his permanent rebellion against the Creator.[143]

John Paul II witnesses to the fact that "Christ drew close above all to the world of human suffering through the fact of having taken *this suffering upon His very self.*"[144] As such, Jesus transforms the meaning of human suffering and associates intimately with the vulnerability of the human person in experiencing the overwhelming conditions that we can endure. In His own humanity, Christ becomes "sensitive to every human suffering, whether of the body or of the soul."[145]

So, too, through His suffering, Jesus is sensitive to the ultimate anguish of rejection and separation from those He loved, including the sense of being abandoned by the Father, as He cries out from the Cross, "*Eloi, Eloi, lama sabachthani?*" meaning, "My God, my God, why has thou forsaken me?" (Mt 27:46)

By embracing the depths of human suffering, Jesus gives us a way to unite to Him in our pains and struggles. As John Paul II further teaches, "*In suffering there is concealed* a particular *power that draws a person interiorly close to Christ*, a special grace."[146]

Suffering is an experience we share with the God-Man that uniquely binds us in love to Him and to the Father. As such, suffering has the power to convert and transform us, particularly from the inside; the effect of this conversion is "not only that the individual discovers the salvific meaning of suffering, but above all that he becomes a completely new person. He discovers a new dimension, as it were, of *his entire life and vocation.*"[147]

If you recall from Chapter One of Part Two, in the aftermath of loss, unforeseen and extraordinary graces can result from our experience of grief. We can discover "new capacities, wisdom, unrecognized strengths, new and meaningful relationships, and broader perspectives."[148]

It's reminiscent of the words from Viktor Frankl, the Austrian psychologist and Holocaust survivor. In his book *Man's Search for Meaning*, he recounts his search for meaning in the suffering he experienced and witnessed while interred at Auschwitz, writing that "even the helpless victim of a hopeless situation, facing a fate he cannot change, may rise above himself, may grow beyond himself, and by so doing change himself. He may turn a personal tragedy into a triumph."[149]

When our suffering and grief is united with the suffering of Jesus Himself, how much greater is our potential for wisdom, strength, and more meaningful relationships? In this way, our suffering can bring us into an intimate union with Christ that is a foretaste of Heaven. For this reason, some have compared the suffering of grief to the effects of the "dark night of the soul," as described in classic spiritual theology by St. John of the Cross and others.

Your grief is not an affliction of your own making. It has been imposed on you by an event beyond your control, as treated in our first spiritual principle — powerlessness over the loss of our loved one and its effects upon us.

However, by trusting in Jesus (our second principle), we can then move to an integrated grief that unites us more closely with God, the most important relationship for which we were created. Reflecting on the meaning of human suffering, Pope Benedict XVI writes, "It is not by sidestepping or fleeing from suffering that we are healed, but rather by our capacity for accepting it, maturing through it, and finding meaning through union with Christ, who suffered with infinite love."[150]

In your current state of mind, this may seem like a very hard teaching to accept. However, we know that in His humanity, Christ endured intense suffering and death, and thereby gave new meaning to our suffering — including the most senseless kind of suffering, such as from the loss of your loved one to suicide. It may be easier to appreciate the paradox of embracing pain and suffering when you consider what happens when we avoid our crosses. As Pope Benedict explains:

> It is when we attempt to avoid suffering by withdrawing from anything that might involve hurt ... that we drift into a life of emptiness, in which there may be almost no pain, but the dark sensation of meaninglessness and abandonment is all the greater.[151]

Recall again the experience of Sammie and her family, when grief overwhelmed them after getting the shock of their lives. They felt as if they could barely keep their heads above water. Having lived through the emptiness and darkness that ensued when she turned away from God amidst the pain of loss from her miscarriage years earlier, Sammie realized that in their current affliction, her family's "only hope was to cling to the cross as to a life preserver."

In the Cross of Christ, Sammie found the strength to endure her trials, which in turn led to a greater capacity for love and a deeper understanding of life's purpose — loving God here on earth so we can be eternally united with Him and our loved ones in Heaven. As we will discuss in the final chapter, the great paradox of the Cross is that it can bring a greater good out of the evils that an imperfect, fallen world can impose upon us.

It's important to note here that our suffering with Christ is not only unitive; we can also participate redemptively in His suffering for the sake of His Body, the Church (see Col 1:24). The merits of redemptive suffering can be applied to those who are in need of Christ's grace and mercy when we choose to unite our suffering with Christ's Passion. In this way, a greater dignity is bestowed upon the sufferer, as they receive the merits from our sharing in Jesus' redemptive love.

As we saw in Part One, these merits can also be applied for the salvation and sanctification of the one you mourn. Again, the great paradox of the Cross is on full display, showing us how God used Jesus' agonizing death to bring victory out of seeming defeat. By uniting your suffering to Christ's and applying the merits of that suffering back in time, the pain inflicted upon you by the death of your loved one can, in turn, bring forth the graces that will move them to embrace Divine Mercy at the moment of their death.

In other words, *the very suffering caused by your grief can be the means by which your loved one embraces salvation.* How amazing and paradoxical! *This is the power of Divine Mercy,* which can be appropriated for the good of your loved one through your suffering in union with Christ. With Pope John Paul II, we can exclaim:

> Even though the victory over sin and death achieved by Christ in His Cross and Resurrection does not abolish temporal suffering from human life ... it nevertheless *throws a new light* upon this dimension and upon every suffering: the light of salvation.[152]

*H*OUR OF *MERCY*. Jesus' suffering reaches its culmination in the final moments of His life, of which we are reminded every time our clocks strike 3 p.m. The 3 o'clock hour commemorates the hour of Jesus' death upon the Cross, when the soldier's spear pierced His side and the source of eternal life gushed forth from the depths of His divine Heart. According to the revelations of Jesus to St. Faustina, the 3 o'clock hour is a special time of grace and mercy for us. On two different occasions, Jesus petitioned St. Faustina:

> **At three o'clock, implore My mercy, especially for sin-ners; and if only for a brief moment, immerse yourself in My Passion, particularly in My abandonment at the moment of agony. This is the hour of great mercy ... In this hour I will refuse nothing to the soul that makes a request of Me in virtue of My Passion** (*Diary*, 1320).
>
> **As often as you hear the clock strike the third hour, immerse yourself completely in My mercy, adoring and glorifying it; invoke its omnipotence for the whole world, and particularly for poor sinners; for at that moment mercy was opened wide for every soul. In this hour you can obtain everything for yourself and for others for the asking; it was the hour of grace for the whole world — mercy triumphed over justice** (*Diary*, 1572).

With these words, Jesus again does everything within His power to instill in us a profound trust and confidence in His loving mercy. He assures us that *nothing* will be refused to those who petition Him at the Hour of Mercy, if what we ask is compatible with God's will. We can obtain *everything* that we ask for ourselves and for others in virtue of His Passion. We should seize this great pledge of grace as a steadfast promise of hope from Jesus' own lips, imploring His mercy upon our deceased loved one and ourselves even in the midst of our feelings of agony and loss. Every day at the 3 o'clock hour, your redemptive suffering, united with the source of all mercy and grace in Christ's Passion and death, can open the floodgates of Divine Mercy for you and those you love.

Jesus asks us through St. Faustina to make the Stations of the Cross at this hour, if our duties permit, or to step into a chapel to pray before the Blessed Sacrament and implore His mercy. If we are unable to do either, He simply asks that we immerse ourselves in prayer wherever we happen to be, if only for a moment (see *Diary*, 1572). He makes it so easy for us to participate in His redemption. The 3 o'clock hour is the hour that definitively changed the course of human history — taking time at this hour to glorify God's mercy can change the course of our lives, helping to lift us from the affliction we are enduring. At this hour, Jesus' promise to us is especially fitting: "Ask, and it will be given you; seek, and you will find; knock, and it will be opened to you" (Mt 7:7).

*E*UCHARISTIC ADORATION. Throughout this book, we have made frequent reference to Eucharistic Adoration, and for good reason. Along with reception of our Blessed Lord in Holy Communion, it is one of the most powerful means of healing, enlightenment, and transformation offered to us from our Lord's storehouse of Divine Mercy. Recall Fr. Chris' powerful experience before the Blessed Sacrament that led him to conversion, an illuminating General Confession, realization of the potential for his grandmother's salvation, and eventually, his vocation to the priesthood.

Eucharistic Adoration can be likened to radiation therapy. That's because here — in the Presence of our Creator and Redeemer who comes to us under the humble appearance of bread — the invisible rays of Christ's mercy *radiate* through our entire being. Jesus' radiating love fills us with hope and *heals* us.

Saint Faustina, who took the full religious name "Sister Maria Faustina *of the Most Blessed Sacrament*," treasured the intimate time she was able to spend with the Eucharistic Jesus. She often prayed for hardened sinners before the Blessed Sacrament, especially "for those who have lost hope in God's mercy" (*Diary*, 319). Let us turn to her inspired writings, crafted while she was in Adoration, to gain deeper appreciation for Eucharistic Adoration, this precious and powerful means of intimate communion by which our Lord gives Himself to us:

> I adore You, Lord and Creator, hidden in the Blessed Sacrament. I adore You for all the works of Your hands, that reveal to me so much wisdom, goodness and mercy ...
>
> My heart is completely immersed in prayer of adoration. ... Your goodness encourages me to converse with You. Your mercy abolishes the chasm which separates the

Creator from the creature. To converse with You, O Lord, is the delight of my heart. In You I find everything that my heart could desire. Here Your light illumines my mind, enabling me to know You more and more deeply. Here streams of graces flow down upon my heart. Here my soul draws eternal life. ... Here, without searching for words, our hearts understand each other. Here, no one is able to interrupt our conversation (*Diary*, 1692).

As St. Faustina did, simply come to Jesus and allow Him to draw close to your aching heart. You need not say much — but you may want to pour your heart out to Him. There are no right or wrong words. He just wants to be close to you, to love, console, and strengthen you wherever you might be in your healing in grief.

JOURNALING YOUR THOUGHTS, FEELINGS, AND PAIN. To help work through the grieving process, many experts recommend that those in grief write about their thoughts and feelings. As we mentioned previously, it is extremely common to experience guilt, shame, and remorse for actions you took, or didn't take, related to your beloved one. This interior questioning often takes place in the bargaining stage of grief and is to be expected.

When your pain involves a suicide, it may be exacerbated by past words or actions that may have been harmful to the deceased and to you. In addition, regardless of the manner of their death, you may not have had the opportunity to find closure, to say goodbye, or to express your love for the departed. This lack of closure may be the most intense part of your suffering. Questions may persist, demanding answers. When these questions continue to swirl about in our minds, we tend to give them an importance that's disproportionate to the reality of our situation.

Writing down some of these thoughts privately or sharing them with another person, especially in the healing sanctuary of sacramental Confession, can diffuse and transform some of the irrational thoughts that can overwhelm us when we're in the midst of grief. These thoughts are to be expected, as extreme as they may be. However, they need not dominate us, taking on a life of their own. Exercised in the context of our three spiritual principles, writing and even sharing our thoughts and feelings can be a healing means of identifying our pain and to then invite Christ's Divine Mercy to bring us peace.

We may resent others who have some connection with the person we lost. Sometimes we may even blame friends or family for their death. We may blame doctors or nurses for missing signs of their illness, or prescribing certain medications with side effects that include suicidal depression, or for other reasons. We may blame the nagging boss or the unsupportive coworkers at their place of employment, or some other "nemesis."

Once we put these sentiments down on paper, we can better identify why we might have them. Many times they are normal reactions to tragedy, but the simple act of writing them down as a way to vent can give us new, healing insights.

As mentioned earlier, after such a terrible loss, we may have feelings of resentment and anger toward God. Don't be alarmed at these feelings. Remember, God is not offended by our anger at Him. He can handle it! In fact, He wants to hear all about it. It can be helpful to write about our anger at God as well. You may even want to write it in the form of a letter directly addressed to God.

Another practice that can bring us healing and consolation is to write down all the reasons we are grateful for our cherished loved one. Gratitude has immense healing power, and we are bound to have countless memories of them for which we are thankful. We thank God for having put them in our lives and for the hope of being reunited with them again. We again entrust them to the care and protection of His loving mercy as we continue to practice the third spiritual principle in healing from our grief.

CONFESSION. As mentioned in Part One, sacramental Confession is a tremendous source of mercy and healing. We will want to take advantage of the gift of grace that this Sacrament affords. A Sacrament is nothing less than God's own pledge of grace, of Himself, and the Sacrament of Penance and Reconciliation is His pledge of forgiveness and the freedom that it provides. It is considered one of the two "Sacraments of Healing," along with the Anointing of the Sick.

You may have some fear at the thought of going to Confession and sharing your interior thoughts with another person. This is understandable. You are apt to feel vulnerable, which is normal. You have already demonstrated tremendous courage in walking through your pain and grief. If you feel fearful, turn to Jesus and ask Him to remove your fear. Enter the confessional with trust in Jesus, taking His words to heart:

Come to me, all you who are weary and burdened, and I
will give you rest. Take my yoke upon you and learn from
me, for I am gentle and humble of heart, and you will find
rest for your souls. For my yoke is easy and my burden is
light (Mt 11:28-30; NIV).

In your grieving process, it can be particularly beneficial to make
frequent use of the Sacrament of Reconciliation. Perhaps, as Fr. Chris
shared in his personal story, you will want to do a more thorough General Confession that reviews your entire life. Oftentimes, this practice
can bring tremendous consolation, especially if you are moving into
more integrated grief in your daily life. If you opt to make a General
Confession, please make an individual appointment, both for the sake
of your confessor and to avoid keeping others waiting in the confessional line. This in-depth Confession will take some time.

When preparing for your Confession, you can take comfort in
three divine gifts of the Sacrament. First, as Jesus disclosed to Faustina
in His revelations, **"When you approach the confessional, know
this, that I Myself am waiting there for you. I am only hidden by
the priest, but I myself act in your soul"** (*Diary*, 1602).

In the confessional, we are confessing our sins to God, and as
Jesus revealed to St. Faustina, it is He who awaits us under the veil
of His appointed and anointed priest-servant. The grace to forgive
sin comes from God, but Jesus delegates this power to the priest,
His chosen instrument. As He said to His apostles on the eve of His
death, "Truly, truly, I say to you, whoever believes in me will also do
the works that I do; and greater works than these will he do, because
I go to the Father" (Jn 14:12).

What greater work could a man perform on behalf of Christ than
to forgive sins in the name of God? After His Death and Resurrection,
Jesus appeared to His apostles in the upper room and said, "'Peace be
with you. As the Father has sent me, even so I send you.' And when
he had said this, he breathed on them, and said to them, 'Receive the
Holy Spirit. *If you forgive the sins of any, they are forgiven; if you retain
the sins of any, they are retained*'" (Jn 20:21-23; emphasis added).

As we saw in Part One, the assurance of the forgiveness of sins is
one of the primary reasons that Jesus established the priesthood. As
the Church teaches, a priest stands *in persona Christi* (meaning "in the
person of Christ") for us. This tremendous gift to us from God should

bring us consolation, because when the priest absolves us from our sins in the name of the Father, of the Son, and of the Holy Spirit, we hear and know the *promise of forgiveness* that Christ has pledged to us. By the end of a valid Confession, every sin that we have ever confessed (or forgotten) up to that point is gone forever — once and for all.

A second benefit of Confession is that it is "under the seal," meaning that the priest-representative, in the person of Christ, is bound by Church law to sworn secrecy about anything you might disclose, regardless of content. As such, we are granted another guarantee — complete anonymity.

In addition to the seal and the complete forgiveness of sins, a final benefit of Confession is that we are given further grace to live in intimate communion with God, our fellow man, and the created order. God's pledge of "sanctifying grace" is also imparted to us in the Sacrament of Reconciliation. When we carry out the recommended penance that helps to repair any harms our sins have caused us and others, we are given new *power* to live in communion with God.

We should be completely open and honest in the confessional. This will allow us to experience much deeper healing in our grieving process. Oftentimes, the Lord will reveal additional insights about our life during Confession. Our confessor can be a great source of help as well. Remember, Jesus is acting through him — this is the way God operates. As we discussed previously, God invites humanity to participate in His work of redemption.

As a result of our self-disclosure in Confession, we may at times have a profound experience of Divine Mercy in our souls. That is because in Confession, Christ pardons us and calls us back to Himself — which is why the Sacrament is appropriately named "Reconciliation." The *Catechism* teaches that Confession often results in "serenity of conscience" and "strong spiritual consolation" (1468).

In addition, we may experience relief from the constant questions that haunt us in the aftermath of a suicide. After we go to Confession, we may feel "lighter" as we receive the gift of true peace from God. The forgiveness granted us in Confession has the effect of opening our hearts, which in turn empowers us with the grace to forgive others who have done us harm.

*F*ORGIVENESS. Having received God's forgiveness and strengthened your communion with Him in the Sacrament of Reconciliation, it is important to forgive others as well. Oftentimes, this can be very difficult.

You might be thinking. "What? Forgive *them*? They need to ask forgiveness from *me*. Now you're asking the impossible!"

Forgiveness can be very challenging for us when serious harm has been done to us or those we love. Perhaps you have been entirely misunderstood by others in your grief. Unfortunately, this is far too common. Even if we have the strong support of our family, friends, and community, it may be difficult for some to truly grasp the impact your loss has had on you. Usually, they are not to blame. They likely do not understand. Perhaps they have never lost someone close to them, close enough that it strikes to the depths of their soul. We may need to exercise patience with them. If we've been misunderstood or harmed, we should pray for the ability to forgive those who have hurt us.

Perhaps we also feel resentment and anger toward the one whom we've lost for inflicting such great suffering upon us by taking their own life. This is a common phenomenon, which may even cause us to feel guilt and shame for our anger. If we still struggle with forgiving our loved one, we might do well to pray for the grace of willingness to forgive them, knowing they were likely in a state of anguish when they made their decision. We can remember the words of Jesus upon the Cross: "Father, forgive them, for they know not what they do" (Lk 23:34). This might be difficult at first, but we can find the grace if we persist. We are praying for them in part so that we might be free from further pain ourselves.

Often in the case of suicide, we also have to deal with other "hard-to-forgive" people and situations, but forgiveness might not be as daunting as it first appears. Here again, the Sacrament of Reconciliation can be a tremendous aid in grace for us. Let's again consider some insights from St. John Paul II. Regarding the mercy that we receive in the confessional, he taught us:

> This reconciliation with God [in confession] leads ... to other reconciliations, which repair the other breaches caused by sin. The forgiven penitent is reconciled with himself in his inmost being, where he regains his inner-most truth. He is reconciled with his brethren whom he has in some way

offended and wounded. He is reconciled with the Church. He is reconciled with all creation (*CCC*, 1469).[153]

Having experienced the power of forgiveness through the mercy of God in Confession, we are "reborn" in His grace. Our reconciliation with God effects an internal change within us, transforming us to be our truer selves — that is, beings who are created to love. Our reconciliation with God effects reconciliation with our brethren and all of creation. It is God's own grace-filled action within us that *empowers us* to forgive those who have offended us most gravely — those "hard-to-forgive" people. Restored to inner integrity in Confession, would we not want the same liberating experience even for those who have hurt us? Are we not called to extend the same forgiveness and mercy that we received to those who have harmed us?

Saint Paul instructs the Colossians that "as the Lord has forgiven you, so you also must forgive" (Col 3:13). Consider that at every Mass, we pray the prayer that Jesus taught us, which includes, "[A]nd forgive us our trespasses, *as we forgive those who trespass against us.*"

If we are still unwilling to forgive others, then St. Paul's instruction and the words of the Our Father ought to stop us in our tracks. Essentially, we only receive the Father's forgiveness to the extent that we are willing to forgive others. To refuse to forgive others, then, is to refuse God's mercy for ourselves (see Mt 6:14-15). In order to be forgiven, we must forgive. In order to receive mercy, we must show mercy.

The Church in her wisdom also teaches us about this sometimes difficult choice to forgive others that is mandated by the grace we receive in Confession:

> Now — and this is daunting — this outpouring of mercy cannot penetrate our hearts as long as we have not forgiven those who have trespassed against us. ... In refusing to forgive our brothers and sisters, our hearts are closed and their hardness makes them impervious to the Father's merciful love; but in confessing our sins, our hearts are opened to his grace (*CCC*, 2840).

This passage illuminates the means by which we gain the grace to forgive in difficult circumstances. Confession opens our hearts through

God's merciful forgiveness and also gives us the grace to forgive others who have harmed us. If we still balk at forgiving others, we should continue to pray for the necessary grace to forgive, for it is only with God's power that we can do so.

But what exactly does forgiving another mean? Forgiveness does not mean that we forget the wrong that others have done to us. (That would be amnesia!) Forgiveness does not mean that the consequences of another's wrongdoing should be overlooked, and any claim we have on them rendered null and void. For example, if someone has stolen money from me, I can forgive them for the wrongful act and the harm it has caused me. However, restitution for the stolen money is sometimes needed for full reconciliation (although an act of mercy might pardon such a debt). In other words, it is not necessarily wrong to hold that person responsible and expect them to make "satisfaction" for the money that was taken. In fact, it may be spiritually beneficial for them to offer restitution for a wrong act they committed.

Forgiveness does not mean that we need to maintain a harmonious, "feel-good" relationship with the person who has offended us. To forgive means to let them go in peace and not wish any ill upon them. But it does not mean we have to be their "best friend."

Forgiveness *does* mean that we no longer *resent* the person who harmed us. The word "resentment" comes from the French word *ressentir*, whose root comes from the Latin word *sentire*, which means "to feel." With the prefix "re," it means to re-feel something again and again. When we resent, we hold the wrongful action against the offender, replaying it over and over again in our minds. This is a poisonous venom to the soul, doing far greater harm to the one who harbors resentment than to the wrongdoer. From this vantage, "justified anger" really is *not* justifiable.

If you have trouble forgiving, you might also take inspiration from St. Faustina, who wrote, "He who knows how to forgive prepares for himself many graces from God. As often as I look upon the cross, so often will I forgive with all my heart" (*Diary*, 390).

As we follow Jesus' example in order to be faithful children of a loving Father, we become icons of mercy to the world. In the papal document *Misericordiae Vultus* (*The Face of Mercy*), Pope Francis teaches us that we become witnesses to the mercy of God if we are merciful people ourselves. Saint Faustina made a similar observation in the *Diary* when she wrote, "We resemble God most when we forgive our neighbors" (1148).

Let's think again of Sammie's story. She will be the first one to tell you that forgiving the deepest of wounds is difficult. Forgiveness is the opening of the wounds to the presence of the Holy Spirit, who, like isopropyl alcohol, stings because He disinfects the wound from all the pus of bitterness and anger. Heroic forgiveness could involve the willingness to offer our suffering for the other person, rather than holding it against the other person (like Jesus, who offered His suffering precisely for those who caused it). It's a decision that has to be renewed repeatedly, sometimes every day. Forgiveness is a choice made at a specific point in time, yet extending over a lifetime, bending our will into conformity with God's will.

Sammie prayed that she would not become bitter and turn in on herself in her sorrow and loss. Our challenge, for the sake of our own souls, our families, and our communities, is to choose to forgive and love even when we are in the darkness of our grief.

Again, in order to fully receive God's loving mercy, we, ourselves, must be merciful to others. This may not happen instantly. We may need to forgive over and over, as Jesus said, not "seven times, but seventy times seven" (Mt 18:21-22) — which in the language of Jesus' time implies an infinite number of times. But be confident that our Lord will grant you from His merciful Heart the grace to forgive if you seek it, along with the priceless gift of His peace in your own heart.

*H*EALING OF THE *F*AMILY *T*REE. There is a very important part of the Body of Christ who will benefit from your prayers, if you have not prayed for them already — your ancestors. Healing for our ancestors from the consequences of their past sins is something we should always desire. Substantial evidence suggests that these consequences can even be passed down through generations, potentially affecting us in the present. God does not hold future generations responsible for the sins of their ancestors, but He does permit the effects of our evil (and good) deeds to reverberate from one generation to the next. As such, we should want to ensure that our ancestors have completed their time in Purgatory and entered Heaven, while also ensuring that we are free from any negative effects their sins may have brought upon us.

One of the key doctrines of the Catholic faith is that Jesus, by taking on our human nature, unites all of human nature to the divine and opens it up to the possibility of sharing in His divine life. As such, we are all members of the Mystical Body of Christ, all united to the family of God by the grace of our Baptism. Supernaturally, we're all members of the Communion of Saints. We are a body, an organism that can transmit divine life and grace to one another through our connection with Christ. Thus, our prayers and penances offered for our deceased loved ones have the power to effect healing and purification for them, and their intercessory prayers can effect grace in our lives.

Of course, we are also connected to our biological family members. And just as predispositions toward certain diseases — such as hypertension, diabetes, or certain genetic defects — can be transmitted within families, so too can spiritual "diseases" and "defects" be transmitted within families. The sins or the sanctity of our natural family members may impact the other family members.

What does all this have to do with grieving suicide? Whether it's similar to a genetic predisposition to diabetes, or whether it's a particular form of concupiscence or some other form of spiritual woundedness passed down in a family, the presence of suicide in the lives of our ancestors has the potential to cause self-destructive behavior in future generations. Mental health research attests that "it is well known that a family history of suicide places survivors at increased risk for suicide."[154] The same sources demonstrate that the inclination towards suicide has intergenerational connections.[155]

Given this evidence, our families may have had troubles in past generations that are, in some fashion, still unresolved. Your family tree may include people who haven't been prayed for, or who were inclined to particular sins or proclivities that have had ramifications for your family down to the present day. No matter what, a suicide within our family should compel us to make sure that all family members, living and deceased, receive the grace they need for healing, and so break the "chain reaction" between generations.

In this situation, the Mass plays an irreplaceable role, as we've explored elsewhere in this book. Having Masses said, not only for a loved one who's just taken their own life, but for your parents, and your parents' parents — perhaps even going back four or more generations — may do you and your family a world of good. The spiritual aids of Eucharistic Adoration, the Chaplet of Divine Mercy, and the Rosary, which are also connected to the Liturgy (see Chapter Four, Part One), are excellent means for interceding for one's ancestors, as are perpetual enrollments in spiritual benefit societies like the Association of Marian Helpers. (For more on this, see Appendix G.)

Another powerful means of stopping the intergenerational transmission of spiritual (and sometimes physical) maladies is through the consecration of your family to Jesus, which can include particular acts of entrustment to members of His Mystical Body. We would encourage you to use forms of consecration (entrustment) such as that found in *33 Days to Morning Glory*, a book explaining Marian consecration by Fr. Michael Gaitley, MIC, or the consecration through St. Joseph by Fr. Donald Calloway, MIC, two highly efficacious means of breaking the transference of negative intergenerational effects. Also, you can use the prayers of our third spiritual principle (see Chapter Three, Part Two) to consecrate and entrust your entire family tree into God's loving care and protection. It is important to keep your family in your prayers, especially those who may have died tragically — it truly is a work of mercy on behalf of your dearly departed.

*"G*OOD DAYS" AND "THE GOOD OL' DAYS." One of the challenges of developing acceptance and integration in the grief process is that you might feel guilty for having a good day or several good days. Perhaps you are beginning to feel more like yourself again, or you are experiencing some semblance of stability, serenity, laughter, and peace more days than not. Nevertheless, you might find yourself thinking, "How can I smile? How can I laugh? How can I possibly be okay with feeling okay when my beloved has been taken from me?"

These "good days" are a sign that one is beginning to experience healing in their grief. Manageability is becoming an increasing norm in day-to-day life, an indication that one is becoming more "integrated" in their grief.

Sammie shared that her family had similar sentiments of guilt regarding their "good days" without Clare physically present. But she was also able to recall the consoling dream that she had of Clare, one that helped to reorient her toward a confident hope for reunion with her daughter in Heaven one day. Sammie has her sights fixed firmly on her own destiny. Recalling the notion of *telos* from Part One, we know that Heaven — the state of full, eternal communion with God and one another — is the end for which we were created and our ultimate destiny.

This "epiphany of truth" has been a great realization in Sammie's own grief journey. When asked what her life is like now, five years after the death of her precious daughter, Sammie says:

> I will tell you one thing ... I think much more about Heaven than I did before. Actually, I think about it all the time. I look forward to it, but I will live out every day that God gives me. Counting on God's grace and mercy and praying for final perseverance, Heaven is my retirement plan.

This sort of confident hope should bring us great consolation. But it doesn't mean that we are not going to experience the pain of grief again at times in days ahead. There will be days when we miss our loved one terribly. Anniversaries, birthdays, special memories, or a sight, sound, or thought may trigger hurt or anger in us. We might want to deny these reactions or emotions, or even try to block them. We might ask ourselves how we could still feel anger, depression, or grief while reminiscing about former pleasant memories. In these moments, we'll probably find it best not to deny our feelings but to embrace them, renewing our entrustment of ourselves and our loved one to God's care and protection.

Nostalgic memories of those dear to us are going to arise throughout our day, and many times, at night in our dreams. When these recurring memories come, we can thank God for them, gaining deeper appreciation for those joys we shared with those we now miss. We should allow ourselves to experience our emotions and turn our thoughts to God again, while also avoiding the traps of self-pity and remorse. We might ask our Blessed Mother to draw close to us, knowing that her Heart was deeply wounded by witnessing the gruesome death of her Son. We can thank God for the gift of having been able to love another person this deeply, for their lives, for His eternal embrace of them, and for the confident hope that we will be reunited with them again someday.

HELPING OTHERS IN THEIR GRIEF. Another component of living the message of Divine Mercy and showing mercy to others is helping them in their misery and grief, whenever realistically possible. Such acts of mercy have a way of lifting us out of our own pain, helping us become a presence of healing, support, and love for another.

We hope that as a result of your own suffering in grief, you have been able to find, or will find, a new interior strength and become more united with Jesus. If your grief has become an *integrated* grief through practicing the three spiritual principles and other practices of Divine Mercy spirituality, you may have precious experience and hope to offer others undergoing similar circumstances, particularly if they are enduring *acute* or *complicated* grief.

Oftentimes, offering ourselves to another in the midst of their own darkness can be a tremendous grace. Although our own loss still may not make complete sense, it can now take on new meaning — through helping others in their grieving process. This is being Christ-like, because that is exactly what Christ did for us. "[He] comforts us in all our affliction, so that we may be able to comfort those who are in any affliction, with the comfort with which we ourselves are comforted by God" (2 Cor 1:4).

A great friend of the Marian Fathers and a prolific messenger of Divine Mercy, the departed Fr. George Kosicki, CSB, used to say, "Mercy is having pains in your heart for the pains of another, and taking pains to do something about their pain." You are now in a unique position, having shared intimately in the Cross of Christ as you walk through suffering and grief. Like Fr. Chris, you can now share your own epiphany of hope with others as you continue to live the three spiritual principles with trust in Jesus at the heart of your works of mercy.

As Jesus instructed St. Faustina, we are to **"Tell** [all people] ... **that I am Love and Mercy itself. When a soul approaches Me with trust, I fill it with such an abundance of graces that it cannot contain them within itself, but radiates them to other souls"** (*Diary*, 1074).

From a practical standpoint, what might this service to those who grieve look like? Well, you might start by thinking back and asking yourself what was — or could have been — helpful at different stages of your own grief. As mentioned earlier, every person's grief is unique. We will want to listen to the other as they speak from their own pain and suffering. Open, receptive listening is perhaps the greatest gift we can offer and is a consolation in itself. By being attentive listeners first, we also may better discern more personalized and effective ways to assist those who labor under the weight of grief.

When comforting someone, sometimes it is most helpful to say little or even nothing at all. Like the good deacon present with the Wood family at Clare's death, you might simply conclude, "I have no words for what you are going through." Sometimes, generosity will mean simply spending time with a grieving person, recognizing that their pain cannot be "fixed" in an instant. Sometimes, it means allowing that person to have time in solitude with our Lord. It may be more helpful to allow them some space, even refraining from a hug or embrace. Sensitivity in discernment will be key to understanding their needs, which will allow you to detect when a hug or embrace might be welcomed consolation.

Sometimes, those in acute or complicated grief need others to step in and take care of practical details, such as meals, yardwork, or other duties of daily life, duties that might seem to pile up under the cloud of darkness that can surround them. Other times, regular activities and projects can serve as helpful and healthy distractions for those dealing with the constant presence of acute grief. When I recently walked through a painful loss, my dad and I took on a whole entire "grief project" by renovating my kitchen and bathroom. In his wisdom, he knew I needed a focused, healthy project that would bring satisfaction and reward as one component of my healing.

It's possible that your grieving friend may need medical, psychological, or spiritual assistance, particularly if their grief is complicated and prolonged. Again, discernment is key. If you remain prayerfully open and listen to them, you will be guided by the Spirit of mercy and your personal experience to assist in your friend's needs. Patience and steadfast, merciful love should be your guiding principles in helping others to find hope.

*F*ROM DARKNESS TO LIGHT. Once we have begun to incorporate into our lives the three spiritual principles with the support of some additional spiritual aids listed in this chapter, certain "epiphany of hope" effects will often follow. We may experience a whole new freedom of spirit. We may begin to emerge from our seemingly endless fog. We will still miss — sometimes deeply — that special person who meant so much to us, but we will often begin to see how our experience can help others undergoing similar circumstances. The acceptance stage is likely to become a more frequent state of mind, moving us more toward integrated grief. We may begin to recognize with full and grateful hearts that Jesus, the Divine Mercy, can do all things in us, far beyond what we had previously thought possible (see Eph 3:20).

In addition, we will frequently begin to live more and more with a new sense of hope and begin to see light through the darkness. We may often begin to feel a new peace replacing the shame, remorse, and pain of the past. Living on this new spiritual plane of hope, we trust in God's infinite love and mercy because He is true to Himself and His Word. Regardless of the degree to which you may or may not *feel* the experience of these effects, be assured that God's healing grace is objectively at work in you.

As we will see in the following chapter, we may also gain greater appreciation for the hope of eternal life for ourselves, a life in union with those we love. With this anticipated hope in mind, please take your time with the next chapter. It contains rich content that ties together several themes discussed throughout this book, and is intended to lead you further in your "epiphany of hope" experience.

CHAPTER FIVE

Hope for Them and Hope for You — Together in Eternity

There are no quick answers. The mystery of God is too great, and our minds are too small, too limited to understand his ways. But I cannot and will not doubt the love of God for every person, a love that is warm, intimate, and true. I shall trust him, even when I find no human grounds for doing so.

Left with the question "Why?" I discover a light that begins to shine in the darkness, just a flicker but enough for me to say: "I know where to look when still unable to see clearly." I look to the figure of Christ dying on the cross. I know that if I look long enough, I shall begin to see that his passion and death have a powerful message to convey. When God became man, he accepted that he would be like one of us and would experience our darkest moments and greatest pain. What many humans have to endure, he endured.[156]

— Cardinal Basil Hume

The loss of someone with whom we shared love, joy, and purpose is one of life's harshest realities, particularly when it is unexpected or perceived to be premature. We might feel that it simply isn't fair and wonder why God would allow such a thing to happen. Sometimes, there are no easy answers to satisfy us.

The problems of evil, suffering, and loss are real and valid ones that are not easily addressed by pithy platitudes. These problems fall into the realm of mystery, which requires a new kind of sight that transcends the natural and touches the supernatural. Mystery confronts our humanity, forcing us to acknowledge that we are limited persons, incapable of seeing the panoramic view from the divine perspective. As John Paul II showed us, "[I]n order to perceive the true answer to the 'why' of suffering, we must look to the revelation of divine love

... the richest source of the meaning of suffering, which is always a mystery."[157]

As Christians who follow the true Light shining forth in a world of darkness, a Light that the darkness cannot overcome, we center our existence and purpose in the Cross and Resurrection of Jesus Christ. There we see that, even with objective evil and wrong in our lives, God can transform these experiences into a greater good, including the losses that make absolutely no sense to us in the moment. He can ultimately make everything work for the good (see Rom 8:28) if we turn to Him with confident trust. We know this from the seemingly ugly, objective evil of Jesus' death on the Cross, from which sprang forth the greatest good that humanity could ever wish for — eternal life with God and one another. Through the Death and Resurrection of Jesus Christ, we are given *THE great epiphany of hope.*

RETURN TO THE BRIDGE OF TRUST.

The eloquence of the cross and death is ... completed by *the eloquence of the resurrection.* Man finds in the resurrection a completely new light which helps him to go forward through the thick darkness of humiliations, doubts, hopelessness and persecution.[158]

— Pope St. John Paul II

Throughout this book, we have made reference to the "bridge of trust." At the end of Part One, we encouraged you to take this bridge with a confident hope that your loved one will have eternal life in God through the intercessory power of your prayers and the prayer of the Church, particularly through the power and efficacy of the Paschal Mystery, which we celebrate in every single Mass.

In our discussion of the second spiritual principle, we encouraged you to take the bridge of trust in Christ, the Divine Mercy, to bring you to the shores of hope in the midst of the grief you experienced from your painful and tragic loss. Now, once again, we are asking you to take this bridge with complete trust that Jesus will fulfill His promise of eternal life for you and your loved one.

We have already established our powerlessness over the loss we are enduring and its effects upon our lives. Yet in our powerlessness, we come to trust in a power greater than ourselves: Jesus, the Divine

Mercy. He is the bridge that leads us into the depths of love in the Holy Trinity, an infinite communion of love that is life eternal. Therefore, we entrusted our lives, our wills, and our loved one into the care and protection of God, knowing that He is the good Father who desires to give every good gift to His children, in and through His Son. Jesus tells us, "I did not come to judge the world but to save the world" (Jn 12:47). In His high-priestly prayer to the Father, we discover that Jesus has not lost one of those whom the Father has entrusted to Him (see Jn 17:12, 18:9). That should give you great hope when wondering about the salvation of your deceased loved one.

In the Gospel of John, the verb form of the word "to believe" in the original Greek is *pisteuo*, which is often better translated in the Johannine passages as "to trust" or "to entrust." It is used 98 times, compared to 34 times in the other three Gospels combined.

On the night He was betrayed and entered into His unimaginable Passion for us, Jesus encouraged His disciples in the midst of the storm that was about to break over them, telling them, "Let not your hearts be troubled; believe [trust] in God, believe [trust] also in me" (Jn 14:1). Here Jesus is telling His closest friends, just before all but one of them desert Him, not to let their hearts be troubled over His impending departure from them, from a loss that will send them into hiding. Rather, He instructs them to *trust* in God and *trust* in Him. Jesus' mission is coming to fulfillment as He is about to enter into His Passion and death, the "hour" of His glory, as John describes it.

Yet the apostles are already feeling the pangs of separation from Jesus. They are incapable of understanding what is about to take place, of what their Lord and God is about to do for them. Like Nicodemus, they, too, are perplexed. Believing that they have found the Holy One of God, the Messiah who was prophesied to come, they bargain with Him, grappling to understand the meaning of His departure. How can He leave them now? He has become their ultimate hope; they believe He can transform not only their own lives, but the entire world.

We may also wonder how God can apparently abandon us when we had hope that He would not let our loved one be taken from us. Yet Jesus assures us — as He assured His beloved friends — that He is going to prepare a place for them with the Father: "In my Father's house there are many rooms; if it were not so, would I have told you that I go to prepare a place for you? And when I go and prepare a place for you, I will come again and will take you to myself, that where I am you may be also" (Jn 14:1-3). We have confident hope that Jesus has also prepared a place for our loved one and for us as well, allowing us to be reunited with them some day in Paradise.

In the midst of impending darkness, Jesus gives words of encouragement to His disciples to solicit trust in Him and in God's divine plan of salvation. Still, the apostles do not know what He is saying. They do not yet realize that Christ will traverse the valley of death and darkness to open the door to a new kind of existence that they never could have imagined.

We have an unshakeable new hope through Jesus' Death and Resurrection. The place He is preparing for them, and for us, is a state of deepest communion with the Father, a communion that the Only Begotten Son shares by His very nature and is about to open to all those whom the Father has given to Him by grace. This is eternal life. In His high-priestly prayer to the Father on the night commencing His Passion, Jesus discloses the nature of Heaven: "And this is eternal life, that they know you the only true God, and Jesus Christ whom you have sent ... that all of them may be one, Father, just as you are in me and I am in you" (Jn 17:3, 21; NIV).

Heaven is not some geographical location up in the clouds where fat little cherubim flap around on rainbows and stars, while the old man God sits on a big cushy armchair, passively observing in delighted amusement. It is an entirely new state of being. Fundamentally, it is a *relationship with infinite Love*, that is, *being* in relation with a God who is Love and Mercy itself. Eternal life means to be — along with those we love — wedded to, enveloped by, and embedded in the infinite, boundless union of Love that is the communion of the Trinity. This is what awaits us after death, even a tragic death.

Pope Benedict XVI insightfully describes eternity as follows:

[E]ternity is not an unending succession of days in the calendar, but something more like the supreme moment of satisfaction, in which totality embraces us and we embrace totality ... It would be like plunging into the ocean of infinite love, a moment in which time — the before and after — no longer exists.[159]

Throughout this book, we have seen how the merits and graces of Christ's Passion, Death, and Resurrection are not bound to space and time. In the following section, "Theological Underpinnings," we will discuss a mode of being called *kairos*, which transcends the everyday realm of our senses. *Kairos* can be thought of as the realm of the human spirit, where space and time as we know them are able to be transcended by human beings, who are spiritual as well as physical. In this realm, the human person is able to "touch the eternal" and commune with God in spirit in the here and now.

In *kairos*, "sight" takes on new dimensions, whereby the human person is capable of seeing with the "eyes of the heart," having spiritual sight, as we described in the earlier section on Heaven. It could be considered another dimension of existence for the human person, beyond space and time, much like the apostles experienced in their encounters with the Risen Christ.

When Jesus assumes humanity and unites it with His divinity, this entirely new dimension is opened up for the human person, as He bridges the gap of eternity and enters space and time to redeem and transform all of creation. Once Jesus perfects humanity, He "inserts" it into the Holy Trinity through His Resurrection and Ascension into Heaven — that is, into the eternal communion of the Father, Son, and Holy Spirit. Humanity can now live "in God" in a fashion it never had before.

The barrier to the Garden of Eden, representing intimate communion with God, has been removed. With the salvific death of Christ on the Cross, the veil of the Temple is torn in two and the Holy of Holies — that is, the inner sanctuary of communion with the Triune God — is now accessible to the human person in and through His first-born and only-begotten Son. This is what God did to give you and your loved one eternal life and to allow you to be reunited one day. This is why we have hope for them and for you. Astonishingly, we don't have to wait for death for this reunion to take place — at least in the spiritual realm. This communion with them, through God, is available to us right now, in part, in the Communion of Saints.

We see in Sacred Scripture that, once they have received the Holy Spirit at Pentecost, Jesus' disciples are able to commune in a more intimate way with God and one another. With this new grace, the apostles are able to do the works of Jesus, and greater works, because He has gone to the Father and has elevated humanity into Paradise, where He has prepared "many rooms" for us (Jn 14:2). Through our

Baptism into Christ, we can experience a foretaste of Heaven while here on earth (which takes place most powerfully in every Liturgy and Eucharistic Adoration). Sin and death, which tend to lock us into a worldly perspective that often despairs of hope, no longer need impede our communion with God and the realm of the saints, of which we have confident hope your loved one is a part.

In this way, you are able to commune with your deceased loved ones in the Communion of Saints, that is, in and through the Spirit of God. Although your tragic loss to suicide is incalculably devastating (because you, too, are a spiritual being), you may find solace in knowing you may still share in communion with your loved one, provided they have accepted Christ's mercy and forgiveness at the moment of their death. You can have great hope that they made this decision, because your prayers in the present touch the eternal.

R*ESURRECTION CHANGES EVERYTHING.* Turning to Pope Benedict's writing, we discover that Christ's Resurrection unveiled an entirely new reality to the disciples and witnesses of the Risen Lord. He writes, "Jesus' Resurrection was about breaking out into an entirely new form of life, into a life that is no longer subject to the law of dying and becoming, but lies beyond it — a life that opens up a new dimension of human existence ... a new kind of future for mankind."[160] In other words, the Resurrection breaks through the barrier imposed by sin and death to open us to a new communion with God and one another.

The capacity of *being* of the human person is changed in the Resurrected Christ. As Pope Benedict explains in regard to the disciples who witnessed the Resurrected Christ firsthand, "It was such an overwhelmingly real happening, confronting them so powerfully, that every kind of doubt was dispelled, and they stepped forth before the world with an utterly new fearlessness in order to bear witness: Christ is truly risen."[161] We, too, can and should have this kind of fearless faith.

Jesus' mode of existence is unlike anything that His friends had ever experienced previously. Think about it. Those who had walked with Him every single day do not recognize the Risen Christ when they first meet Him. His post-resurrected state of being defies and transcends the order of space and time as we know it. The resurrected Jesus is real. He has a real body of flesh and blood. He is not a ghost. He eats fish and bread with His disciples after the Resurrection. Yet

He walks through the door of the Upper Room and reveals Himself to doubting Thomas, who touches Jesus and places his finger in the nail marks of His hands and puts his own hand in the wound in Jesus' side, that mark of Divine Mercy. Thomas sees and believes.

Jesus walks bodily with the disciples on the road to Emmaus. But they do not recognize Him at first sight. Pope Benedict observes: "His presence is entirely physical, yet he is not bound by physical laws, by the laws of space and time ... he is the same embodied man, and he is the new man, having entered upon a different manner of existence."[162] So, we pray, will our loved ones be someday — what an incredible point to ponder, one that gives joy and hope to us who are left behind.

Jesus' Resurrection changes *everything* for humanity. When He ascends into Heaven, the disciples are filled with *joy* at His departure. They have witnessed resurrected life in their Lord and God. He truly *is* the Messiah, come to save, redeem, and transform them so they can now participate in an eternal communion in God, fulfilling the original destiny of humanity. Therefore, in a paradoxical kind of way, we should have this same kind of joy in consideration of the eternal bliss our departed loved ones can now experience.

Pope Benedict writes that "man was created for greatness — for God himself; he was created to be filled by God. But his heart is too small for the greatness to which he is destined. It must be stretched."[163] He goes on to explain that a primary means of this stretching — even when it appears senseless — is through suffering, which "requires hard work and is painful, but in this way alone do we become suited to that for which we are destined."[164]

Thus, the Cross and Resurrection are always linked together. We cannot have the joy and glory that comes with the resurrected state without first enduring the Cross that Christ bore. The servant is not greater than the Master, and the bride (the Church) must resemble her betrothed (Christ), if we are to share in His fullness. It is through Christ's Passion and death — and not just His Resurrection — that we are now sons and daughters of the Father. "Now if we are children, then we are heirs — heirs of God and co-heirs with Christ, if indeed we share in his sufferings in order that we may also share in his glory" (Rom 8:17; NIV).

This doesn't mean that God wills the terrible suffering that comes from the tragic loss caused by a suicide, but He will use that suffering (with His grace) as a means to prepare your heart to receive the fullness of His glory. A share in His glory, a share in Him, is the inheritance of eternal life, which is born in pain and suffering, regardless of the circumstances that cause your suffering while on earth. He takes an evil that is not of Him and transforms it into the occasion through which you are able to receive His love in a greater way, through your own suffering.

Moreover, when your suffering is united with Christ's Passion, the same joy that the apostles experience in the Risen Christ also awaits you in communion with God. And if you confidently trust in His loving mercy, you will experience this joy with your loved one in the fullness of eternity. "As a result of Christ's salvific work, man exists on earth *with the hope* of eternal life and holiness."[165] It means that **your suffering can help transform you into a saint.** But you can also have this joy, in part, while on earth as a member of the Mystical Body of Christ — that is, in the Communion of Saints — which, we pray, includes your beloved departed.

The apostles were devastated when they learned of the death of Jesus, the one whom they loved so dearly. Can you imagine how much they must have been tempted to give up hope? Can you imagine how they must have felt, as if *everything* were lost? You might have reacted in the same way upon learning of the death of your loved one. Maybe you felt the same kind of despair that the apostles did. Maybe you felt all was lost. But reflect on what happened to the apostles after Christ's death — how all their hopes were actually fulfilled. They learned that they had not lost their beloved Jesus. He was alive again!

Not only that, but He had also prepared a place for them to join Him one day in Paradise, where they would be united in eternal bliss. This is how God brought a greater good out of what appeared to be the ultimate tragedy. This is the same hope you can have, the hope that your loved one is not dead, but alive again in a new and more profound way. And you can have the confident hope that you will join them again someday, with God, in the unimaginable beauty that is Heaven.

We may have indeed found this great hope. Oftentimes, however, the pain resulting from a devastating loss such as suicide weighs so heavily upon us that we lose our spiritual sight. We despair, thinking *all is lost*. Death has the final say. But we cannot give in to this temptation. When our sorrow burdens and overwhelms us, we must turn with complete trust to ask for light in the darkness, like blind Bartimaeus when he cried out, "Jesus, Son of David, have mercy on me!"

When Jesus asks what He might do for him, Bartimaeus responds, "Master, let me receive my sight." Moved with compassion, Jesus responds to him, "Go your way, your faith [trust] has made you well." Immediately, Bartimaeus received his sight and followed Him (see Mk 10:46-52). We, too, need to ask Jesus to help us see again, so that we might receive healing through faith in His loving mercy for us.

Pope Benedict's encyclical letter *Spe Salvi* offers us further encouragement to hope even in our darkest moments:

> It is important to know that I can always continue to hope, even if in my own life, or the historical period in which I am living, there seems to be nothing left to hope for. Only the great certitude of hope that my own life and history in general, despite all failures, are held firm by the inde-structible power of Love, and that gives them their meaning and importance, only this kind of hope can then give the courage to act and to persevere.[166]

Human persons tend to think in terms of the immediate present, but we need to consider that our baptized state allows us to participate in the eternal while still on earth — to share in the joy that the disciples experienced when encountering a transformed humanity in the presence of the Risen Christ. Otherwise, it is all too easy to fall into despair.

Yes, our joy is only partial now, but the glory that awaits us is beyond our comprehension. "[N]o eye has seen, nor ear heard, nor the heart of man conceived, what God has prepared for those who love him" (1 Cor 2:9). Therefore, our present sufferings, as intense as they are, are still "not worth comparing with the glory that is to be revealed to us" (Rom 8:18). Our sights are fixed upon the promises of Christ — promises that apply both now and in eternity. *This is our true epiphany of hope,* now and forever in Christ.

A MOTHER'S HOPE REVISITED. Earlier, I mentioned the spiritual bond I'd forged with Sammie Wood through the grief we share in losing a loved one. In a very short time, I have been honored to come to know, to some small degree, the profound depths of her spirituality. Like the Beloved Disciple, she lives close to Jesus, fluent in His spiritual language of the heart. I knew that she had to be part of this narrative of hope after she endured a tragedy of the worst kind — the death of her own child.

When I reached out to Sammie, the connection was instantaneous. She opened herself to share how God enabled her to bring strength out of pain, hope out of sorrow, and healing out of grief. I had to ask her several hard questions, which made me uncomfortable at first. Then, in a way that I have come to know as "Sammie just being Sammie," she put my spirit at ease.

I asked her two tough questions. I asked, "How is life five years later after the loss of Clare?" And much more awkwardly, with a lump in my throat, I asked, "Can you see any 'greater good' from this experience?"

Let's listen to how Sammie answered these questions in a way that only she could:

> So how is life today without Clare? We will always, always, always miss her. I tell her many times a day in my heart that I love her and that I miss her. I pray for her always, especially the Chaplet. In the life of our family, we've had lots happen since she left … many happy, wonderful things. Her sister had a beautiful baby boy. Her brother, her best friend, got married and they have a new baby boy. There are so many things that she would have loved being a part of. She would have been the greatest aunt to those two little boys. This side of eternity, they will not have the pleasure of knowing her.
>
> We will never see her live out her vocation. All our joys have the added color of missing her, but maybe we also have a deeper appreciation for those joys. We certainly don't take as much for granted as we once did.
>
> We've had heartbreaks since she has been gone, too, and she would have been a consolation during those times. I know completely that she is with us and that she prays for us. I feel her with us often, but we miss her physically here with us, too. She was a big, beautiful, colorful part of our lives.
>
> I know losing Clare has changed all of us. It has changed me. I'm not as naive as I used to be, and I've lost some of my innocence. I never dreamed something like this could happen. I hope and pray I'm more compassionate, but I'm not sure if I am. I think for sure my faith is stron-

ger. I'm sure (and rightly so) that losing Clare has humbled me. I used to think I had things figured out, and now I'm absolutely certain I don't know much at all. Thankfully, I *do* know God is in control — I *do* know that He has it figured out! I'm thankful for the great gift of eternity and thankful for His Infinite Mercy.

Sammie continues, addressing the question of possibly "seeing a greater good" in the loss of Clare:

I can't say I have seen the greater good, but I trust that it is there. I believe pain has a purpose in God's great plan, and any pain that is offered up to Him has infinite value. I know that the greater good is there, because God promises that all things work together for good for those who love Him, and I know that I love Him. I don't have to see the good ... I just have to trust His plan. Even on those days when I don't feel the trust, I have to bend my will to keep on trusting. Our feelings aren't always in line with truth, so we have to tap into what *is* Truth!

I will tell you one thing ... I think much more about Heaven than I did before. Actually, I think about it all the time. I look forward to it, but I will live out every day that God gives me. Counting on God's grace and mercy and praying for final perseverance, Heaven is my retirement plan. My priorities have definitely changed. I pray they aren't as silly and frivolous as they used to be. I hope I'm less sensitive to my own feelings and more sensitive to the needs of others.

There are always a zillion blessings and things to be thankful for ... I hope that comes through in what I say.

As far as the greater good ... if some young person decides to live out the other side of despair, if our story provides consolation for another family, if someone feels less alone in their suffering ... those are all good. Sometimes I think the greater good is only seen from Heaven's view. Maybe it's not always ours to see here. We just have to wait and trust. Thank you, Jesus, for your sacrifice and for loving us so much!

Another great thing is that I have met some wonderful people from Stockbridge, Massachusetts, with the Marian Fathers, and I believe they will use many stories, including ours, to help others. That is a wonderful and good thing.

I think it is hard for a parent to sometimes come up with a greater good when on one side of the scale is their child. I know God will use our Clare and her story powerfully because, despite her very bad choice, she loves Him deeply.

Sammie and I took a pause to reflect on our exchange for a few days. With a very long phone conversation and several emails, there was much to digest. We later resumed our correspondence. She added:

I *know* the finished project of this book will be a blessing to so many people ... a balm to so many hurting souls. I have prayed and prayed for this project, and I'm so thankful that you are working on it! You guys are always in my prayers! I'm so happy you have felt Clare. I know she would love that you are working on this.

Upon reading Sammie's thoughts again, I sit speechless in awe at our Lord's majesty. Her words are worth every moment of prayerful reflection. From the depths of a mother's sorrowful heart, she reveals her epiphany of hope in grief and sorrow, and looks with trust to *the ultimate hope* of an everlasting eternity with those she loves.

*E*PIPHANY OF TRUST. Through the loss and grief we've endured, we can hopefully arrive at yet another epiphany, one that brings us to a deeper relationship with God. We know in the depths of our hearts that there is one fundamental response we can make to our suffering — *trust in Jesus.*

When the storms of life come, and they will, trust in Jesus. When pain wrenches our hearts to the core of our being, trust in Jesus. If we feel alone, afraid, resentful, or rejected, trust in Jesus. If we are consoled, feel loved, secure, and happy, trust in Jesus. If things go our way, trust in Jesus. If things don't go our way, trust in Jesus. He is the Way, the Truth, and the Life. If we fulfill the one primary task given to us in life — trust in Jesus — then His way is our way, and our way is His way. Then we live Truth. Then we live Life. Then all else fits into the pattern of the greater good, to the glory of God the Father. *Jesus, I trust in You!*

The journey of our "epiphany of hope" started in a manger, with the Magi discovering the light of the world in a tiny, innocent babe. It has taken us through deserts of pain, grief, and sorrow, allowing for our own epiphanies of hope along the way. We've seen how God is ever-present and ever-transcendent in space, time, and eternity. We've gained new hope for the salvation of our loved ones and blessed communion with them in Heaven.

We've gained new hope for ourselves in the aftermath of our loss and grief, recognizing and admitting our powerlessness over the loss of our loved one and its effects on us. We've gazed upon Jesus in the Image of Divine Mercy, through the lens of His Cross and Resurrection that impart to us His divine life. We've entrusted ourselves and our loved ones to this compassionate and merciful God. With confident trust, we've arrived at a new epiphany of hope in life everlasting — for them, and for us — knowing that in all things, God works for the good of those who love Him (see Rom 8:28).

As we close with hearts full of trust in His loving mercy, we want to share the following words that seem to capture our message of hope for you. These words are attributed to Jesus by a Benedictine monk — for the Word Himself shall always be the first and last Word, the Alpha and the Omega:

> **These words confirm My promise to you, My promise of a new beginning and of years of holiness, blessing and peace. Cling to these words and hold them in your heart ... Trust Me in all things. Allow me to do for you what you cannot do ... Be abandoned to Me in obedience and in trust, and you will not be disappointed in your hope.**[167]

~ POSTSCRIPT ~

Theological Underpinnings:
Eternity, Time, and Power

Now that you have gained hope for your loved one and a newfound hope for yourself, we want to look deeper into the claim that God is outside of time and can apply our present prayers to past events to aid in the salvation of our departed loved ones. Establishing this claim on solid ground will require some theological and philosophical discussion.

To begin our discussion, we need to introduce the term "speculative theology." This is commonly understood as theology founded on, or fundamentally influenced by, speculation or metaphysical philosophy. What does this mean and why is it allowed by the Church? While the common understanding of the meaning of *speculation* is to make an "educated best guess," that is not our approach here. Our conclusions are based on rational, metaphysical philosophy, and fortified by divine revelation entrusted to the Church. It is not a guess; it is based upon the certainty of God's own revelation of Himself — a God who is *omniscient, omnipotent, all-loving, and all-merciful.*

Nothing in the following material is in the slightest way contrary to the teachings of Holy Mother Church. We draw only from her foundational doctrines. However, just as one cannot indisputably prove one's love for another, our conclusions cannot be absolutely proven by citing defined Church doctrine. Points presented by the authors are therefore to be considered mainly in the context of speculative theology.

Any determinations arrived at are based upon the authors' deepest conviction of God's unlimited, fathomless love and mercy. You don't have to accept our conclusions, but none of them are contrary to the faith, and so we are allowed to hold such beliefs. Although "speculative" in one sense, all the conclusions we have derived from Scripture and Catholic Tradition are reasonable because, as mentioned, all sound theology is based upon God's revelation of Himself. Therefore, our thoughts are not exclusively speculative, but have their roots in dogmatic theology, as well.

To begin this discussion, let's look at the concepts of time and eternity.

*G*OD IS OUTSIDE OF TIME. Eternity is a mind-bending notion when you take the time to contemplate it. But it's important for us to have at least some basic grasp of the eternity of God if we're going to grasp how we can pray for those whom God puts on our hearts today, even though they may well have died long ago. To start, we need to understand that eternity and infinity are two different things. Eternity doesn't just mean that God is immortal. Eternal life isn't just a very, very long time. Eternal life is life *outside* of time.

People often ask, "Well, what came before God?" But "before" presumes time. And time itself is a created thing. God made time and as I've mentioned, He is outside of it. Sound unlikely? Interestingly enough, modern physics agrees with theology on this point. Time goes with space, and space goes with time. Where there is no space, there is no time. Even atheist physicist Stephen Hawking speaks of "space-time" in his book *A Brief History of Time*.

Thus God, who is pure spirit and doesn't take up any space, is by His very nature outside of our time — He is in *sacred* time. We, on the other hand, take up physical space and live in physical time, or *cosmic* time. But in the "fullness of time" (see Gal 4:4), God became incarnate in Jesus Christ, and so stepped into physical time. That's when things really got interesting.

Father Robert Spitzer, SJ, who hosts the popular EWTN show "Fr. Spitzer's Universe," states, "While it is true that physical time does not work the same way as sacred time, sacred time works because God wills it to be so. If one believes that God is beyond all time (and that time exists through the mind of God), then God can do anything He wants — He can bring a future event into the present, and He can bring the reality of a past event into the future — which is what Jesus expects He will do when He commands His disciples to 'Do this in remembrance of me.'"[168]

Father Spitzer then asserts that Jesus collapsed time at the Last Supper, specifically so that His suffering, Death, and Resurrection was already completed at the Last Supper. Christ was holding His resurrected body in His hands even though the Resurrection hadn't happened yet (in physical time). Prior to that, time was collapsed in the womb of St. Anne when all the merits of Christ's salvific work were applied to Mary at conception, although Christ had not yet been conceived in time Himself.[169]

We can perhaps get a better grasp on this topic in the *Catechism*. On the topic of the Paschal Mystery — the saving events of Christ's Passion, Death, and Resurrection — the *Catechism* teaches:

> The Paschal mystery of Christ ... cannot remain only in the past, because by his death he destroyed death, and all that Christ is — all that he did and suffered for all men — participates in the divine eternity, and so transcends all times while being made present in them all. The event of the Cross and Resurrection *abides* and draws everything toward life (1085).

That's an incredibly rich passage, and is worth praying over and contemplating. The events of the Paschal Mystery — indeed, all the events of Christ's life — *abide*, meaning they do not pass away. They do not remain in the past. For instance, the Paschal Mystery is "re-presented," or made present, sacramentally in a uniquely powerful way at every Mass.[170]

The mysteries of Christ are accessed again and again throughout history every time a believer prays the Rosary or the Stations of the Cross, every time we practice *lectio divina* (divine reading) with the Gospels, every time we contemplate the events of Christ's life, and every time we suffer and lovingly unite that suffering with the Cross of Christ. Again, all the mysteries of the life of Christ *abide*: They transcend all times, are made present in them all, and are present in the divine eternity "once for all" (Heb 9:26).

Joseph Cardinal Ratzinger (the future Pope Benedict XVI) said, "All time is God's time. When the eternal Word assumed human existence at his Incarnation, he also assumed temporality. He drew time into the sphere of eternity. Christ is himself the bridge between time and eternity."[171]

Some may agree with the statement that God is outside of time, but apply it no further. They may say, "Yes, God is outside of time, but we are not. So our prayers cannot be effective in a manner that transcends time." In response, we can say that when we, with faith, hope, and love, approach Christ — who stepped into our reality — in a certain way we enter into *His* reality, the divine eternity. In other words, just as God, out of His love for us, stepped into "space-time" at the Incarnation, we enter in a certain way into His "spaceless and timeless" eternity through our baptismal faith and the Mass. How does this affect our life of prayer? It means that we don't just look at Jesus in His mysteries; He is also looking back at us. As the *Catechism* puts it:

> Jesus knew and loved us each and all during his life, his agony, and his Passion, and gave himself up for each one of us: "The Son of God ... loved me and gave himself for me" (478).

Similarly, in Jeremiah 1:5, God says, "Before I formed you in the womb I knew you." If God "knew us" before we were even in the womb, couldn't one conclude that He also knew our prayers before we were in the womb? Yes, God is *omniscient* and has knowledge of every prayer we will ever make before we make it. He is also *omnipotent*, so He has the power to take those prayers into account and apply them to the past, present, or future — especially when they are for someone's salvation.

Since God desires our salvation more than anything else, why would anyone doubt that He would allow our prayers to assist those we love? Doesn't God want us to be charitable? Our intercessory prayers on behalf of another are the ultimate expression of charity. Why, then, would God not accept them and apply the graces of those prayers to those most in need at the most critical time of their lives — the moment of their death? If someone doubts God's ability and willingness to do this, it would seem they are limiting His mercy. And we know from Christ's words to St. Faustina that His mercy is infinite, and He is clamoring to pour it upon us (see *Diary*, 294, 379, 400, 687).

Therefore, our prayers can have a powerful effect; they have power or Christ would not have commanded us to "pray constantly" (see Lk 18:1, 21:34-36; 1 Thess 5:16-18; Eph 6:18). I mentioned previously that we enter into the divine eternity through faith, hope, and love. Those theological virtues (and our prayers rooted in those virtues) are supernatural powers that we have possessed since we became supernatural beings.[172]

When do we actually become "supernatural beings?" Some may argue that this doesn't occur until we get to Heaven. But in reality it occurred when Christ saved each of us, personally.

Continuing this train of thought, we can now ask, "So when did God save you and me?" A born-again Christian will say it happened when we accepted Jesus into our hearts as our personal Lord and Savior. We Catholics would say, while the exercise of faith certainly strengthens the supernatural life in us, that life actually begins with our Baptism.

Through Baptism, we are divinized! We literally are "baptized into Christ [and] have put on Christ" to become "sons of God through faith" (Gal 3:26-27). As St. Peter proclaims, we have become "partakers of the divine nature" (2 Pet 1:4). Since we have truly become part of the Body of Christ, we can act with divine power. Through prayer, we have the power to transcend space-time and enter into the divine eternity, especially at the Mass.[173] It seems to logically follow that we can therefore merit future graces, or reach back in time to affect others through prayer.

As I shared earlier, I believe my future prayers made a difference at the moment of my grandmother's death. And that's not because I'm some sort of super "prayer warrior," but because I'm a supernatural being. I am a member of the Body of Christ, a person who has supernatural power through the exercise of my faith in prayer, especially at the Mass and through my suffering.

You could even go so far as to say that when we pray, Jesus prays, and when we suffer, Jesus suffers, because we are the Body of Christ (see Acts 9:4). You could say that through us, His saving act (which affects all of human history) is complete; in other words, our prayers as members of the Body of Christ can affect people who have already died and those who have not even been born yet.

A powerful example of this comes from St. Faustina. The novena that Jesus gave her to pray includes several passages revealing how our behavior in the present affected His experience of suffering during His Passion. These portions of the Divine Mercy Novena show that our prayers can transcend time and are effective, even when applied to the past:

SECOND DAY
Today bring to me the souls of priests and religious,
and immerse them in My unfathomable mercy. It was

they who gave Me the strength to endure My bitter Passion (*Diary*, 1212).

THIRD DAY

Today bring to Me all devout and faithful souls, and immerse them in the ocean of My mercy. These souls brought Me consolation on the Way of the Cross. They were that drop of consolation in the midst of an ocean of bitterness (*Diary*, 1214).

FOURTH DAY

Today bring to Me the pagans and those who do not yet know Me. I was thinking also of them during My bitter Passion, and their future zeal comforted My Heart (*Diary*, 1216).

SIXTH DAY

Today bring to me the meek and humble souls and the souls of little children, and immerse them in My mercy. These souls most closely resemble My Heart. They strengthened Me during My bitter agony. I saw them as earthly Angels, who would keep vigil at My altars (*Diary*, 1220).

As these examples illustrate, what we do now — our fidelity or infidelity, our love or our indifference, our sanctity or our sins — was visible to Jesus back at the time of His Passion. It always humbles me to contemplate the fact that as Jesus was sweating blood during His Agony in the Garden, some of His anguish came from seeing my future personal sins. What we do now has an eternal impact. Conversely, He also saw all the good that each of us will do in our lifetime, especially through our prayers, as we saw in the above passages from St. Faustina's *Diary*.

Now let's take a look at a few more examples of how our prayers can reach across time.

*T*HE WITNESS OF PADRE PIO AND OTHER EXAMPLES. Father Alessio Parente, OFM Cap, Padre Pio's personal assistant, recounts the following conversation between Padre Pio and his physician:

Padre Pio: "[I] can pray even now for the happy death of my great-grandfather."

Doctor: "But he has been dead for many, many years."

Padre Pio: "For the Lord, the past doesn't exist; the future doesn't exist. Everything is an eternal present. Those prayers had already been taken into account. And so I repeat that even now I can pray for the happy death of my great-grandfather!"[174]

The reason we can surmise that our prayers can make a difference regarding the eternal destiny of people who died years ago is because God doesn't receive our prayers after their death. That is, for God, my grandmother's suicide didn't happen over a decade ago. Everything is present to Him at once.

I was delighted to see a story in the *National Catholic Register* by Jimmy Akin, senior apologist for Catholic Answers, who also cited this example of Padre Pio and underscored the same point, that God is outside of time and so our prayers can affect the past. In his article, Akin explains why we can hold this speculative theological viewpoint. He states:

[I]f God is bound by time the way we are, it would make no sense to pray for [a] person to be saved in the moment he died. He either was or wasn't. ... [However] God is not bound by time. He is completely outside of time. All of history is simultaneously present to [God] like a giant mural.

From his eternal perspective outside of time, God simultaneously knows everything that exists, whether in the past, the present, or the future.

He is also capable of interacting with history at any point. This is illustrated by the fact that he not only created the universe in the beginning, he also — from his eternal perspective — sustains it at every moment of its existence. ...

If God is aware of everything in history then he knows it if on April 15 I am praying for a man who died on April 12.

Further, if he is capable of interacting with every point in history, he can give his grace to that man — as he is dying on April 12 — in light of the request I make on April 15.

It thus can make sense for me to pray for the salvation of someone who is already dead.

Usually, our prayers concern the future, but they can also concern the present, and as this illustration shows, they can even concern the past. ...

This principle has a special application to the dying.

We can't objectively tell whether a person is in a state of grace at the point of death. ...

It thus makes sense, whenever someone has died, to ask God to have given the person the graces he needed for salvation at the moment of death.[175]

*D*OROTHY DAY AND C.S. LEWIS. Servant of God Dorothy Day, the great American Catholic activist, journalist, and founder of the Catholic Worker Movement, once wrote a column where she recounted her sorrow and consternation when, shortly after her conversion to Catholicism, the son of a friend died by suicide. She went to speak with her confessor, a kindly and wise priest by the name of Fr. Zachary, who ministered at "the little church on Fourteenth Street, Our Lady of Guadalupe" in New York City, and asked him how she should pray for this young man. He answered her with these words:

There is no time with God. All the prayers you will say in the future for this soul will count. God has said, "ask and ye shall receive." He has promised this. If you keep on asking for God's mercy for that soul, you can be sure your prayers are answered. At the moment of death, when the soul is released from the down drag of the body, there is given a choice — "do you prefer darkness to light, evil to good, denial rather than assent?"[176]

Dorothy Day found that to be very consoling, and so do I!

World-renowned apologist C.S. Lewis (arguably one of the greatest Christian writers of the 20th century) also weighed in on this matter. In his book *Miracles*, Lewis states:

To Him [God] all the physical events and all the human acts are present in an eternal Now. ... In this sense God did not

create the universe long ago but creates it at this minute —
at every minute. ... But then to God (though not to me)
I and the prayer I make in 1945 were just as much present
at the creation of the world as they are now and will be a
million years hence. ...

[W]hen we are praying about the result, say, of a battle
or a medical consultation the thought will often cross our
minds that (if only we knew it) the event is already decided
one way or the other. I believe this to be no good reason for
ceasing our prayers. The event certainly has been decided
— in a sense it was decided "before all worlds." But one of
the things taken into account in deciding it, and therefore
one of the things that really cause it to happen, may be this
very prayer that we are now offering. Thus, shocking as it
may sound, I conclude that we can at noon become part
causes of an event occurring at ten a.m. ...

"Then if I stop praying can God go back and alter
what has already happened?" No. The event has already
happened and one of its causes has been the fact that you
are asking such questions instead of praying. It will ask,
"Then if I begin to pray can God go back and alter what has
already happened?" No. The event has already happened
and one of its causes is your present prayer. Thus something
does really depend on my choice. My free act contributes to
the cosmic shape. That contribution is made in eternity or
"before all worlds"; but my consciousness of contributing
reaches me at a particular point in the time-series.[177]

Now, let's look at one clarification and a couple of questions that
I am often asked regarding the "epiphany of hope."

WHEN IS IT APPROPRIATE TO PRAY FOR THINGS IN THE PAST?
It is ordinarily true that we pray for people who are alive now
and for events that are occurring in the present moment. However,
God may desire that in some cases we pray for someone or something
in the past — things that pertain directly to us, such as family members
or close friends. The Lord entrusts certain things to us to pray for, but
perhaps not all things, such as world events that happened centuries
ago. For instance, we would not pray today that the terrorist attacks

of September 11, 2001, never happened, but we could certainly pray today for God's mercy on those who died during the attacks.

Let's return briefly to Jimmy Akin's article, "Is It Possible to Pray Across Time?" In that article, Akin raises the question of when it is appropriate to pray for things in the past. He states:

> It is not appropriate to pray for [things we know didn't happen]. The reason is that we know it was God's will to allow our history to unfold in a way that didn't include them. To pray for something we know didn't happen [like an avoidance of World War II or that our friend did not die in a car accident, asking God to change the history He has already unfolded] would be to pray contrary to God's known will. ... In the same way, it would be inappropriate for us to pray contrary to things we know *will* happen in the future (e.g., that the end of the world not happen [or that our children will never die]).[178]

It is appropriate, however, to pray for things that we are uncertain about.

> In this case, you don't know whether it was or wasn't God's will, so you're neither praying against God's known will nor praying for something you already know happened. That's the situation we're in with most of our prayers: We don't know whether God will grant them or not, but he encourages us "always to pray and not lose heart" (Luke 18:1). ...
>
> We can't objectively tell whether a person is in a state of grace at the point of death, so this knowledge is by its nature inaccessible to us. It thus makes sense, whenever someone has died, to ask God to have given the person the graces he needed for salvation at the moment of death.
>
> I do, however, have a note of caution: God has designed us as time-bound creatures to be principally oriented toward the future, not the past. There is a sense in which, like St. Paul, we need to be "forgetting what lies behind and straining forward to what lies ahead" (Phil. 3:13).[179]

This is a great article, and I do agree with Akin — spending too much time thinking only about the past can lead us to neglect the attention we need to give to present and future concerns. Akin says he can't "rule out that some might grow closer to God by praying for something they *know* God allowed to happen in the past, but it's easy to see how this kind of prayer could become a spiritual distraction from more urgent [present or future] concerns."[180]

Returning to C.S. Lewis and his book *Miracles*, we see a similar argument. Lewis states:

> The following question may be asked: If we can reasonably pray for an event which must in fact have happened or failed to happen several hours ago, why can we not pray for an event which we know *not* to have happened? e.g. pray for the safety of someone who, as we know, was killed yesterday. What makes the difference is precisely our knowledge. The known event states God's will. It is psychologically impossible to pray for what we know to be unobtainable, and if it were possible the prayer would sin against the duty of submission to God's known will.
>
> [T]he Christian is not to ask whether this or that event happened because of a prayer. He is rather to believe that all events without exception are *answers* to prayer in the sense that whether they are grantings or refusals the prayers of all concerned and their needs have all been taken into account. ... When the event you prayed for occurs your prayer has always contributed to it. When the opposite event occurs your prayer has never been ignored; it has been considered and refused, for your ultimate good and the good of the whole universe.[181]

Overall, C.S. Lewis and Jimmy Akin make very compelling arguments that it is possible to pray across time. Following the logic of their arguments, one can see why I am offering prayers to assist my grandmother at the moment of her death, but I am not praying to God that she never took her life. That fact cannot change. That event was allowed by God's permissive will, and for me to pray against that would be inappropriate. However, her eternal destiny is uncertain to me (in other words, I do not know the result of God's judgment upon her soul), so her salvation is something I can absolutely pray for, even in the future.

I should also make an important point of clarification here: *Through my prayers to assist my grandmother in the past, I am not helping to release her from hell.* That cannot happen. Once a soul is in hell, that is its final state for all eternity and can never be changed. What we've been talking about here is that our prayers of intercession can aid a person at the moment of their death because God is outside of time, omniscient, and omnipotent.

At the moment of death, these prayers, regardless of when they were made, give a person more grace to possibly say "yes" to God (again, it is their *yes* and not ours) before they make the final decision to reject Him and ultimately end up in hell. At that point, their decision cannot be undone. The prayers that we offer for our loved one are applied to them at the moment of their death so that they don't in fact choose hell. Whether or not they accept the grace is a mystery that will only be revealed in eternity.

It is a beautiful consolation knowing that this principle applies to all of our loved ones who have died, not just those who died by suicide. To summarize, I have real hope not only because of the magisterial teaching of the Church, but because of the witness of the saints, especially St. Faustina's description of the mercy of God, a God who desires us to be united with Him. Having made this clarification, let's now turn to another question I am often asked when telling people about my epiphany of hope.

*W*HO ELSE SUPPORTS THIS CLAIM THAT MY PRAYERS CAN HAVE AN ETERNAL EFFECT? Let us now return to the objection mentioned earlier, that "God is outside of time but we are not, so our prayers cannot transcend time."

In his book *Everything You Ever Wanted to Know about Heaven ... But Never Dreamed of Asking*, Peter Kreeft touches on the eternal power of prayer. He explains that "eternity is not spread out like time. It is simultaneously present all at once, not piece by piece in passing" nor "dispersed into past and future."[182] If we ask the question, "What time is it in eternity?" the answer is "now," since all things are present at once. Therefore, Boethius' definition of eternity makes sense: "the simultaneous possession of all perfection in a single present."[183]

Kreeft then observes that the time we measure each day, clock time (*chronos* in Greek), is not the only kind of time we experience in this world. He says, "We live in *kairos*: lived time, or life-time. *Kairos* is time *for* something, time relative to human purpose. ... At the moment of death, according to very widespread testimony, your whole lifetime often flashes before you in vivid detail, in perfect order, and in a single instant. All your *kairos* does not take a single minute of *chronos*, for the boundary, the *chronos*-limit, is removed."[184]

Kreeft then ties time to the three levels of reality: the human (humanity), the superhuman (God), and the subhuman (the material world). "Each has its own kind of duration that is natural to it: eternity for God, *kairos* for humanity, *chronos* for the world."[185] Thus, the reason that our prayers can make a difference, even for a past event, is because "our human time (*kairos*) touches both superhuman time (eternity) and subhuman time (*chronos*), both the divine and the material, just as our subjective spirit touches both objective spirit (God) and objective matter (the world)."[186]

The human person is capable of touching eternity because, having a spiritual nature, he has the quality of transcendence. Through the modality of human-spirit time, or *kairos*, he can transcend the limits of the *chronos* and participate in the superhuman "time" of God, which is eternity.

According to Kreeft, "Our *kairos* includes as one of its dimensions the world's *chronos*, for time is part of our experience. And our *kairos* is included in God's eternity" because "God is not an ingredient in our experience; we are ingredients in God's experience. The meaning of our life's time is in God's eternity. The point of *kairos*, the point of our lives, what it all points to, is eternity."[187] So "*chronos* never touches eternity, but *kairos* does."[188]

Thus, one can conclude that it is through this very means that the prayers that come from the depths of our soul, from our *kairos*, can have an eternal effect. "Only the soul, which lives in *kairos*, touches eternity and can take the body and even the universe with it to eternity through the Resurrection [of Christ]."[189] In other words, "God is in humanity (Christ) so that humanity can be in God (Christians)."[190] And this gives our prayers an eternal, timeless dimension. Kreeft states:

> The "present" of *chronos*, the chronological now, is a mere point separating past and future. In *chronos* there is only

past and future; nothing is present. In *kairos*, all is present; past and future are dimensions *of* the present. This is because *kairos* touches eternity. Eternity includes all pasts and futures in the living present. Only eternity can "redeem the time," can heal the separation of time by touching past and future, Alpha and Omega, together.

A startling consequence is that eternity can change the past! Eternity causes everything; we in time cause only future things. The causality of eternity does not work horizontally along the time line from past to future or from present to future, but along the vertical line from eternity to time, including all time, past as well as future. The past is open to eternity, as open as the future.[191]

Therefore, the reason our prayers can obtain this eternal, timeless dimension is because "in eternity, all time is alive. The past is present." And according to our faith, "what is present can be changed, redeemed." Thus, Kreeft says, "All the sins and mistakes and missed opportunities of the past, all the unsolvable problems and dead ends, even death itself, can be made to work backwards from eternity."[192] He continues:

Eternity makes regret impossible because there is nothing to regret when nothing is past, just as there is nothing to fear when nothing is future. Regret is possible only when in time we look at the dead, unchangeable past, when we say, "I believe in yesterday."[193]

Now let's return to the question of the efficacy of our prayers and whether or not they can transcend time. In addressing this point, Kreeft offers a powerful personal example:

"Prayer changes things," past as well as present, by touching eternity. Let me give an example from my own experience. When my daughter was misdiagnosed as having a fatal, malignant brain tumor, I asked my friends to pray for her, and the prayers "worked": the tumor, surprisingly, turned out to have been benign. A skeptical friend whom I thanked for his prayers said to me, "You realize, of course, that our prayers couldn't have changed anything, really; the doctor said the tumor had been in her for years, and was benign from the beginning." I replied, "Your prayers *did* change things. God, eternally foreseeing all those prayers, decided to give her a benign tumor instead of a malignant one when He created her. Thank you."[194]

Wow! We see as in previous examples that through God's omniscience and omnipotence, He both knew that those prayers were going to be made and had the power to apply the graces from them back at the moment of the child's creation. As Kreeft notes:

"With the Lord one day is as a thousand years, and a thousand years as one day"; and just as He plays time like an accordion, expanding and contracting it at will, so can we when we live in Him. As an author can move backward or forward in a story, God can move in time; and so can we, once we get out of the story and into the Author.[195]

Thus, prayers can transcend time if they are made in Christ. Like Jimmy Akin and C.S. Lewis, Kreeft states that we can pray for anything we do not know the definitive, historical result of, past or present, because the One we pray to is not bound by time. To God, "all time is simultaneously present in eternity, as all the events in the novel are present in the mind of its author."[196]

*R*EAL HOPE, EVEN FOR THE GREATEST SINNER. As we've seen through these examples, there are real-world consequences to the fact that God is outside of time and stepped into time through the Incarnation. There are real consequences to the fact that we who have been baptized are members of the Body of Christ. There are real consequences to the fact that our prayers today can still assist those we love who have died in the past.

In other words, there is real hope. I have hope, not because God's grace comes *from* me, but because it can go *through* me. Indeed, whether or not our deceased loved ones accept the grace of Divine Mercy when Jesus makes a last appeal to them, and whether or not they can hear the still, small whisper of the Holy Spirit through the sound and fury of their depression, or whatever brought them to suicide, may depend on the prayers and the Masses we offer for them now, even years later. We can see that God wills us to be active participants in His work of Redemption. We are not meant to be passive and uninvolved spectators.

Since Jesus is eternal, His actions have an eternal character in which our prayers and good works share when we are joined to Him through sanctifying grace. As the *Catechism* teaches, "[B]ecause in his incarnate divine person he has in some way united himself to every man, 'the possibility of being made partners, in a way known to God, in the Paschal mystery' is offered to all men" (618).

This means that all of humanity throughout history (including us) have the opportunity to be joined to the Paschal Mystery through prayer. Because of this, we may pray with confidence for the salvation of those who have died in the past, or will die in the future. Thus, those we love are not beyond our assistance and certainly not beyond the mercy of God.

If you are like me, however, you may sometimes wonder if you are "holy enough" to have your prayers answered by God. Or you may wonder if the one you lost was holy enough to receive the graces from those prayers. If you are in that category, you should look again at the above entry from the *Catechism*, which tells us that the grace of being made partners with Christ is "offered to *all*." Well, we are *all* great sinners. Here we should also be reminded of Jesus' words to St. Faustina: **"Encourage souls to place great trust in My fathomless mercy. Let the weak, sinful soul have no fear to approach Me, for even if it had more sins than there are grains of sand in the world, all would be drowned in the immeasurable depths of My mercy"** (*Diary*, 1059).

Think about that. *More sins than there are grains of sand in the whole world!* Have you ever gone to the beach, taken a big scoop of sand in your hand, and allowed it to pour slowly through your fingers? There are literally *hundreds of thousands* of grains of sand in just one handful. Imagine the *trillions upon trillions* of grains of sand that exist in the entire world! This is the magnitude of the *fathomless* Divine Mercy that Jesus impresses upon St. Faustina to share with the world. His Divine Mercy drowns out every imaginable sin ever committed, even if they were as plentiful as all the grains of sand of the whole entire world! They would be completely absorbed and drowned out, as though the ocean's waters were washing away every single grain of sand in the world.

So let us respond to Jesus' fathomless Divine Mercy with unreserved confidence, hope, and trust in His infinite goodness. No matter what sins you or your deceased loved ones have committed, His mercy is always there to forgive. He is always ready to answer your prayers for your departed ones, and to offer salvation to all who come to Him. Thus, there is hope for *them* and there is hope for *you*. And this hope can make all the difference in the world.

Saint Stanislaus Papczynski, Founder of the Marian Fathers of the Immaculate Conception and patron saint of those in mortal danger, pray for us!

Prayer to Obtain Graces Through The Intercession of St. Stanislaus Papczynski

Saint Stanislaus,
gracious intercessor before God,
defender of the oppressed,
and patron of those in mortal danger,
you always zealously served Jesus
and His Immaculate Mother
for the salvation of immortal souls,
and you took pity on every misery.
Trusting in your intercession,
I have recourse to you,
and I ask that you
do not deny me your help.
By your earnest prayers,
obtain for me from God the grace
for which I beg you with trust:

(*say your intentions here*)

Help me, all my life long,
to fulfill the will of the Heavenly Father.
Amen.

APPENDICES

APPENDIX A:

Warning Signs and Risk Factors of Suicide[197]

SUICIDE WARNING SIGNS

Talk
If a person talks about:

- Killing themselves
- Feeling hopeless
- Having no reason to live
- Being a burden to others
- Feeling trapped
- Unbearable pain

Behavior
Behaviors that may signal risk, especially if related to a painful event, loss or change:

- Increased use of alcohol or drugs
- Looking for a way to end their lives, such as searching online for methods
- Withdrawing from activities
- Isolating from family and friends
- Sleeping too much or too little
- Visiting or calling people to say goodbye
- Giving away prized possessions
- Aggression
- Fatigue

Mood

People who are considering suicide often display one or more of the following moods:

- Depression
- Anxiety
- Loss of interest
- Irritability
- Humiliation/Shame
- Agitation/Anger
- Relief/Sudden Improvement

SUICIDE RISK FACTORS

Health Factors

- Mental health conditions
  - Depression
  - Substance use problems
  - Bipolar disorder
  - Schizophrenia
  - Personality traits of aggression, mood changes and poor relationships
  - Conduct disorder
  - Anxiety disorders
- Serious physical health conditions including pain
- Traumatic brain injury

Environmental Factors

- Access to lethal means including firearms and drugs
- Prolonged stress, such as harassment, bullying, relationship problems or unemployment
- Stressful life events, like rejection, divorce, financial crisis, other life transitions or loss
- Exposure to another person's suicide, or to graphic or sensationalized accounts of suicide

Historical Factors

- Previous suicide attempts
- Family history of suicide
- Childhood abuse, neglect or trauma

APPENDIX B:

Recent Statistics on U.S. Suicide

Suicide, one of the most tragic, distressing forms of death for loved ones to grieve, continues to overwhelm our society. These statistics suggest that, at the very least, you do not grieve alone.

- In the U.S. in 2017, more than 47,000 people took their own lives. That's one person every 11.1 minutes.[198]

- "Within the past year [2017-2018] ... 1.3 million adults have attempted suicide, 2.7 million adults have had a plan to attempt suicide and 9.3 million adults have had suicidal thoughts."[199]

- Death by suicide has even surpassed death by homicide in annual statistics.[200]

- For each suicide, researchers estimate that more than six people suffer what researchers consider "a major life disruption" as a result (presumably close family and friends). Some researchers refer to those in this category as "loss survivors."[201]

- It affects the elderly. Those over 85 years old have the highest suicide rate.[202]

- It affects the young. Death by suicide places second in the leading causes of death for those ages 15-24, behind only accidental injury.[203]

- Suicide comes mostly by way of firearms, but also suffocation, hanging, cutting, poisoning, drowning, and in many other tragic ways. But suicide is merely the end result — the culmination of hours, days, weeks, months, years, perhaps even decades of mental agony. Research suggests that 54 percent of those who die by suicide did not have a known mental health condition.[204]

- About 14 percent of high school students have considered suicide, while almost seven percent have attempted it. Furthermore, victims of bullying have a two to nine times more likely chance of considering suicide than non-victims.[205]

- In the U.S., physician-assisted suicide is legal in California, Colorado, the District of Columbia, Hawaii, New Jersey, Oregon, Vermont, and Washington.[206]

- "Since September 11, 2001, more than 3,000 service members have died by suicide (USA Today, 2014). In 2012 and 2013, suicide was the leading cause of death for service members."[207]

- The U.S. Department of Veterans Affairs estimates that PTSD afflicts about 30 percent of Vietnam veterans, about 12 percent of Gulf War veterans, and about 11 to 20 percent of veterans of the wars in Iraq and Afghanistan.[208]

Appendix C

How to Pray the Chaplet of Divine Mercy

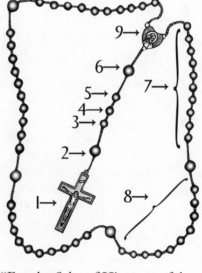

1. Make the Sign of the Cross.

2. Say the optional Opening Prayer.

3. Say the "Our Father."

4. Say the "Hail Mary."

5. Say the "Apostles' Creed."

6. Say the "Eternal Father."

7. Say 10 "For the sake of His sorrowful Passion" on the "Hail Mary" beads.

8. Repeat for four more decades, saying "Eternal Father" on the "Our Father" bead and then 10 "For the Sake of His sorrowful Passion" on the following "Hail Mary" beads.

9. At the conclusion of the five decades, on the medallion say the "Holy God," the concluding doxology, three times.

10. Say the optional Closing Prayer.

Prayers of the Chaplet of Divine Mercy

1. *The Sign of the Cross:* In the name of the Father, and of the Son, and of the Holy Spirit. Amen.

2. *Opening Prayers (optional):* You expired, Jesus, but the source of life gushed forth for souls, and the ocean of mercy opened up for the whole world. O Fount of Life, unfathomable Divine Mercy, envelop the whole world and empty Yourself out upon us (*Diary*, 1319).

   O Blood and Water, which gushed forth from the Heart of Jesus as a fount of mercy for us, I trust in You! (*three times*) (*Diary*, 84).

3. *The Our Father:* Our Father, who art in heaven; hallowed be Thy name; Thy kingdom come; Thy will be done on earth as it is in heaven. Give us this day our daily bread; and forgive us our trespasses as we forgive those who trespass against us, and lead us not into temptation; but deliver us from evil. Amen.

4. *The Hail Mary:* Hail Mary, full of grace. The Lord is with thee. Blessed art thou among women, and blessed is the fruit of thy womb, Jesus. Holy Mary, Mother of God, pray for us sinners, now and at the hour of our death. Amen

5. *The Apostles' Creed:* I believe in God, the Father almighty, Creator of Heaven and earth, and in Jesus Christ, His only Son, our Lord, who was conceived by the Holy Spirit, born of the Virgin Mary, suffered under Pontius Pilate, was crucified, died, and was buried; He descended into hell; on the third day He rose again from the dead; He ascended into Heaven, and is seated at the right hand of God the Father almighty; from there He will come to judge the living and the dead. I believe in the Holy Spirit, the holy catholic Church, the Communion of saints, the forgiveness of sins, the resurrection of the body, and life everlasting. Amen.*

6. *On the "Our Father" bead before each decade:* Eternal Father, I offer You the Body and Blood, Soul and Divinity of Your dearly beloved Son, Our Lord Jesus Christ, in atonement for our sins and those of the whole world (*Diary*, 476).

7. On the "Hail Mary" beads of each decade: For the sake of His sorrowful Passion, have mercy on us and on the whole world.

8. Repeat "Eternal Father" and "For the Sake of His sorrowful Passion": (Number 6 and 7) Prayers for four more decades.

9. After five decades, the concluding doxology (three times): Holy God, Holy Mighty One, Holy Immortal One, have mercy on us and on the whole world.

10. Closing Prayer (optional): Eternal God, in whom mercy is endless, and the treasury of compassion inexhaustible, look kindly upon us, and increase Your mercy in us, that in difficult moments, we might not despair, nor become despondent, but with great confidence, submit ourselves to Your holy will, which is Love and Mercy Itself. Amen (*Diary*, 950).

*The wording of the Apostles' Creed conforms with the Roman Missal.

Appendix D

Suicide Prevention and
Grief Support/Postvention Resources

Suicide Prevention

If you are experiencing suicidal thoughts or temptations, call the National Suicide Prevention Lifeline at 1-800-273-8255. Available 24 hours every day.

Also, Crisis Text Line (text 741741) provides free, 24/7, confidential support via text message to people in crisis.

People 60 years and older who are contemplating suicide can call the Institute on Aging (IOA) 24-hour, toll-free Friendship Line at 800-971-0016. IOA also makes ongoing outreach calls to lonely older adults.

Resources recommended by Dr. Melinda Moore:

• American Foundation for Suicide Prevention (AFSP)

   This group raises funds for research into suicide prevention and has expanded its mission to become the largest U.S. organization concerned with the needs of suicide survivors. Beyond postvention, AFSP sponsors several million dollars' worth of research into the causes and prevention of suicide and maintains an active advocacy effort on behalf of suicide prevention and postvention. See afsp.org for more information on AFSP.

• National Action Alliance for Suicide Prevention (NAASP)

   NAASP is a public-private partnership dedicated to reducing suicide in America. Among its activities have been the issuing of an updated U.S. National Strategy for Suicide Prevention (U.S. Department of Health & Human Services, Office of the Surgeon General & National Action Alliance for Suicide Prevention, 2012), and the formation of a Survivors of Suicide Loss Task Force. See actionallianceforsuicideprevention.org/ for more information on NAASP.

Grief Support/Postvention

For help in building resilient communities, capable of persevering through tragedy and trauma, please see the work of Dr. Mollie Marti's National Resilience Institute (nationalresilienceinstitute.org).

Resources recommended by Dr. Melinda Moore:

- American Foundation for Suicide Prevention (AFSP)
  See afsp.org for more information on AFSP.

- Survivor-initiated programs:
  - Heartbeat, begun by LaRita Archibald in Colorado
  - Friends for Survivors, begun by Marilyn Koenig in California
  - The LINK Counseling Center, begun by Iris Bolton in Georgia
  - Baton Rouge Crisis Intervention Center, begun by Dr. Frank Campbell

- Development of postvention in the United States:
  - American Association of Suicidology.
    - Please visit suicidology.org to learn more about their work, find further resources on suicide prevention and suicidology, and more.

APPENDIX E

Conversation of the Merciful God with a Despairing Soul

Jesus: **O soul steeped in darkness, do not despair. All is not yet lost. Come and confide in your God, who is love and mercy.**

— But the soul, deaf even to this appeal, wraps itself in darkness.

Jesus calls out again: **My child, listen to the voice of your merciful Father.**

— In the soul arises this reply: "For me there is no mercy," and it falls into greater darkness, a despair which is a foretaste of hell and makes it unable to draw near to God.

Jesus calls to the soul a third time, but the soul remains deaf and blind, hardened and despairing. Then the mercy of God begins to exert itself, and, without any co-operation from the soul, God grants it final grace. If this too is spurned, God will leave the soul in this self-chosen disposition for eternity. This grace emerges from the merciful Heart of Jesus and gives the soul a special light by means of which the soul begins to understand God's effort; but conversion depends on its own will. The soul knows that this, for her, is final grace and, should it show even a flicker of good will, the mercy of God will accomplish the rest.

My omnipotent mercy is active here. Happy the soul that takes advantage of this grace.

Jesus: **What joy fills My Heart when you return to Me. Because you are weak, I take you in My arms and carry you to the home of My Father.**

Soul (as if awaking, asks fearfully): Is it possible that there yet is mercy for me?

Jesus: **There is, My child. You have a special claim on My mercy. Let it act in your poor soul; let the rays of grace enter your soul; they bring with them light, warmth, and life.**

Soul: But fear fills me at the thought of my sins, and this terrible fear moves me to doubt Your goodness.

Jesus: **My child, all your sins have not wounded My Heart as painfully as your present lack of trust does — that after so many efforts of My love and mercy, you should still doubt My goodness.**

Soul: O Lord, save me Yourself, for I perish. Be my Savior. O Lord, I am unable to say anything more; my pitiful heart is torn asunder; but You, O Lord...

Jesus does not let the soul finish but, raising it from the ground, from the depths of its misery, he leads it into the recesses of His Heart where all its sins disappear instantly, consumed by the flames of love.

Jesus: **Here, soul, are all the treasures of My Heart. Take everything you need from it.**

Soul: O Lord, I am inundated with Your grace. I sense that a new life has entered into me and, above all, I feel Your love in my heart. That is enough for me. O Lord, I will glorify the omnipotence of Your mercy for all eternity. Encouraged by Your goodness, I will confide to You all the sorrows of my heart.

Jesus: **Tell me all, My child, hide nothing from Me, because My loving Heart, the Heart of your Best Friend, is listening to you.**

Soul: O Lord, now I see all my ingratitude and Your goodness. You were pursuing me with Your grace, while I was frustrating Your benevolence. I see that I deserve the depths of hell for spurning Your graces.

Jesus (interrupting): **Do not be absorbed in your misery — you are still too weak to speak of it — but, rather, gaze on My Heart filled with goodness, and be imbued with My sentiments. Strive for meekness and humility; be merciful to others, as I am to you; and, when you feel your strength failing, if you come to the fountain of mercy to fortify your soul, you will not grow weary on your journey.**

Soul: Now I understand Your mercy, which protects me, and like a brilliant star, leads me into the home of my Father, protecting me from the horrors of hell that I have deserved, not once, but a thousand times. O Lord, eternity will hardly suffice for me to give due praise to Your unfathomable mercy and Your compassion for Me (*Diary*, 1486).

APPENDIX F

The Seven Sorrows Rosary

"More than ever, the world needs the Seven Sorrows Rosary."
(Visionary Marie Claire of Kibeho, Rwanda)

This devotion goes back to the Middle Ages but has gained new popularity following the Church-approved Marian apparitions in Kibeho, Rwanda, in the 1980s. In her apparitions, Our Lady of Kibeho recommended that people pray the Rosary (or Chaplet) of the Seven Sorrows.

Let us answer Our Lady of Kibeho's call and make the Seven Sorrows Rosary a regular part of our prayer life.

How to pray on the Seven Sorrows Rosary Beads

1. Make the Sign of the Cross. Say the Introductory Prayer and an Act of Contrition.

2. Say three Hail Marys in honor of the tears of Our Sorrowful Mother.

3. Announce the First Sorrow, then say the Our Father.

4. Say seven Hail Marys while meditating on the Sorrow.

5. Say "Most merciful Mother, remind us always about the sorrows of your Son, Jesus" or the Glory Be.

6. Announce the Second Sorrow; then say the Our Father. Repeat 4 and 5. Continue with the Third through Seventh Sorrows in the same manner.

7. Say the Queen of Martyrs prayer on the medal after the five decades are completed. Conclude with "Mary, who was conceived without sin and who suffered for us, pray for us" three times.

The Seven Sorrows of Our Lady

1. The prophecy of Simeon (Lk 2:22-35)
- One Our Father
- Seven Hail Marys
- "Most merciful Mother, remind us always about the sorrows of your Son, Jesus" or the Glory Be.

2. The flight into Egypt (Mt 2:13-15)
- One Our Father
- Seven Hail Marys
- "Most merciful Mother, remind us always about the sorrows of your Son, Jesus" or the Glory Be.

3. The loss of Jesus in the Temple (Lk 2:41-51)
- One Our Father
- Seven Hail Marys
- "Most merciful Mother, remind us always about the sorrows of your Son, Jesus" or the Glory Be.

4. Mary meets Jesus on the way to Calvary (Lk 23:27-31)
- One Our Father
- Seven Hail Marys
- "Most merciful Mother, remind us always about the sorrows of your Son, Jesus" or the Glory Be.

5. Mary stands at the foot of the Cross (Jn 19:25-27)
- One Our Father
- Seven Hail Marys
- "Most merciful Mother, remind us always about the sorrows of your Son, Jesus" or the Glory Be.

6. Mary receives the dead body of Jesus (Jn 19:38-40)
- One Our Father
- Seven Hail Marys
- "Most merciful Mother, remind us always about the sorrows of your Son, Jesus" or the Glory Be.

7. Jesus is laid in the tomb (Jn 19:41-42)
- One Our Father
- Seven Hail Marys
- "Most merciful Mother, remind us always about the sorrows of your Son, Jesus" or the Glory Be.

Prayers

1. Introductory Prayer: My God, I offer you this Rosary for Your glory, so that I can honor Your Holy Mother, the Blessed Virgin, and share and meditate upon her suffering. I humbly beg You to give me true repentance for all my sins. Give me wisdom and humility so that I may receive all the indulgences contained in this prayer.

2. Act of Contrition: O my God, I am heartily sorry for having offended You, and I detest all my sins, because I dread the loss of Heaven and the pains of hell, but most of all because they offend You, my God, You who are all good and deserving of all my love. I firmly resolve, with the help of Your grace, to confess my sins, do penance, and amend my life. Amen.

3. Our Father: Our Father, who art in heaven; hallowed be Thy name; Thy kingdom come; Thy will be done on earth as it is in heaven. Give us this day our daily bread; and forgive us our trespasses as we forgive those who trespass against us, and lead us not into temptation; but deliver us from evil. Amen.

4. Hail Mary: Hail Mary, full of grace. The Lord is with thee. Blessed art thou among women, and blessed is the fruit of thy womb, Jesus. Holy Mary, Mother of God, pray for us sinners, now and at the hour of our death. Amen.

5. Glory Be to the Father: Glory be to the Father, and to the Son, and to the Holy Spirit. As it was in the beginning, is now, and ever shall be, world without end. Amen.

6. Closing prayer: Queen of Martyrs, your heart suffered so much. I beg you, by the merits of the tears you shed in these terrible and sorrowful times, to obtain for me and all the sinners of the world the grace of complete sincerity and repentance. Amen.

Mary, who was conceived without sin and who suffered for us, pray for us. (3x)

With Ecclesiastical Approval.
According to Fr. Leszek Czelusniak, MIC, this version of the Seven Sorrows Rosary was given by Our Lady at Kibeho.

Appendix G

Spiritual Opportunities

Prayer is so important because God is the Divine Physician and the ultimate Source of healing. In fact, there's no better gift for someone, especially someone hurting, than the gift of prayer. As Providence would have it, Fr. Chris serves as the director of the Association of Marian Helpers, a Catholic spiritual benefit society whose 1.5-million members answer God's invitation to participate in His divine plan by means of intercessory prayer. By taking up one another's burdens through prayer, Marian Helpers multiply God's grace in tremendous ways for the benefit of those who are suffering.

Officially established in 1944, the Association began as a small group of friends who believed in and supported the work of the Marians. Now some 1.5-million members strong, the Association is a spiritual benefit society that continues to prayerfully and financially support the priests and brothers of the Congregation of Marian Fathers of the Immaculate Conception.

What are the spiritual benefits of membership?

As a Marian Helper, a person shares in the benefits of all the daily Masses, prayers, and good works of Marian priests and brothers all over the world. In addition, members of the Association receive a specific remembrance in the following ways:

- A daily Holy Mass celebrated for Marian Helpers

- A Holy Mass offered for members on the First Friday and First Saturday of each month

- A Holy Mass offered for deceased members on All Souls Day

- A special Mass offered on each feast day of Our Savior and His Blessed Mother, including the Presentation (February 2), the Annunciation (March 25), the Assumption (August 15), the Birth of Mary (September 8), and the Immaculate Conception (December 8)

- The continuous Novena to the Divine Mercy at the National Shrine of The Divine Mercy in Stockbridge, Massachusetts

- The daily prayers offered by workers at the National Shrine of The Divine Mercy and the Marian Helpers Center

Call 1-800-4MARIAN (1-800-462-7426)
or visit marian.org/enrollments
to arrange for Masses or to enroll yourself and your
loved ones in the Association of Marian Helpers.

Endnotes

[1] Hope is one of the three theological virtues (along with faith and love) that are described as *supernatural*, meaning that God infuses them into our soul at Baptism. So they are purely a gift from God, and we cannot acquire these virtues on our own.

Hope is a combination of the desire for something and the expectation of receiving it. While faith is a function of the intellect, hope is an act of the will, so we can make a conscious effort to exercise this infused virtue given by God. That is the goal of this book: for you to rediscover hope in the midst of suffering and tragedy.

In his *Summa Theologica*, Thomas Aquinas says hope is the theological virtue by which we aspire with confidence to grace and Heaven, trusting God, and being resolved to use His help (ST II-II, 17.1). Aquinas says hope, in the strict sense of the word, is in a person and for himself. But, since love unites those who have it, a person may be said to hope for his beloved as for himself; in this sense it is possible for one person to hope on behalf of another (ST II-II, 17.3).

As the Church has always taught, the virtue of hope will be fulfilled in Heaven. Our hope for God and Heaven gives us certainty that we shall attain what we hope for if we do our part! The certainty of this hope rests on the unfailing goodness and mercy of God, and on His absolute fidelity to His promises (ST II-II, 17.4). We know this from Hebrews 10:23, where St. Paul says, "Let us hold fast the confession of our hope without wavering, for he who promised is faithful."

[2] Unless otherwise stated, all biblical quotations are taken from the *Revised Standard Version — Catholic Edition* (RSVCE).

[3] John R. Jordan, "Grief After Suicide: The Evolution of Suicide Postvention," in *Death, Dying, and Bereavement: Contemporary Perspectives, Institutions, and Practices*, eds. Judith M. Stillion and Thomas Attig (New York, NY: Springer, 2015), pp. 349-62, cited in Dr. Melinda Moore, correspondence with the authors, June 30, 2019.

[4] "[T]he term coined by Edwin Shneidman for the efforts after a suicide to help the survivors and to mitigate its deleterious impact." Jordan, "Grief After Suicide," in Stillion and Attig, *Death, Dying, and Bereavement*, p. 349.

[5] William Feigelman et al., "Suicide Exposures and Bereavement Among American Adults: Evidence from the 2016 General Social Survey," *Journal of Affective Disorders* 227 (2018): 1-6, https://doi.org/10.1016/j.jad.2017.09.056, cited in Christopher W. Drapeau and John L. McIntosh, American Association of Suicidology, "U.S.A. Suicide 2017: Official Final Data," December 10, 2018, https://www.suicidology.org/Portals/14/docs/Resources/FactSheets/2017/2017datapgsv1-FINAL.pdf.

[6] Sarah Zhang, "More Americans Are Dying From Suicide," *The Atlantic*, June 8, 2018, accessed February 26, 2019, https://www.theatlantic.com/health/archive/2018/06/more-americans-are-dying-from-suicide/562406/. The statistics are drawn from the Centers for Disease Control and Prevention (CDC), "Trends in State Suicide Rates — United States, 1999–2016 and Circumstances Contributing to Suicide — 27 States, 2015," *Vital Signs*, June 8, 2018, accessed February 26, 2019, https://www.cdc.gov/mmwr/volumes/67/wr/mm6722a1.htm?s_cid=mm6722a1_w.

[7] Sally C. Curtin and Holly Hedegaard, "Suicide Rates for Females and Males by Race And Ethnicity: United States, 1999 and 2017," National Center for Health Statistics (NCHS) Health E-Stat, page last reviewed June 20, 2019, https://www.cdc.gov/nchs/data/hestat/suicide/rates_1999_2017.pdf.

[8] Maggie Fox, "More Teens Are Attempting Suicide. It's Not Clear Why," NBC News, May 16, 2018, accessed February 26, 2019, https://www.nbcnews.com/health/

health-news/more-kids-especially-girls-are-attempting-suicide-it-s-not-n874481.

[9] Lisa Schlein, "More People Die from Suicide Than From Wars, Natural Disasters Combined," Voice of America, September 4, 2014, accessed May 7, 2019, https://www.voanews.com/a/more-people-die-from-suicide-than-from-wars-natural-disasters-combined/2438749.html; see also Yuval Noah Harari, "Nationalism vs. Globalism: The New Political Divide," "TED Dialogues" (February 2017), accessed May 7, 2019, https://www.ted.com/talks/yuval_noah_harari_nationalism_vs_globalism_the_new_political_divide, minute 3:53-3:43.

[10] Leo Shane III, "VA: Suicide Rate for Younger Veterans Increased by More Than 10 Percent," *Military Times*, September 26, 2018, accessed March 5, 2019, https://www.militarytimes.com/news/pentagon-congress/2018/09/26/suicide-rate-spikes-among-younger-veterans.

[11] Drapeau and McIntosh, "U.S.A. Suicide 2017: Official Final Data."

[12] Ibid.

[13] Richard Morgan, "Artificial Concern for People in Pain Won't Stop Suicide. Radical Empathy Might," *Washington Post*, June 15, 2018, accessed February 27, 2019, https://www.washingtonpost.com/outlook/artificial-concern-for-people-in-pain-wont-stop-suicide-radical-empathy-might/2018/06/15/3145d508-6f52-11e8-bd50-b80389a4e569_story.html.

[14] Colin Pritchard and Lars Hansen, "Examining Undetermined and Accidental Deaths as Source of 'Under-Reported-Suicide' by Age and Sex in Twenty Western Countries," *Community Mental Health Journal* 51, no. 3 (2014): 365-72, doi:10.1007/s10597-014-9810-z; see also World Health Organization (WHO), "Suicide," August 24, 2018, accessed February 27, 2019, https://www.who.int/news-room/fact-sheets/detail/suicide, see also "Mental Health: Suicide Data," accessed February 27, 2019, https://www.who.int/mental_health/prevention/suicide/suicideprevent/en/.

[15] The "Werther effect" is named for the supposed consequences of the famous 19th-century German author Goethe's novel *The Sorrows of Young Werther*, in which the titular protagonist completes suicide. According to urban legend at the time, the novel inspired a wave of copycat suicides. See also Patrick Devitt, "*13 Reasons Why* and Suicide Contagion: What Science Shows about the Dangers of Suicide Depictions," *Scientific American*, May 8, 2017, accessed February 27, 2019, https://www.scientificamerican.com/article/13-reasons-why-and-suicide-contagion1.

[16] Marissa Martinelli, "*13 Reasons Why*'s Controversial Depiction of Teen Suicide Has School Counselors Picking up the Pieces," *Brow Beat: Slate's Culture Blog*, May 1, 2017, accessed January 31, 2018, http://www.slate.com/blogs/browbeat/2017/05/01/school_counselors_talk_netflix_s_controversial_teen_suicide_drama_13_reasons.html.

[17] Kalhan Rosenblatt, "Suicide Searches Increased After Release of '13 Reasons Why'," NBC News, July 31, 2017, accessed March 1, 2019, https://www.nbcnews.com/health/health-news/suicide-searches-increased-after-release-13-reasons-why-n788161.

[18] Jeffrey A. Bridge et al., "Association Between the Release of Netflix's *13 Reasons Why* and Suicide Rates in the United States: An Interrupted Times Series Analysis," *Journal of the American Academy of Child & Adolescent Psych*, published online April 28, 2019, DOI: https://doi.org/10.1016/j.jaac.2019.04.020, accessed August 5, 2019, https://www.jaacap.org/article/S0890-8567(19)30288-6/fulltext.

[19] As I write this, season two has been recently released on Netflix and the book is #1 on Amazon in the "Teen & Young Adult: Literature & Fiction: Social & Family Issues: Suicide" section.

[20] ReportingOnSuicide.org, "Recommendations for Reporting on Suicide," 2015, accessed June 16, 2018, http://reportingonsuicide.org.

[21] Netflix, the streaming service that produced the show, has since edited out the depiction of Hannah's suicide — but the damage has already been done.

[22] U.S. National Library of Medicine, "Opioid Abuse and Addiction," MedlinePlus (page last updated June 10, 2010; topic last reviewed June 10, 2019), accessed June 16, 2018, https://medlineplus.gov/opioidabuseandaddiction.html.

[23] Eric D. Hargan, Acting Secretary, Department of Health and Human Services, "Determination That a Public Health Emergency Exists," October 26, 2017, accessed June 16, 2018, https://www.hhs.gov/sites/default/files/opioid%20PHE%20Declaration-no-sig.pdf.

[24] National Institute on Drug Abuse, "Opioid Overdose Crisis," revised January 2019, accessed July 2, 2019, https://www.drugabuse.gov/drugs-abuse/opioids/opioid-overdose-crisis.

[25] Travis Rieder, "The Agony of Opioid Withdrawal — And What Doctors Should Tell Patients about It," *TEDxMidAtlantic*, October 2017, minute 10:39ff, accessed March 1, 2019, https://www.ted.com/talks/travis_rieder_the_agony_of_opioid_withdrawal_and_what_doctors_should_tell_patients_about_it?language=en.

[26] Melinda Smith, Jeanne Segal, and Lawrence Robinson, "Suicide Prevention," *Help Guide*, Last updated: June 2019, accessed August 7, 2019, https://www.helpguide.org/articles/suicide-prevention/suicide-prevention.htm.

[27] Kristen Fuller, "5 Common Myths About Suicide Debunked," National Alliance on Mental Illness (NAMI) Blog, September 6, 2018, accessed August 8, 2019, https://www.nami.org/Blogs/NAMI-Blog/September-2018/5-Common-Myths-About-Suicide-Debunked.

[28] Lisa Firestone, "How Can You Stop a Suicide?" *Psychology Today*, September 3, 2018, accessed August 7, 2019, https://www.psychologytoday.com/us/blog/compassion-matters/201309/how-can-you-stop-suicide.

[29] "How to Help Those Considering Suicide," accessed August 7, 2019, https://careersinpsychology.org/how-help-those-considering-suicide/.

[30] Ibid.

[31] Fuller, "5 Common Myths About Suicide Debunked."

[32] Centers for Disease Control and Prevention Newsroom, "Suicide Rates Rising Across the U.S.: Comprehensive Prevention Goes Beyond a Focus on Mental Health Concerns," press release, June 7, 2018, https://www.cdc.gov/media/releases/2018/p0607-suicide-prevention.html.

[33] Ibid.

[34] CareersInPsychology.org, "How to Help Those Considering Suicide," https://careersinpsychology.org/how-help-those-considering-suicide.

[35] Pope St. John Paul II, Encyclical Letter *Evangelium Vitae (The Gospel of Life)*, March 25, 1995, see especially n. 12.

[36] Nicene Creed.

[37] Ericka Andersen, "Is God the Answer to the Suicide Epidemic? Someone Who Attends Religious Services is Significantly Less Likely to Kill Himself," *The Wall Street Journal*, July 11, 2019, accessed July 22, 2019, https://www.wsj.com/articles/is-god-the-answer-to-the-suicide-epidemic-11562885290.

[38] Third Plenary Council of Baltimore, "Lesson First: On the End of Man, Question 6," in *Baltimore Catechism No. Two* (Charlotte, NC: TAN Books, 2010), p. 8.

[39] St. Augustine, *Conf.*, 1, 1, 1: PL 32, 659-61.

[40] Kanita Dervic et al., "Religious Affiliation and Suicide Attempt," *American Journal of Psychiatry*, published online December 1, 2004, https://doi.org/10.1176/appi.ajp.161.12.2303.

[41] See, for instance, her address at the National Prayer Breakfast, CSpan.org, February 3, 1994, https://www.c-span.org/video/?54274-1/national-prayer-breakfast.

[42] cf. *Sir* 5:8.

[43] St. Thomas Aquinas, *Summa Theologiae* II-II, 35, 4 ad 2.

[44] Alex Johnson, "Parkland Shooting Suspect Nikolas Cruz Spoke of 'Voices,' Says He Attempted Suicide," NBC News, August 6, 2018, accessed March 1, 2019, https://www.nbcnews.com/news/us-news/parkland-shooting-suspect-nikolas-cruz-spoke-voices-says-he-attempted-n898151.

[45] The Church teaches that physician-assisted suicide is also grave matter. Do not assume that just because a doctor might suggest that one "should" end a family member's suffering by ending their life, it is ethical or within Church teaching to do so. Nor should assisted suicide be encouraged. Only God is the Author of life. Neither we nor any other human person ought to usurp His role, even out of a misplaced sense of mercy or compassion. Essentially, when we take such life decisions upon ourselves, we play God. This may be difficult because we believe that it may be "merciful" to assist someone's passing into eternity, but we have other, more effective, merciful means of assisting those who are dying. Having said that, there are grounds for removing extraordinary means of treatment or medical intervention for a dying person, but that is not the same as actively taking their life. In each unique situation, please seek the spiritual counsel of a knowledgeable priest or Church authority on such matters.

[46] It is interesting to note here that these conditions apply to anyone, not just those who died by suicide. So, even if we have lost someone we love by any means (natural causes, car accident, etc.) who appeared to have been living in a state of mortal sin, all three conditions may not have been present while they were alive, therefore giving us the hope for the possibility of their salvation.

[47] Sister Emmanuel of Medjugorje, *The Amazing Secrets of the Souls in Purgatory: An Interview with Maria Simma* (Denver, CO: Children of Medjugorje, Inc., 1997), Chapter 3. The Church is still discerning the authenticity of her private revelations. The authors defer to the final judgment of the Church in this matter.

[48] U.S. Department of Health and Human Services, "Does Depression Increase the Risk for Suicide?" Frequently Asked Questions, content last reviewed on September 16, 2014, accessed June 14, 2018, https://www.hhs.gov/answers/mental-health-and-substance-abuse/does-depression-increase-risk-of-suicide/index.html.

[49] American Psychiatric Association, *Diagnostic and Statistical Manual of Mental Disorders: DSM-5*, Section: Depressive Disorders (Arlington, VA: American Psychiatric Publishing, 2013).

[50] CDC, "Risk and Protective Factors: Risk Factors for Suicide," accessed May 8, 2019, https://www.cdc.gov/violenceprevention/suicide/riskprotectivefactors.html, page last reviewed: September 6, 2018; see also Suicide Prevention and Resource Center, "Risk and Protective Factors," accessed May 8, 2019, https://www.sprc.org/about-suicide/risk-protective-factors.

[51] Ilanit T. Young et al., "Suicide Bereavement and Complicated Grief," *Dialogues in Clinical Neuroscience* 14, no. 2 (2012): 177-86, https://www.ncbi.nlm.nih.gov/pmc/articles/PMC3384446/.

[52] Presumption, the polar opposite of despair, is the other deadly condition that leads to an unrepentant heart. It is the condition wherein one thinks they need no help from God and can save themselves, or can hope to obtain God's forgiveness without conversion (see *Catechism*, 2092). In this book, we are careful regarding suicide to keep the balance between not being presumptuous by saying "my loved one is absolutely in Heaven because God would never allow anyone to go to hell" and falling into despair by saying "there is no hope for my loved one because they committed a grave sin and now they are automat-

ically in hell." We can hold neither of these positions.

[53] Fr. Ron Rolheiser, "On Suicide and Despair," *Echoes: A Forum of Catholic Thought*, May 16, 2018, accessed March 4, 2019, https://thebostonpilot.com/opinion/article.asp?ID=182329#.WvzNwMijOEo.mailto.

[54] Fr. Edward McNamara, "Funeral Masses for a Suicide," A Zenit Daily Dispatch, November 15, 2005, accessed March 4, 2019, https://zenit.org/articles/funeral-masses-for-a-suicide/.

[55] Ibid.

[56] Bishop Joseph Osei-Bonsu, "Can Catholics Who Commit Suicide Be Given a Catholic Church Burial?" *The Catholic Standard*, Ghana, reprinted by Vatican Radio, October 22, 2014, accessed July 04, 2019, http://cqrcengage.com/ccdocle/app/document/4808104?0.

[57] The (short) list of those who are not to be permitted Christian burial is given in the *Code of Canon Law*, Canon 1184:

"1. notorious apostates, heretics, and schismatics;

2. those who chose the cremation of their bodies for reasons contrary to Christian faith;

3. other manifest sinners who cannot be granted ecclesiastical funerals without public scandal of the faithful."

"§2. If any doubt occurs, the local ordinary is to be consulted, and his judgment must be followed."

[58] Albert Y. Hsu, *Grieving a Suicide: A Loved One's Search for Comfort, Answers, & Hope* (Downers Grove, IL: Intervarsity Press, 2002), p. 93.

[59] "The path to successful coping with this crucial 'why' question often involves acquiring the capacity to 'hold complexity' (Sands, Jordan, & Neimeyer, 2011). This means being able to see the many elements in the perfect storm, to realistically sort out what was and was not under the survivor's control, to accept the limitations on their ability to influence the outcome, and to forgive themselves for actions that, in hindsight, might have been taken differently." Jordan, "Grief After Suicide," in Stillion and Attig, *Death, Dying, and Bereavement*, p. 356.

[60] Mt 18:18: "Amen, I say to you, whatever you bind on earth shall be bound in heaven, and whatever you loose on earth shall be loosed in heaven" (NABRE); Jn 20:21-23: "[Jesus] said to them again, 'Peace be with you. As the Father has sent me, so I send you.' And when he had said this, he breathed on them and said to them, 'Receive the holy Spirit. Whose sins you forgive are forgiven them, and whose sins you retain are retained'" (NABRE).

[61] *Baltimore Catechism No. Two*, p. 7.

[62] *Catechism of the Catholic Church*, 2nd ed., English translation, (Washington, D.C./Vatican: United States Catholic Conference, Inc./Libreria Editrice Vaticana, 1997), Glossary, p. 881, definition of "happiness."

[63] Saint Augustine also said, "[B]ut that in the Eternal nothing passes away, but that the whole is present; but no time is wholly present; and let him see that all time past is forced on by the future, and that all the future follows from the past, and that all, both past and future, is created and issues from that which is always present? Who will hold the heart of man, that it may stand still, and see how the still-standing eternity, itself neither future nor past, utters the times future and past?" (Augustine, *Confessions*, Book XI, Chapter XI).

[64] This can be any despairing soul, not just those who are contemplating suicide or who have just taken their own life by suicide.

[65] Pope St. John Paul II, "Letter of John Paul II to the Pontifical Academy of Sciences,"

February 1, 2005, accessed March 4, 2019, http://w2.vatican.va/content/john-paul-ii/en/speeches/2005/february/documents/hf_jp-ii_spe_20050201_p-acad-sciences.html, n. 4.

[66] Apparition at Fatima of August 19, 1917, "Fourth Apparition of Our Lady," EWTN. com, accessed March 4, 2019, https://www.ewtn.com/fatima/fourth-apparition-of -our-lady.asp.

[67] Abbé Francis Trochu, *The Curé d'Ars St. Jean-Marie-Baptiste Vianney (1786-1859) According to the Acts of the Process of Canonization and Numerous Hitherto Unpublished Documents,* trans. Dom Ernest Graf, OSB (Rockford, IL: TAN Books and Publishers, 1977), pp. 579-80.

[68] Fr. Michael Gaitley, MIC, *33 Days to Merciful Love: A Do-It-Yourself Retreat in Preparation for Consecration to Divine Mercy* (Stockbridge, MA: Marian Press, 2016), Day 13, p. 62; *Diary of Saint Maria Faustina Kowalska* (Stockbridge, MA: Marian Press, 2005), 47.

[69] Peter Kreeft, *Everything You Ever Wanted to Know about Heaven ... But Never Dreamed of Asking* (San Francisco: Ignatius Press, 1990), p. 92.

[70] Address of Pope John Paul II at the Shrine of Divine Mercy, Krakow, Poland, June 7, 1997, https://w2.vatican.va/content/john-paul-ii/en/travels/1997/documents/hf_jp-ii_spe_07061997_sr-faustina.html.

[71] Jesus promised to give great graces on Divine Mercy Sunday. Specifically, He told St. Faustina:

> On that day [Divine Mercy Sunday], the very depths of My tender mercy are opened. I pour out a whole ocean of graces upon those souls who approach the fount of My mercy. ... On that day all the divine floodgates through which graces flow are opened (*Diary*, 699).

Regarding the graces of Divine Mercy Sunday, Jesus told St. Faustina, **"The soul that will go to Confession and receive Holy Communion shall obtain complete forgiveness of sins and punishment"** (699).

This is an extraordinary promise! This is because when we normally go to Confession, the eternal punishment due to sin (i.e., hell) is removed, but the temporal punishment due to sin (i.e., Purgatory) may remain (see Ps 99:8). Unless we have perfect contrition, or pray, fast, and/or give alms with perfect purity of intention, temporal punishment as a consequence of our sins most likely remains. But all sins and punishment are removed by the grace of Divine Mercy Sunday when we fulfill the conditions of a valid Confession and worthily receive Holy Communion, as long as we have some rectification of the will (meaning that we are sorry and will try to amend our life). In fact, the grace of Divine Mercy Sunday has been compared to the grace of Baptism. It forgives all sins and provides for the removal of all punishment due to sin (even for sins forgotten to be confessed) and is fully effective even if our contrition is less than perfect. What is required is receiving Holy Communion worthily with trust in Jesus' promise.

Unfortunately, a lot of people confuse the great grace of Divine Mercy Sunday with a plenary indulgence. It's not exactly the same thing, however. With a plenary indulgence, not only must we perform the indulgenced act (like reading 30 minutes of Scripture or walking the Stations of the Cross), but we must fulfill four additional conditions: 1) We must receive Holy Communion on the same day that we perform the indulgenced act; 2) we must go to sacramental Confession "about 20 days" before or after doing the indulgenced act, even if we are in the state of grace; 3) we must pray for the intentions of the Holy Father (usually an Our Father, Hail Mary, and Glory Be); and 4) we can have no attachment to sin — even venial sin. Wow! That isn't easy!

To receive the grace of Divine Mercy Sunday, you simply need to go to Confession before or on the day of the Feast — sometime during Lent suffices; be in the state of grace on Divine Mercy Sunday itself (no mortal sin); and receive Holy Communion with the intention of obtaining the promised grace. Another beautiful element of Divine Mercy

Sunday is that the Church also gives us the opportunity to receive a plenary indulgence attached to an act of worship of the Divine Mercy or participation in a Divine Mercy service on the same day (under the normal conditions) that we can offer for ourselves or for a Holy Soul in Purgatory.

[72] Joseph Cardinal Ratzinger, *The Spirit of the Liturgy*, trans. John Saward (San Francisco: Ignatius Press, 2014), 70-71.

[73] Ratzinger, *The Spirit of the Liturgy*, pp. 57, 60.

[74] Fr. Michael Gaitley, MIC, *Divine Mercy Explained: Keys to the Message and Devotion* (Stockbridge, MA: Marian Press, 2013), pp. 15-18.

[75] The authors acknowledge that the historical and theological understanding of the principle of *lex orandi, lex credendi* are much richer than presented herein. For a more thorough treatment of the origin, development, and depth of this principle, see, for example, Kevin Irwin, *Context and Text: Method in Liturgical Theology* (Collegeville, MN: Pueblo/Liturgical Press, 1994).

[76] *Order of Christian Funerals* (Totowa, NJ: Catholic Book Publishing Corp., 1998), No. 44, p. 347.

[77] Ibid., No. 45.

[78] Ibid., No. 3.

[79] Jesus spoke a great deal about the importance and the power of the Divine Mercy Chaplet:

> **Encourage souls to say the Chaplet which I have given you (*Diary*, 1541). Whoever will recite it will receive great mercy at the hour of death (687). [W]hen they say this Chaplet in the presence of the dying, I will stand between My Father and the dying person, not as the just Judge but as the Merciful Savior (1541). Priests will recommend it to sinners as their last hope of salvation. Even if there were a sinner most hardened, if he were to recite this Chaplet only once, he would receive grace from My infinite mercy. ... I desire to grant unimaginable graces to those souls who trust in My mercy (687). Through the Chaplet you will obtain everything, if what you ask for is compatible with My will (1731).**

[80] Apparition at Fatima of August 19, 1917, "Fourth Apparition of Our Lady," EWTN. com.

[81] Fr. George Kosicki, CSB, and Vinny Flynn, *Now is the Time for Mercy* (Stockbridge, MA: Marian Press, 2015), pp. 75-76.

[82] According to a 2010 study, after patients were provided counseling, "there was a significant reduction in severity of symptoms" for anxiety, depression, self-esteem, and quality of life. Source: Roger Baker et al., "A Naturalistic Longitudinal Evaluation of Counselling in Primary Care," *Counselling Psychology Quarterly* 15, no. 4, (2002): 359-73. Counseling can make a significant difference in gaining your life back and maintaining your personal relationships, especially with God, after such a tremendous loss.

[83] Melinda Moore, "Addressing Suicide and Its Aftermath," in Melinda Moore and Daniel A. Roberts, eds., *The Suicide Funeral (or Memorial Service): Honoring Their Memory, Comforting Their Survivors* (Eugene, OR: Wipf and Stock/Resource Publications, 2017), pp. 6-7.

[84] Andersen, "Is God the Answer to the Suicide Epidemic?"

[85] Todd Burpo and Lynn Vincent, *Heaven is for Real: A Little Boy's Astounding Story of His Trip to Heaven and Back* (Nashville, TN: Thomas Nelson, 2010).

[86] *Roman Missal*, English translation according to the third typical edition (Totowa, NJ: Catholic Book Publishing Corp., 2011), Preface of Christian Death, p. 474.

[87] Fr. Donald Calloway, MIC, *Champions of the Rosary: The History and Heroes of a Spiri-*

tual Weapon (Stockbridge, MA: Marian Press, 2016).

[88] Mercy is not opposed to justice but rather expresses God's way of reaching out to the sinner, offering him a new chance to look at himself as God sees him, convert, and believe.

[89] Tim Staples, "What is Heaven?" *Catholic Answers*, February 27, 2015, accessed March 4, 2019, https://www.catholic.com/magazine/online-edition/what-is-heaven.

[90] Ibid.

[91] Ibid.

[92] Sister Emmanuel Maillard, *Scandalous Mercy: When God Goes Beyond Boundaries* (Denver, CO: Children of Medjugorje, Inc., 2017), p. 263.

[93] St. Catherine of Genoa, *Fire of Love! Understanding Purgatory* (Manchester, NH: Sophia Institute Press, 1996), p. 83.

[94] St. Catherine of Genoa, *Treatise on Purgatory*, quoted in Maillard, *Scandalous Mercy*, pp. 264-65.

[95] C.S. Lewis, *The Problem of Pain* (San Francisco: HarperOne, 2001), p. 130.

[96] Fr. William Byron, SJ, "Ask Father: Do People Who Commit Suicide Go to Hell?" *Catholic Digest*, April 1, 2007, accessed June 14, 2018, http://www.catholicdigest.com/faith/200704-01do-people-who-commit-suicide-go-to-hell.

[97] Pope Benedict XVI, Encyclical Letter *Spe Salvi* (*Saved in Hope*), November 30, 2007 (Boston, MA: Pauline Books and Media, 2007), n. 48.

[98] Ignacy Rózycki, the theologian whom Karol Wojtyla used to examine the *Diary* of St. Faustina, states that this promise of the Lord applied solely to Faustina. Since this prayer is so efficacious for the conversion of sinners, as would be any such appeal to the Blood and Water of Christ, placing it into the hands of St. Faustina and asking for her intercession through such a prayer would be exceptionally powerful.

[99] But remember that giving them the grace of conversion does not guarantee their salvation. They still have to accept it, consent to it, and surrender to it.

[100] Young et al., "Suicide Bereavement and Complicated Grief."

[101] Ibid.

[102] Ibid.

[103] Melinda Moore, correspondence with the authors, June 30, 2019.

[104] Young et al., "Suicide Bereavement and Complicated Grief."

[105] Ibid.

[106] Ibid.

[107] Ibid.

[108] Ibid.

[109] Ann M. Mitchell et al., "Complicated Grief in Survivors of Suicide," *Crisis: The Journal of Crisis Intervention and Suicide Prevention* 25, no. 1 (2004): 12-18, http://dx.doi.org/10.1027/0227-5910.25.1.12; see also Amy E. Latham and Holly G. Prigerson, "Suicidality and Bereavement: Complicated Grief as Psychiatric Disorder Presenting Greatest Risk for Suicidality," *Suicide and Life-Threatening Behavior* 34, no. 4 (2004): 350-62, doi:10.1521/suli.34.4.350.53737, cited in Dr. Melinda Moore, correspondence with the authors, June 30, 2019. See also Melinda Moore, "Addressing Suicide and Its Aftermath," p. 4.

[110] S. Sethi and S.C. Bhargava, "Child and Adolescent Survivors of Suicide," *Crisis: The Journal of Crisis Intervention and Suicide Prevention* 24, no. 1 (2003): 4-6, doi:10.1027//0227-5910.24.1.4, cited in Dr. Melinda Moore, correspondence with the authors, June 30, 2019.

111 Latham and Prigerson, "Suicidality and Bereavement," cited in Dr. Melinda Moore, correspondence with the authors, June 30, 2019.

112 Esben Agerbo, "Risk of Suicide and Spouse's Psychiatric Illness or Suicide: Nested Case-Control Study," *The BMJ* 327 (2003): 1025, https://doi.org/10.1136/bmj.327.7422.1025; see also Agerbo, "Midlife Suicide Risk, Partner's Psychiatric Illness, Spouse and Child Bereavement by Suicide or Other Modes of Death: A Gender Specific Study," *Journal of Epidemiology and Community Health* 59, no. 5 (2005): 407-12, doi:10.1136/jech.2004.024950, cited in Dr. Melinda Moore, correspondence with the authors, June 30, 2019.

113 Ping Qin and Preben B. Mortensen, "The Impact of Parental Status on the Risk of Completed Suicide," *Archives of General Psychiatry* 60, no. 8 (2003): 797-802, doi:10.1001/archpsyc.60.8.797, cited in Dr. Melinda Moore, correspondence with the authors, June 30, 2019.

114 Ping Qin, Esben Agerbo, and Preben B. Mortensen, "Suicide Risk in Relation to Socio-economic, Demographic, Psychiatric, and Familial Factors: A National Register-Based Study of All Suicides in Denmark, 1981-1997," *American Journal of Psychiatry* 160, no. 4 (2003): 165-72, doi:10.1176/appi.ajp.160.4.765, cited in Dr. Melinda Moore, correspondence with the authors, June 30, 2019.

115 Chart created by Sammie Wood. Used with permission. For another list of symptoms, please see Crossroads Hospice and Palliative Care, "Why Experts Talk about Symptoms, Not Stages, of Grief," *Blog: Hospice Views*, August 30, 2017, accessed July 8, 2019, https://www.crossroadshospice.com/hospice-palliative-care-blog/2017/august/30/why-experts-talk-about-symptoms-not-stages-of-grief/.

116 While it is held in some academic circles that Kübler-Ross' research is dated and not fully applicable to bereavement due to suicide, in part because her research was conducted with cancer patients, we nonetheless believe her work is foundational regarding grief and identifies important, perennially applicable truths about human nature and the grieving process.

117 Elisabeth Kübler-Ross, MD, and David Kessler, *On Grief and Grieving: Finding the Meaning of Grief Through the Five Stages of Loss* (New York: Scribner, 2014), p. 7. See also Grief.com, "The Fives Stages of Grief," https://grief.com/the-five-stages-of-grief, for summary explanations of the five stages and a free download of the first chapter of *On Grief and Grieving*.

118 Ibid.

119 Ibid., pp. 8-11.

120 Grief.com, "The Five Stages of Grief."

121 Kübler-Ross and Kessler, *On Grief and Grieving*, pp. 12-13, 16.

122 Ibid., p. 16.

123 Ibid., pp. 19-20.

124 Ibid., pp. 20-24.

125 Ibid.

126 Ibid., pp. 25-27.

127 See, for instance, Ps 3-7, 22, 44, 51, 74, 79, 88, and 130.

128 St. Augustine, *Sermo* 241, 2: PL, 38, 1134.

129 Kübler-Ross and Kessler, *On Grief and Grieving*, p. 102.

130 Ibid., p. 104.

131 Tristan Gooley, *How to Connect with Nature (The School of Life)* (London: Macmillan UK, 2015), p. 128.

[132] Jennifer Nelson, "New Research Shows that Petting Dogs is Like a Drug for Our Brains," IHeartDogs.com, https://iheartdogs.com/new-research-shows-that-petting-dogs-is-like-a-drug-for-our-brains.

[133] Alliance of Therapy Dogs, "The Benefits of Therapy Dogs in Classrooms and on College Campuses," https://www.therapydogs.com/therapy-dogs-classrooms-campuses.

[134] Nelson, "New Research Shows that Petting Dogs is Like a Drug for Our Brains."

[135] Spe Salvi, n. 6.

[136] Eucharistic Prayer of the Mass, Roman Missal, Third Edition of the English translation (Washington, DC: International Commission on English in the Liturgy Corporation, 2010).

[137] Pope St. John Paul II, Apostolic Letter Salvifici Doloris, "On the Christian Meaning of Human Suffering," February 11, 1984 (Boston, MA: Pauline Books and Media, 1984), n. 25.

[138] Ibid.

[139] Saint John Paul II used the language of "spiritual crucifixion" to describe Mary at the foot of the Cross on numerous occasions, including in the Encyclical Letter Redemptoris Mater (Mother of the Redeemer). Her unique participation in the salvific mission of her Son warrants the recognition of the title "Coredemptrix," meaning that Mary participated uniquely with her Son in the redemption of humanity as the "New Eve." John Paul II applied the term "Coredemptrix" to Mary on no less than five occasions in his pontificate.

[140] Salvifici Doloris, n. 26.

[141] See Joseph Ratzinger, Jesus of Nazareth: Holy Week: From the Entrance into Jerusalem to the Resurrection, (San Francisco: Ignatius Press, 2011), pp. 220-22.

[142] Salvifici Doloris, n. 26.

[143] Ibid.

[144] Ibid., n. 16.

[145] Ibid., n. 16.

[146] Ibid., n. 26.

[147] Ibid., n. 26.

[148] Young et al., "Suicide Bereavement and Complicated Grief."

[149] Victor Frankl, Man's Search for Meaning (Boston: Beacon Press, 2006), 146.

[150] Spe Salvi, n. 37.

[151] Ibid, n. 37.

[152] Salvifici Doloris, n. 15.

[153] JP II, RP 31, 5.

[154] Jane G. Tillman, "The Intergenerational Transmission of Suicide: Moral Injury and the Mysterious Object in the Work of Walker Percy," Journal of the American Psychoanalytic Association, June 6, 2016, https://journals.sagepub.com/doi/abs/10.1177/0003065116653362#.

[155] Ibid.

[156] Cardinal Basil Hume, The Mystery of the Cross (Brewster, MA: Paraclete Press, 2000), p. 13.

[157] Salvifici Doloris, n. 13.

[158] Ibid, 20.

[159] Spe Salvi, n. 12.

[160] Ratzinger, Jesus of Nazareth: Holy Week, p. 244.

[161] Ibid, p. 248.

[162] Ibid, p. 266.

[163] *Spe Salvi*, n. 33.

[164] Ibid., n. 33.

[165] *Salvifici Doloris*, n. 15.

[166] *Spe Salvi*, n. 35.

[167] *In Sinu Jesu* (Brooklyn, NY: Angelico Press, 2016), pp. 45-46. This book is from a collection of alleged private revelations to a Benedictine monk and is having an enormous impact on renewing the priesthood in the life of the Church in our present time. The authors and Marian Press always and ultimately submit to the Church's motherly discernment of the validity and inspiration of any such revelations.

[168] Fr. Robert Spitzer, SJ, "The Sacred Eucharistic Liturgy," *Credible Catholic Big Book*, Volume 9 (Magis Center, 2017), accessed March 4, 2019, https://www.crediblecatholic.com/pdf/M9/BB9.pdf#P1V9, p. 7.

[169] Fr. Robert Spitzer, SJ, conversation with Fr. Chris, February 14, 2019.

[170] Another explanation of this mystery is given by Brant Pitre. He states that the Eucharist is an event that transcends time. In some mysterious way, just as the old covenant, Passover, brought the Jewish people back in time to that first Exodus, so, too, the new Passover of the Eucharist takes us back to the night when Jesus died for us. It takes us back to the night of the Last Supper. It takes us back to His Passion and all the way to the Cross. For more, see Brant Pitre, *Jesus and the Jewish Roots of the Eucharist: Unlocking the Secrets of the Last Supper* (New York: Doubleday, 2011).

[171] Ratzinger, *The Spirit of the Liturgy*, p. 92.

[172] Fr. Michael Gaitley, MIC, *The 'One Thing' is Three: How the Most Holy Trinity Explains Everything* (Stockbridge, MA: Marian Press, 2012), pp. 79-84.

[173] For more on all this, see Gaitley, *The 'One Thing' is Three*, especially Point Two, Chapter Two, "Transforming Communion with Christ through Faith and the Sacraments."

[174] Fr. Alessio Parente, OFM Cap, *The Holy Souls: "Viva Padre Pio"* (Edizione Padre Pio da Pietrelcina, 2011), pp.178-79.

[175] Jimmy Akin, "Is It Possible to Pray Across Time?" *National Catholic Register*, January 5, 2018, accessed March 4, 2019, http://www.ncregister.com/blog/jimmy-akin/is-it-possible-to-pray-across-time. © 2019 EWTN News, Inc. Reprinted with permission from the National Catholic Register — www.ncregister.com.

[176] Dorothy Day. "There is No Time with God," *The Catholic Worker*, Nov. 1953, 1, 7, accessed July 4, 2019, https://www.catholicworker.org/dorothyday/articles/657.html.

[177] C.S. Lewis, *Miracles* (San Francisco: HarperOne, 2001), Appendix B, pp. 288-92.

[178] Akin, "Is It Possible to Pray Across Time?"

[179] Ibid.

[180] Ibid.

[181] Lewis, *Miracles*, Appendix B, pp. 292-94.

[182] Kreeft, *Everything You Ever Wanted to Know about Heaven*, pp. 154-55.

[183] Boethius, quoted in ibid., p. 154.

[184] Kreeft, *Everything You Ever Wanted to Know about Heaven*, p. 57.

[185] Ibid., p. 155.

[186] Ibid.

[187] Ibid., p. 156.

[188] Ibid., p. 157.

[189] Ibid., p. 158.

[190] Ibid., p. 160.

[191] Ibid., pp. 165-66.

[192] Ibid.

[193] Ibid., p. 167.

[194] Ibid., p. 168.

[195] Ibid., pp. 168-69.

[196] Ibid., pp. 158-59.

[197] American Foundation for Suicide Prevention, "Risk Factors and Warning Signs," accessed August 6, 2019, https://afsp.org/about-suicide/risk-factors-and-warning-signs/.

[198] Drapeau and McIntosh, "U.S.A. Suicide 2017: Official Final Data."

[199] Fuller, "5 Common Myths About Suicide Debunked."

[200] Drapeau and McIntosh, "U.S.A. Suicide 2017: Official Final Data."

[201] Ibid.

[202] Ibid.

[203] Ibid.

[204] National Alliance on Mental Illness, "Risk of Suicide," accessed March 5, 2019, https://www.nami.org/learn-more/mental-health-conditions/related-conditions/risk-of-suicide.

[205] Bullying Statistics, "Bullying and Suicide," accessed March 5, 2019, http://www.bullyingstatistics.org/content/bullying-and-suicide.html.

[206] Death with Dignity National Center, "Death with Dignity Acts," accessed July 8, 2019, https://www.deathwithdignity.org/learn/death-with-dignity-acts.

[207] Moore and Roberts, *The Suicide Funeral*, p. 3.

[208] U.S. Department of Veterans Affairs, "PTSD: National Center for PTSD," last updated September 24, 2018, accessed March 5, 2019, https://www.ptsd.va.gov/understand/common/common_veterans.asp.

Acknowledgments

All glory and thanksgiving to our Almighty God for His steadfast, merciful love upon us, who has supplied every grace in superabundance, enabling us to complete this work through the hands of our Immaculate Mother.

To all who suffer the loss of a loved one, especially to suicide, our hearts, prayers, and sacrifices poured into this book are offered for your consolation and healing.

Special thanks to all who contributed directly to this project — first and foremost, the Wood family. Sammie, Chip, Gus, and Sally, your story of courageous hope inspired this endeavor to the very end. Sammie, your raw transparency is a gift offering hope to readers of this book. You are all true family, and we could not have done this without you. With love and humble appreciation — thank you.

We must thank a special friend, sister in Christ, and coworker in the vineyard, Colleen. This project could never have happened without you. The tapestry Our Lady is weaving with us together is a thing of beauty and will touch many lives — thank you.

We express our deepest gratitude to an extraordinary Marian Press publishing team. Chris Sparks, your countless hours of editorial contribution and dedication are appreciated more than you know — thank you. Mary Clark and Tad Floridis, your objective guidance yielded a final manuscript far superior than where we started — thank you. Bob French and Felix Carroll, now we know why *we* are not copy editors and *you* are. You made us much better — thank you. Dr. Robert Stackpole and Fr. Thaddeus Lancton, MIC, for hours of theological labor and insight in making sure "we got it right" — thank you. Kathy Szpak, for your beautiful design and layout "artistry" — thank you. Brother Mark Fanders, MIC, your meticulous attention to detail in formulating such a fitting cover is greatly appreciated. And to all the employees of the Marian Helpers Center who endured our weaknesses and offered your prayerful and loving support to help us cross the finish line — thank you.

Sincerest appreciation to Fr. Robert Spitzer, SJ, and Dr. Peter Kreeft. Your theological expertise helped confirm that our theological speculations are in line with orthodox Christian teaching on God's eternity and our participation therein. In addition, thanks to all the others who graciously offered their endorsements of this book.

To all our Marian brothers for your prayers, patience, and support in helping us to see this project through. Special thanks to our provincial superior, Fr. Kazimierz Chwalek, MIC, and to one of the great teachers of Divine Mercy, Fr. Seraphim Michalenko, MIC. Your spiritual (and theological) wisdom and counsel brought us through some of the most difficult times — thank you. Special thanks to Fr. Michael Gaitley, MIC, for your advice and contribution to the content of this book, as well as Fr. Ron McBride, MIC, and Fr. Richard Drabik, MIC, for providing us the environment conducive to thoughtful writing. Additional thanks to all those visitors to the National Shrine of The Divine Mercy for your invaluable prayers and support.

SPECIFIC THANKS FROM FR. CHRIS

The prayers, support, and love from friends and family are far too great to mention. Special thanks to my parents, who have given the most supportive help in my greatest times of need. To Pam, who experienced a devastating loss herself and is the best sister a man could ever ask for. I am deeply honored to be your little brother. To all my family who endured the loss of our grandma, I pray this book may be a source of hope and healing. To all my friends, your words of love and encouragement have given me strength to persevere through all the challenges of this journey. To my special friend and co-author Jason: Man, I could not have done this without you! Finally, to Grandma: I am sorry that I wasn't there for you in your time of need. I miss you tremendously, but I have confident hope that I will see you again. I love you.

SPECIFIC THANKS FROM JASON

To my "circle of trust": Mom and Dad — I have no words that could ever articulate the depths of my love and gratitude for you. You know the "whole story," and have been my unfailing rock of support. To Chadie — my brother, your heart is golden and you inspire me in hope; Billie, Mary, and Kurt — your experience, strength, and support helped bring me through the darkest hours; Fr. Thomas Nau — your unconditional fatherly direction helped bring me to where I am today;

and Charlie Bear —your puppy-lovin' spirit makes you the best "daddy's boy" I could ever hope for. To Russell and Brooke, for providing an oasis of peace and friendship that allowed for healing and reflective writing. The deepest gratitude to my co-author and close friend, Chris — what a journey it has been, my brother. Only you and the Lord know what's gone into this! Thank you for the invitation to join the trek for the love of Christ, the Church, and our tender Mother.

In grateful, loving memory of Papa Mark Garrow, MIC, a true father and brother whose life has taught me to discover the deepest meaning of the *Via Dolorosa*. Your personal sacrifice continues to bear abundant fruit.

About the Authors

FATHER CHRIS ALAR, MIC, is a member of the Marian Fathers of the Immaculate Conception, the religious community entrusted with spreading the message and devotion of Divine Mercy. He wrote and produced the popular "Divine Mercy 101" DVD, and is an international speaker and a regular host and guest on EWTN. He also hosts the online "Divine Mercy Matters" series at DivineMercyMatters.org. He currently serves as "Fr. Joseph, MIC," the director of the Association of Marian Helpers, and is the head of Marian Press, located in Stockbridge, Massachusetts, home of the National Shrine of The Divine Mercy.

JASON LEWIS, MIC, is a member of the Marian Fathers of the Immaculate Conception and directs the Special Projects department for the Marian Helpers Center. He has delivered theological reflections on EWTN's 13-part series "The Cenacle of Divine Mercy II" and "EWTN Live." He has made numerous radio appearances and delivered talks around the country on the Blessed Virgin Mary and the message of the Divine Mercy.

Jason completed his STL coursework at Catholic University of America and is conducting his thesis research on Divine Mercy and its intrinsic relationship to the Paschal Mystery. He has a master's degree in theology from Catholic University and completed his master's work in philosophy at the Franciscan University of Steubenville.

Father Chris and Jason are available for interviews, speaking engagements, and conferences.

To arrange a visit, please call 800-462-7426 or 413-298-1349 or email parishmissions@marian.org

MORE FROM THE
MARIAN FATHERS

Memorialize Your Lost Loved One Online at

SuicideAndHope.com

Join other bereaved in praying
for each other and for those
who have taken their own lives.

Join the

Association of Marian Helpers,

headquartered at the
National Shrine of The Divine Mercy,
and share in special blessings!

An invitation from
Fr. Joseph, MIC, director

**Marian Helpers is an Association of
Christian faithful of the Congregation of
Marian Fathers of the Immaculate Conception.**
By becoming a member, you share in the
spiritual benefits of the daily Masses,
prayers, and good works of the Marian
priests and brothers.

This is a special offer of grace given to you by the Church through
the Marian Fathers. Please consider this opportunity to share in these
blessings, along with others whom you would wish to join into this
spiritual communion.

1-800-462-7426 • marian.org/join

Spiritual Enrollments & Masses

Enroll your loved ones in the Association of Marian Helpers, and they will participate in the graces from the daily Masses, prayers, good works, and merits of the Marian priests and brothers around the world.

Request a Mass to be offered by the Marian Fathers for your loved ones

Individual Masses
(for the living or deceased)

Gregorian Masses
(30 days of consecutive Masses for the deceased)

1-800-462-7426 • marian.org/enrollments • marian.org/mass

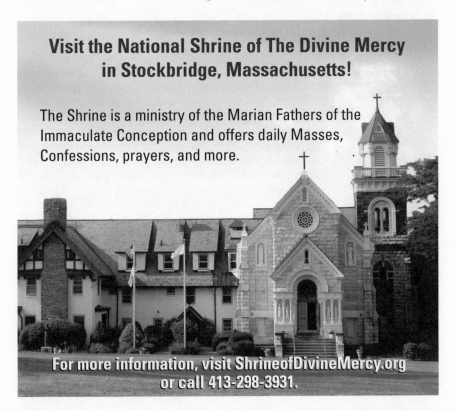

Visit the National Shrine of The Divine Mercy in Stockbridge, Massachusetts!

The Shrine is a ministry of the Marian Fathers of the Immaculate Conception and offers daily Masses, Confessions, prayers, and more.

For more information, visit ShrineofDivineMercy.org or call 413-298-3931.

Diary of Saint Maria Faustina Kowalska:
Divine Mercy in My Soul

Large Paperback:
Y86-NBFD
Compact Paperback:
Y86-DNBF
Deluxe Leather-Bound
Edition: Y86-DDBURG
Audio *Diary* MP3
Edition: Y86-ADMP3

Also available
as an ebook —
Visit ShopMercy.org

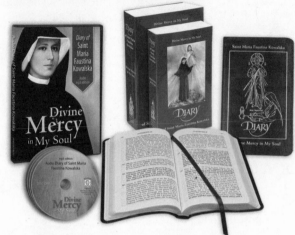

The *Diary* chronicles the message that Jesus, the Divine Mercy, gave to the world through this humble nun. In it, we are reminded to trust in His forgiveness — and as Christ is merciful, so, too, are we instructed to be merciful to others. Written in the 1930s, the *Diary* exemplifies God's love toward mankind and, to this day, remains a source of hope and renewal. Keep the *Diary* next to your Bible for constant insight and inspiration for your spiritual growth! Also available in Spanish.

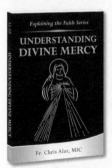

Explaining the Faith Series
Understanding Divine Mercy
by Fr. Chris Alar, MIC

Pope St. John Paul II said there is nothing the world needs more than Divine Mercy, yet few people understand exactly what Divine Mercy is and why it is so critical for our times. Now there's one book that summarizes it all in an easy-to-understand way! Have you ever wondered "What exactly is Divine Mercy and who is St. Faustina?" Would you like to know how to receive the extraordinary promise Jesus offers only one day a year, on Divine Mercy Sunday? Have you ever asked, "How could a merciful God allow so much suffering in the world?" If you answered yes to any of these questions, *Understanding Divine Mercy* by Fr. Chris Alar, MIC, is for you. In this first volume of his *Explaining the Faith* series, Fr. Chris shares, in his engaging style, the elements of the Divine Mercy message and devotion and explains why Jesus told St. Faustina that Divine Mercy is "mankind's last hope of salvation." Paperback. 184 pages. Y86-EFBK

Divine Mercy 101 DVD
The popular presentation by Fr. Chris Alar, MIC, is better than ever: all the basics of Divine Mercy in a clear, one-hour presentation. Also available as a CD.
Y86-DM102 Audio CD: Y86-NE101

For our complete line of books, prayer cards, pamphlets, Rosaries, and chaplets, visit ShopMercy.org or call 1-800-462-7426 to have our latest catalog sent to you.

Invite a Marian Father to speak at your parish or event!

The Marian Fathers of the Immaculate Conception offer talks and missions on Divine Mercy, Our Lady, the Holy Souls in Purgatory, and much more.

CONTACT THE MARIAN EVANGELIZATION TEAM
413-298-1349 • email parishmissions@marian.org

DivineMercyArt.com

Top Quality Religious Art ... at *Merciful* Prices!

Handmade at the National Shrine of The Divine Mercy with top-quality wood, canvas, and inks.

- Lowest prices
- Many sizes available
- Framing options

Canvas images starting at $19.95!

Y86-PV10GW

Y86-PH10GW

Y86-PB10GW

DivineMercyArt.com or call 1-800-462-7426
Prices subject to change.